Edwd. P. Chapin

THE

ONE HUNDRED AND SIXTEENTH

REGIMENT OF

NEW YORK STATE VOLUNTEERS:

BEING

A COMPLETE HISTORY OF ITS ORGANIZATION AND OF ITS NEARLY THREE YEARS OF ACTIVE SERVICE IN THE GREAT REBELLION.

TO WHICH IS APPENDED

MEMORIAL SKETCHES, AND A MUSTER ROLL OF THE REGIMENT, CONTAINING THE NAME OF EVERY MAN CONNECTED WITH IT.

By ORTON S. CLARK,

Late Captain Co. H, 116th Regiment New York State Volunteers.

BUFFALO:

PRINTING HOUSE OF MATTHEWS & WARREN,

Office of the "Buffalo Commercial Advertiser."

1868.

THIS VOLUME IS

Most Affectionately Dedicated

TO

EVERY MAN, WHATEVER HIS RANK,

WHO

BORE AN HONORABLE PART IN THE HISTORY
HERE RECORDED;

BUT ESPECIALLY TO THE

Hallowed Memory of our Dead.

PREFACE.

THE members of the organization whose history is recorded in the following pages, have always felt and often expressed a desire that the scenes through which it passed, during the nearly three years of its service, should be written and preserved, not only for their own satisfaction, but for future generations.

They felt that a record of its services, embracing, as it must, experience as varied as that of any portion of our army, extending from Virginia to Texas, and including a siege as protracted and campaigns as severe as any in the history of the war, could not but be of interest to the general reader, while to themselves it would be of inestimable value.

In the fall of 1867, it was determined among some half dozen of the old officers, that such a work should be undertaken, and the undersigned was prevailed upon to enter upon it. He did so with many misgivings as to his ability to produce a book worthy of the regiment and its history; but it has been a labor of love, entered upon with pleasure and prosecuted amid the cares of business.

It is not offered to the public for criticism, as the compiler lays no claim to the name of author. Errors of a literary nature will undoubtedly be found, and he asks a generous allowance for such imperfections; but so far as regards facts, he feels confident that it may be relied upon.

Every possible exertion has been made to secure memorial sketches of Capt. David W. Tuttle and Lieut. Timothy J. Linahan, who were both killed in action. For some reason they have not been provided, and Appendix I. is therefore incomplete.

Appendix II., containing a complete muster-roll of the regiment, is the result of much careful research, and must add materially to the value of the work. Some imperfections may be found, but the responsibility for them rests with the company officers who made out the rolls from which it is compiled.

No attempt has been made to spin out the story, and but very little moralizing upon the war, its causes and results, has been indulged in. Personalities have been avoided as far as was possible, for the reason that such matters are only interesting to relatives, and only excite unpleasant comparisons.

The thanks of the undersigned are due to Gen'l H. L. Lansing, Gen'l Love, Col. Weber, Col. Sizer, Surgeon Hutchins, Captains Morgan and Kinney, and Sergeant Oatman, for valuable services.

With these remarks, by way of introduction, the reader is invited to a perusal of the book.

Orton S. Clark.

CONTENTS.

CHAPTER I.

CHAPTER II.

CHAPTER III.

CHAPTER IV.

CHAPTER V.

CHAPTER VI.

CHAPTER VII.

CHAPTER VIII.

CHAPTER IX.

CHAPTER X.

CHAPTER XI.

CHAPTER XII.

CHAPTER XIII.

CHAPTER XIV.

CHAPTER XV.

CHAPTER XVI.

CHAPTER XVII.

CHAPTER XVIII.

CHAPTER XIX.

CHAPTER XX.

CHAPTER XXI.

CHAPTER XXVII.

CHAPTER XXVIII.

CHAPTER XXIX.

APPENDIX I.

APPENDIX II.

HISTORY OF THE

ONE HUNDRED AND SIXTEENTH

NEW YORK VOLUNTEERS.

CHAPTER I.

BUT few, if any, of the people of the North had the remotest idea, in 1860, that the threats of a disruption of the Union, in case Abraham Lincoln was elected President, with which the South were wont to assail their ears, were anything more than bombast. They could not conceive but that, as soon as it was decided that Mr. Lincoln was, by a majority of the votes of the electoral college, selected for that high and honorable position, they would cease their threats, and, with as good a grace as possible, submit themselves to the declared will of the majority, as became good citizens.

The North did not then know, as they now do, that ample preparation had been made, by Federal officials in high station, by sending our little navy to the remotest portions of the world, and by scattering our standing army far and wide; nor had they any idea that most of our forts and arsenals in the Southern States, were even then in the possession of those ready to write themselves traitors.

The wonderful discovery that the men who had made these threats meant what they said, and were prepared to act accordingly, was made on the 12th day of April, 1861, when, all over the Northern States, the wires flashed the news that our flag at Fort Sumter, in Charleston harbor, had been fired upon. Who that lived on that day, will ever forget the mingled feelings of amazement and vengeance which thrilled every heart?

A call for seventy-five thousand men was made by the President, on the 15th day of April, 1861, and then began the offering of freemen on the altar of their country. Very many considered the number called for too great by far, and few thought there would be need of any more. But how little we knew the path of blood upon which we had entered! Other calls were made, and still defeat was ours, during many months, oftener than victory. More men must be had, and on the 2d day of July, 1862, the President issued a call for 300,000 volunteers for three years, or during the war, and this was the call to which the One Hundred and Sixteenth New York Volunteers responded.

CHAPTER II.

The quota of the State of New York, by the provisions of this call, was sixty thousand; and on the 7th inst., His Excellency, Gov. Morgan, issued General Order No. 52. It divided the State into Regimental Districts, corresponding to the Senatorial Districts; and directed a camp to be organized in each, to which all recruits were to be sent. A commandant, adjutant, quartermaster and surgeon, were to be appointed, so soon as selections could be made. Each company was to be organized as follows:

MINIMUM.	MAXIMUM.
1 Captain,	1 Captain,
1 First Lieutenant,	1 First Lieutenant,
1 Second Lieutenant,	1 Second Lieutenant,
1 First Sergeant,	1 First Sergeant,
4 Sergeants,	4 Sergeants,
8 Corporals,	8 Corporals,
2 Musicians,	2 Musicians,
1 Wagoner,	1 Wagoner,
64 Privates.	82 Privates.
83 Aggregate.	101 Aggregate.

When ten companies were complete, they were to be organized into a regiment as follows:

MINIMUM.	MAXIMUM.
1 Colonel,	1 Colonel,
1 Lieut.-Colonel,	1 Lieut.-Colonel,
1 Major,	1 Major,
1 Adjutant,	1 Adjutant,
1 Quartermaster,	1 Quartermaster,
1 Surgeon,	1 Surgeon,
1 Asst. Surgeon,	1 Asst. Surgeon,
1 Chaplain,	1 Chaplain,
1 Sergt.-Major,	1 Sergt.-Major,
1 Quartermaster Sergeant,	1 Quartermaster Sergeant,
1 Commissary Sergeant,	1 Commissary Sergeant,
1 Hospital Steward,	1 Hospital Steward,
2 Principal Musicians,	2 Principal Musicians,
830 Company officers and men.	1010 Company officers and men.
844 Aggregate.	1024 Aggregate.

By an Act of Congress, passed about this time, this number was increased by the allowance of another assistant surgeon to each regimental organization.

The whole work of recruiting and organizing, in each district, was to be done under the supervision of a committee of citizens appointed by the Governor. Erie County, by this order, was constituted the Thirty-first District; the camp located at Buffalo; and the following named gentlemen were appointed the military committee by His Excellency:

Brig.-Gen'l Henry L. Lansing,	Henry M. Kinne, Esq.,
Hon. Geo. W. Clinton,	John G. Deshler, "
" Nathan K. Hall,	Philip Dorsheimer, "
" Wm. G. Fargo,	Asaph S. Bemis, "
" John Ganson,	E. S. Warren, "
Jacob Beyer, Esq.,	S. G. Austin, "

Alexander W. Harvey, Esq.

The Committee held its first meeting at the office of General Lansing on the 10th day of July, 1862, and organized by the election of General Lansing as chairman, and Mr. Harvey as secretary.

Their first duty was the selection of a commandant, a task of very great importance and requiring great care, which they at once entered upon.

At their second meeting, held July 11th, the command was tendered to Mr. John Wilkeson, of Buffalo, but was declined by him. Mr. Henry W. Rogers was then waited upon, and the same tender made to him; but in view of his advanced age and poor health, he preferred that some one else should be selected; promising, however, that should the committee be unable to do better, he would take the position and discharge the duties to the best of his ability. Captain Perry, a graduate of West Point, was then named; but in answer to the enquiries of the committee, he stated that he was unable to obtain the permission of his superiors.

At this stage of the proceedings Mr. Rogers appeared before the committee, and urged the appointment of Major Edward P. Chapin, of the Forty-fourth N.Y.Vols., then in Buffalo on recruiting service for that regiment, he having been wounded at the battle of Hanover Court House, and unable to endure the fatigue of an active campaign.

The suggestion of Mr. Rogers was favorably received by the committee, and in accordance therewith Major Chapin was invited to assume command of the new regiment about to be organized. After due consideration, the Major accepted the position and at once entered upon the work before him. Major Chapin, although not born in Buffalo, was considered a Buffalo boy, his life having been identified more or less intimately with its history. At the breaking out of the rebellion he was quietly practising his profession—that of a lawyer—in Buffalo, and at once made himself familiar with the science of war, putting his theory into practice, both as captain and major of the Forty-fourth N.Y.Vols. He came, therefore, well qualified by experience as well as by study to take charge of this new offering of Erie County. Looking back now upon his short but remarkably brilliant career, we who learned to reverence him as our colonel, and to love him as a man, almost wonder at a Providence which took him from us and from his country, when both we and it needed him so much.

Immediately on his acceptance, Maj. Chapin recommended Lieut. John B. Weber, also of the Forty-fourth N. Y. Vols., as adjutant, and he was at once selected for that position. Mr. James Adams, one of the prominent business men of Buffalo, was appointed quartermaster, and Dr. Chauncey B. Hutchins, also of Buffalo, received the appointment of surgeon. Thus a beginning was made, which could not have been improved; all the selections were admirable, and gave promise of a faithful execution of the duties involved.

In the meantime, recruiting had been going on to a limited extent, and it only remained to raise funds, secure more recruiting officers, and push on the good work to a speedy consummation. Every means was devised to raise the needful funds, and most nobly did the citizens of Erie County, and especially of Buffalo, respond. A horse exhibition was inaugurated by which some hundreds of dollars were added to the treasury; the Messrs. Meech, of the Metropolitan Theatre, gave an entertainment for the same purpose; Parson Brownlow came and lectured, and quite a sum was realized, besides which a large amount was raised by subscription. Henry Martin, Esq., was appointed by the committee to receive and disburse the money obtained from these sources, and five thousand six hundred and fifty dollars ($5,650) was expended by him in defraying the necessary expenses attending the recruiting of the regiment. Many of our business men closed their places of business at three o'clock in the afternoon, that they and their employees might by every means in their power help to increase the number of our country's defenders.

The inducements for enlisting, as regards bounty, were very meagre, compared, at least, with what was offered at a later period. For each accepted volunteer for three years or the war, a premium of two dollars was allowed by the government, and twenty-five of the one hundred dollars bounty given to all volunteers, was paid in advance; the State paid fifty dollars, and some wards and towns paid a further sum of twenty-five or fifty dollars. By these figures it will be seen that nothing but pure patriotism induced the men who formed the One Hundred and Sixteenth to enter the service.

The ground selected for the camp was Fort Porter, about a mile and a half from the centre of the city of Buffalo, although within its limits. In honor of the Governor it was called "Camp Morgan," and a more beautiful spot could not have been found. Situated on Prospect Hill, immediately on the banks of the Niagara river, a fine view was had of this noble stream, with Canada on the opposite bank, and the ruins of old Fort Erie in the distance; while as far as the eye could reach in a south-westerly direction, nothing could be seen but the blue waters of Lake Erie.

The fort itself was used only for storing purposes, but the castle, a large stone building, occupied in part by the keeper of the premises, was used by the colonel, adjutant, quartermaster and surgeon, as offices. A mess house had been erected some time before, sufficiently large to comfortably seat nearly one thousand men, where Mr. S. W. Carpenter, who had been given the contract for subsisting the men, dealt out to them a supply of good clean food. It was not strange, however, that coming from well-filled larders at home, where "mother's bread and butter, pies and doughnuts," were heaped up, that a deal of grumbling was heard about the bill of fare; nor was it startling that after we entered active service in the field, a wish was often expressed for the potatoes, mush, etc., with which Mr. Carpenter furnished us at Camp Morgan.

Barracks for the accommodation of the men had also been erected, and in these we were quartered after being thoroughly examined by Surgeon Hutchins as to our fitness, physically, for soldiers, solemnly sworn by Adjt. Weber to support the Government of the United States, and entirely metamorphosed by Quartermaster Adams into "boys in blue." A regular Camp Guard was instituted, with its accompanying Guard-house, Guard-mounting, etc., which, with dress parade and some attempt at drilling, gave the camp quite a military look.

When Maj. Chapin had been selected to command the new regiment, and had signified his acceptance of the position, the committee at once notified the Adjutant General at Washington, and requested that he might be granted a leave of absence until such time as he should receive a commission as colonel. On the 2d of August a reply was received refusing the request. Upon its receipt they waited upon him, and learned from him that under the circumstances he could no longer consider himself commandant. Capt. Robert Cottier, then recruiting for the regiment, was at once placed in temporary command, and on the 6th, Col. Henry K. Viele, an old resident of Buffalo, received from the committee the appointment of commandant, *vice* Chapin.

The next day he assumed command at Camp Morgan, but instituted few new regulations, carrying out in the main the plan pursued by Maj. Chapin.

The friends of Maj. Chapin were not content, however, that matters should remain thus, and strenuous efforts were made to secure for him the position. These efforts were at length successful, and on the 16th, he once more appeared at Camp Morgan, taking command of the One Hundred and Sixteenth N. Y. Vols., as we had been designated in orders, by virtue of a commission as colonel from Gov. Morgan.

At this time five hundred and seventy-seven men were reported mustered into the United States service, and recruiting was progressing with such rapidity as to dissipate all fears of a failure. Everything looked well for a speedy entrance into active service.

On the 18th, six hundred and eight men were reported as mustered, and on the 22d, seven hundred and forty-six. On the 25th, the paymaster arrived, and the day was consumed in paying to each man one month's pay and the advance bounty.

On the 26th, seven hundred and eighty-seven were reported duly mustered; on the 30th, eight hundred and forty-seven, and on the 3d day of September, nine hundred and twenty-nine. This—as but very few, if any more, were enlisted—was the number of men with which the One Hundred and Sixteenth entered the service; but they were men, every one of them, fit for the duty upon which they were about to enter!

Too much credit cannot be given Surgeon Hutchins for the strictness with which he examined every man who presented himself as a volunteer, and it is not saying too much, to assert, that the very small per centage of men on our sick list wherever we went, compared with other regiments, was due to him.

On this same day, Lieut. Shelden Sturgeon, U. S. A., mustering officer at Buffalo, appeared at Camp Morgan, and it having been decided that the individual muster of each man by Adjt. Weber only secured them to the State, mustered the regiment, by companies, into the United States service, for three years or during the war.

The work of officering the regiment was one of much

trouble, requiring great care and no small amount of tact. Permits had been given to twice as many recruiting officers as could by any possibility receive commissions ; and their several squads had to be so consolidated as to secure the best officers, and yet give as little cause for complaint, to those necessarily left out, as possible. It was soon found that, should the wishes of all parties be listened to, and an attempt made to harmonize them, much valuable time would be lost, and an order to move at once would find us entirely unprepared. Col. Chapin therefore assumed the responsibility of recommending to the Governor for the different positions, such officers as he deemed best, and they were accordingly commissioned, thereby making the following the roster of the One Hundred and Sixteenth when it left for the seat of war:

FIELD OFFICERS.

Colonel—EDWARD P. CHAPIN. *Lieut.-Colonel*—ROBERT COTTIER.
Major—GEORGE M. LOVE.

STAFF OFFICERS.

Adjutant—JOHN B. WEBER. *2d Asst. Surg.*—CAREY W. HOWE.
Surgeon—C. B. HUTCHINS. *Quartermaster*—JAMES ADAMS.
1*st Asst. Surg.*—URI C. LYNDE. *Chaplain*—WELTON M. MODDESIT.

NON-COMMISSIONED STAFF.

Sergt.-Major—ORTON S. CLARK. *Qr.-Mast. Sergt.*—ALEX. GOSLIN.
Commis.-Sergt.—J. L. CLAGHORN. *Hosp.-Stew.*—C. F. A. NICHELL.

COMPANY A.

Captain—Ira Ayer.
1*st Lieut.*—J. C. Thompson.
2*d Lieut.*—Warren T. Ferris.

COMPANY B.

Captain—Albert J. Barnard.
1*st Lieut.*—Leander Willis.
2*d Lieut.*—Daniel Corbett.

COMPANY C.

Captain—David W. Tuttle.
1*st Lieut.*—Robert F. Atkins.
2*d Lieut.*—Edward J. Cornwell.

COMPANY D.

Captain—John Higgins.
1*st Lieut.*—Chas. F. Wadsworth.
2*d Lieut.*—Elisha W. Seymour.

COMPANY E.
Captain—Richard C. Kinney.
1st Lieut.—James McGowan.
2d Lieut.—Thomas Notter.

COMPANY F.
Captain—Geo. G. Stanbro.
1st Lieut.—Wilson H. Grey.
2d Lieut.—Clinton Hammond.

COMPANY G.
Captain—John M. Sizer.
1st Lieut.—Timothy Linahan.
2d Lieut.—George Peterson.

COMPANY H.
Captain—William Wuerz.
1st Lieut.—David Jones.
2d Lieut.—Fred. Sommers.

COMPANY I.
Captain—P. R. Stover.
1st Lieut.—Geo. W. Carpenter.
2d Lieut.—Edward Irwin.

COMPANY K.
Captain—James Ayer.
1st Lieut.—P. W. Gould.
2d Lieut.—John W. Grannis.

Nearly every day witnessed the presentation of some article necessary to a soldier's outfit to some one. Col. Chapin was the recipient of a splendid black stallion, the gift of Capt E. P. Dorr, of Buffalo, and the officers of the regiment. He was a thorough-bred Kentucky horse, the pride of the Colonel and the envy of all. The services of Tim Flanigan, his former groom, were secured; and if ever an army horse received good care, that horse was "Dan." Tim was a character deserving of more than mere mention. Leaving Buffalo with the regiment, he came home with it, and except for some three months, was with it during its entire term of service. A good deal of a wag, with a large share of Irish wit, no one attempted a joke upon him who did not get more than a fair return. Upon the march he was everywhere present, and soon came to be known by almost every man in the brigade, division or army, and was always liked.

Lieut.-Col. Cottier received a horse from Isaac Holloway and Allen M. Adams; Maj. Love received one from Chandler J. Wells, Capt. D. P. Dobbins and some others; and Adjt. Weber received a similar gift from L. H. Flersheim and others. Quite a number of line officers received from their companies or friends, swords, belts, revolvers, &c.

Anxiety for marching orders was now felt by nearly all: by the officers, because the near proximity of Camp Morgan to the city, made it a difficult matter to keep such men as were inclined to visit saloons, etc., from excesses, which would add nothing to our good name at home; and by the men, because of a desire to taste the sweets of a soldier's life. This anxiety was soon set at rest, by the reception of an order to proceed at once to Washington. Co. "K" had but just arrived at Camp Morgan, and as no preparation had been made by its members before leaving home, in expectation of being permitted a short furlough to settle up business matters, it was arranged that the whole company should be furloughed, with instructions to join the regiment with as little delay as possible.

At Camp Morgan all was hurry and confusion, on the 5th day of September, 1862. The news that marching orders had been received soon spread itself throughout the city and surrounding country, drawing together an immense throng to witness the departure of the regiment.

Soon after noon, the Adjutant's call was sounded, the drums beat the assembly, and the companies formed in front of their respective barracks. The line was formed the Colonel gave the command to face to the right, and the One Hundred and Sixteenth took up its line of march for the depot, leaving Camp Morgan to be returned to after nearly three years service. Following Sixth street for a short distance, we turned into Niagara, moved down Niagara to Court, through Court to Main, down Main to the churches, followed by an eager crowd.

At this point we were halted, and presented by the Hon. Henry W. Rogers, in the name of the citizens of Buffalo, with a stand of colors. Mr. Rogers said: "I am commissioned to present you, in the name of the citizens of Buffalo, this banner, with the hope and confidence that you will never desert it, or allow its folds to gather dust at the feet of the foe;" to which Col. Chapin replied, "that so long as an officer or man remained to uphold it, it should never be trailed in the dust or be dishonored by the contaminating touch of traitors."

When the ceremony was concluded, we moved down Main street to Exchange, and down Exchange to the depot of the Erie Railway. An escort, composed of the "Tigers," Capt. Wardwell; the "Light Guard," Lieut. Avery; the "Eagle Zouaves," Capt. McLeish; and the "Continentals," Capt. Millard Fillmore, with Miller's band, had accompanied us, and as we approached the depot, they were halted, and saluted us as we passed them.

A train of twenty-one passenger coaches was found already made up, and with as much despatch as possible the regiment was placed on board. Many sad hearts were there, as dear ones parted perhaps forever, from husbands, sons, brothers or lovers; but at last every parting word was spoken, the iron horse whistled a warning, and at five o'clock in the afternoon of the fifth day of September, 1862, amid the shouts of the multitude, the One Hundred and Sixteenth moved out of the depot and was off for the wars.

CHAPTER III.

OUR ride to Elmira was unenlivened by anything remarkable. At Lancaster, Alden and Attica, large crowds were congregated to give us their parting cheers as we whirled past them, but darkness soon prevented any more such expressions of sympathy, and all prepared to make themselves as comfortable for the night as circumstances would allow.

About four o'clock on the morning of September 6th, we arrived at Elmira, and amid the darkness, turned out of the passenger coaches to find prepared for us a train of cattle cars. This was the first experience of the regiment in real soldier's fare, and such shouts of derision, such hooting in imitation of driving cattle as woke the echoes of Elmira, had seldom been heard. They must have caused those of its inhabitants who were awake, to imagine that beef would be very plenty in the morning. Many expressions of indignation from the more staid and sober ones were heard, and yet in our after experience such a train of cattle cars, which would have saved a fatiguing march, would have been hailed with delight.

Some two hours were spent in getting the regiment and its arms and equipments, which were already boxed for us, on board the new train, and just as the day was breaking, the One Hundred and Sixteenth once more started, this time on the Northern Central Railroad for Baltimore.

To most of us this was an entirely new country, and as its picturesque scenes opened to our view as we wound around rocky curves, or glided along easy grades, on one side the still waters of the Susquehanna, on the other the bold heights of the Alleghanies, the fact that we were soldiers, hastening perhaps to bloody battle-fields, was lost sight of, and many thought themselves enjoying a delightful pleasure trip. It needed, however, only a glance at the accommodations with which we were provided, to convince such imagined tourists of their error.

At Williamsport a short stop was made, and with good appetites we partook of the hospitalities of its kind-hearted ladies. During the day our ride was relieved in a measure of its tediousness by the constantly changing scenes; but the long night which followed, made our near approach to Baltimore the next morning very acceptable. On the morning of Sunday, September 7th, we found ourselves in Baltimore, of which we had heard much and imagined more, and when, not long after our arrival, we were marched into the rooms of the Soldiers' Relief Association, and found so bountiful a supply of food prepared for us, and learned that every regiment, that entered the city, was in like manner provided for, our feelings toward it materially changed, and we thought it could not be so very bad a place after all.

Our orders when we left Buffalo were to proceed to Washington, but the movements of the rebels, which looked like an advance into Maryland and Pennsylvania, made a change necessary. We soon found that for the present, at least, Baltimore was to be our abiding place. The whole day was spent in the vicinity of the rooms of the Relief Association, and night found us without orders where to proceed for a camping ground. Close at hand were the ruins of the Camden Station Depot, burned but a short time before, and in and around this, the men of the One Hundred and Sixteenth lay down in their blankets and rested as best they could.

Bright and early Monday morning, Col. Chapin proceeded, with an aide of Maj. Gen'l Wool, in whose command we now were, in search of a suitable ground for a camp. He soon returned, and much to our satisfaction (for we had become tired of inaction), gave the command to "fall in," which we obeyed, and proceeded out Eutaw street some two miles to grounds selected, near Druid Hill Park. We found it a very pleasant spot, some distance from the street, well shaded with trees, and not far from a stream of water. "A" tents had been procured for the men, and wall tents for the officers, by Quartermaster Adams, and, as we were entirely ignorant of the manner of pitching them, some very amusing failures occurred. However, by the exercise of a deal of patience, they were all pitched in some shape before night, and the One Hundred and Sixteenth prepared to take its first nights rest beneath the canvass.

Before leaving Buffalo, Col. Chapin had received the assurance of one of Gov. Morgan's staff, then in the city, that there were just enough Springfield muskets at Elmira to arm one regiment, and that he would secure them for the One Hundred and Sixteenth, have them boxed, marked, and on board the train we were to occupy on our trip from Elmira to Baltimore. Relying on this assurance and congratulating us on our good fortune, the Colonel only satisfied himself when we reached Elmira that the arms were on board the train, and waited a more convenient season to see them. This happened soon after our arrival in Baltimore. Chagrin and indignation were blended in the good Colonel's countenance when the fact was brought to light, that instead of the new and beautiful Springfield muskets, his regiment were to be armed with plain Enfield rifles, of foreign manufacture and with clouded barrels. However, as there was no help for it, all made the best of it, and when we learned that the muskets we had expected to get, were issued to the One Hundred and Fourteenth N. Y. Vols., encamped within a stone's throw of us, we were glad they had fallen into such good hands.

The next day the camp was laid out in strict conformity to army regulations, each company street being ditched and graded to carry off all surface water. While all this necessary work was being done, and every effort made to secure and keep a clean healthy camp, the one great need of our present life, was the main care of Col. Chapin. No commanding officer ever more fully realized the absolute necessity of strict discipline, the utter impossibility of the One Hundred and Sixteenth being a first-class regiment, unless every man was made to understand that unquestioning obedience to the orders of a superior was his first and only duty, than did he; and hard as was the lesson, our teacher was stern and inexorable, and it was learned ere we left "Camp Chapin," as the camp had been named. He knew also the worth of a well-drilled regiment, and as the officers with few exceptions, were guiltless of any knowledge of tactics, he instituted a school, giving certain portions of the United States Army Regulations and Tactics to be learned and repeated to him, and every morning before breakfast, all the line officers of the regiment, were ordered to appear armed with muskets at the Colonel's tent, where they were instructed, either by him or Adjt. Weber, in the manual of arms for one hour; and drilling by squad, by company, and by battalion, occupied some eight or nine hours each day. At half-past five o'clock every morning reveille was sounded, when the roll was called in each company street. From six to seven o'clock we had company drill. An hour and a half was then allowed for breakfast, and at half-past eight, guard-mounting—upon which we always prided ourselves—took place; after this the companies were again drilled until half-past eleven o'clock. By this time a good appetite called loudly for rations, and tired limbs for rest. Two hours and a half sufficed for this, and at two o'clock the whole regiment again turned out for battalion drill, which generally occupied two hours. Time was then allowed for a little rest and for cleaning up, in preparation for dress parade, the great event of the day.

It could not be otherwise, than that we should improve under such thorough drilling as this; and it is no wonder that the One Hundred and Sixteenth soon became very proficient in all that goes to make good soldiers.

One thing more there was, the careful execution of which Col. Chapin knew would help wonderfully in our schooling, and that was guard duty. A strong camp guard was detailed every day in command of an officer, which was posted around the camp, to prevent the admission of venders of sickly pies and stale gingerbread, as well as the departure of any members of the regiment without permission from head-quarters. The orders to this guard were very strict, and the duty was no light one, especially at night. An officer of the day who had entire charge of the guard, visited each post many times during the night, and at midnight made the "Grand Rounds," challenging each sentinel in due form, to which challenge he must reply correctly in every particular.

Many amusing incidents occurred, of course, among green hands as we all were; but it was persevered in, until guard duty was performed as perfectly by the One Hundred and Sixteenth, as by any regiment in the service.

To show the manner in which the men had learned to obey orders in the performance of this duty, it will only be necessary to give one instance. Among our number were some who could not resist the desire to visit the city, and darkness best suited their purpose. It was their practice after quiet had settled over the camp, to steal out of their tents, and in the darkness run the guard. After a stay in the city, sufficiently prolonged to satisfy them, they would return to camp, and in the same sly manner regain their quarters. To such an extent was this practised, that orders were given the guard to prevent it at whatever cost, and but few after this attempted it. One man, however, succeeded in getting out of camp by eluding the vigilance of the guard. After some hours absence, he returned to try his fortune in getting back. Cautiously he advanced, but the quick eye of one of the sentinels caught sight of him. "Who comes there!" was demanded; no answer was given, and still he advanced. Again he was commanded to "halt," but with a rush he attempted to pass the sentinel, whose bayonet pierced his heart, and his days of disobedience were over. This sad occurrence cast a gloom for a time over the regiment, but its effect was beneficial in the last degree, showing as it did that disobedience of military law brought speedy punishment, and emphasizing, thus early in our experience, the hardest lesson a soldier has to learn, that the will of another is law to him.

About this time, Co. "K," which it will be remembered was left behind, with orders to join the regiment as speedily as possible, arrived at Camp Chapin, thus completing our organization.

On the 9th day of October, up to which time we had reported directly to Maj. Gen'l Wool, an order was received, organizing a brigade, under the command of Brig. Gen'l Wm. H. Emory, composed of the One Hundred and Tenth, One Hundred and Fourteenth, One Hundred and Sixteenth, One Hundred and Twenty-eighth N. Y. Vols., Thirty-eighth Mass. Vols., and Sixth N.Y. Artillery; and not many days after we were all assembled at what purported to be a brigade drill, but which was simply a review. The regiments were all full, and presented as soldierly an appearance as our recent entrance into the service would permit, and composed really as fine a command as any brigadier general need desire. On one or two subsequent occasions the review was repeated, and the hard work we had been doing in the intervals at drilling, gave us a perceptible advantage over some of the other regiments, which we were not slow to understand and appreciate.

The constant recurrence of these same duties, day after day, soon lost the charm of novelty, became monotonous in the extreme, and led us to wish for more active service. We longed to participate in the stirring scenes of real warfare, and were not content to bide our time, which we might have known would come soon enough. The duties which seemed so irksome were really worth more to us in preparing us for that real warfare, than premature participation in those stirring scenes could have been. We learned this in after time. Whatever of service the One Hundred and Sixteenth rendered in the crushing of the rebellion, whatever success attended its after movements, was due almost wholly to the preparatory work performed while we remained in Baltimore, and to Col. Chapin, who saw not only that it was done, but well done.

About midnight, October 11th, a mounted orderly from Gen'l Emory's Headquarters, rode furiously into Camp Chapin, with an order to cook three days' rations, and prepare to move at a moment's notice. The news soon spread itself among all the men, and although it was raining terribly, the whole regiment were soon astir, busily engaged in making preparations for its first campaign, which was afterwards known, by some as the "Gettysburg," but by most of us as the "Apple Butter" campaign. Every tent was struck, every ration cooked, and some of them eaten, too, before the final order to move was received, which was at ten o'clock, A. M., October 12th.

We proceeded down Eutaw street to the depot of the Baltimore and Harrisburg Railroad, but as nearly all our brigade were under orders for the trip, it was found difficult to procure cars sufficient to accommodate all. Hour after hour we waited, expecting every moment that our train would be ready; but it was fully nine o'clock, P. M. before we were enabled to get aboard and start for Harrisburg. Nothing was known, except by rumor, of the object of our expedition; but as the rebel Gen'l Stuart was reported on a raid of very extensive proportions, and had already entered Pennsylvania, we credited the rumor this time, and believed ourselves in for a show at real fighting.

Early the next morning, October 13th, we reached Hanover Junction, and took the road for Gettysburg, where we arrived about three o'clock in the afternoon. We heard constantly, as we passed people assembled at the stations, of the depredations the rebels had committed, and judging from these accounts, one would have supposed that Gen'l Lee's army would never more lack for horses. Almost every man had lost a number of valuable animals, and such as had succeeded in saving these, had lost many other things equally valuable. At every point where a stop was made, we were informed that we were just too late, and our blood-thirsty desire to avenge the wrongs of these sons of Pennsylvania would find expression in expostulations to hurry up.

However, as has been stated, we reached Gettysburg at three o'clock, still too late, our Dutch friends told us. That night we remained on board the cars, and the next morning marched some five miles to a small place, which for some good reason, no doubt, though we were unable to ascertain what, was called "Cashtown." Here we bivouaced for the night in an open field. A plentiful supply of beef, pork, chickens, etc., etc., were obtained, all secured, as the cattle dealers say, "on the hoof," from which it may be presumed that no one "turned in" hungry that night. Our approach, or some other equally good reason, had scattered the enemy, and we were not molested, but enjoyed a good night's rest. Awaking on the morning of October 14th, we received orders to re-enter the cars, and return to Baltimore. We passed Hanover about noon, and at Hanover Junction found our further progress disputed by a broken bridge, which caused our detention that night and the whole of the next day. On the morning of Oct. 16th, the bridge having been repaired we proceeded on our way, arriving at Baltimore at three o'clock, P. M. Our camp equipage had been sent after us, but, upon learning of our failure and consequent return, it was turned back, and when we arrived at Camp Chapin we found everything in readiness to proceed at once to housekeeping. A very short time sufficed to pitch our tents and make everything wear a home-like aspect again.

It is astonishing how soon a soldier becomes domesticated. At this time, only about six weeks had passed since we left Buffalo, and but a little over four of these had been spent in Camp Chapin; yet I venture to say, that more real joy would not have been felt by the most of us, could we have seen the old home in Erie County, than was experienced when we marched into our old camp.

Our trip had been a pleasant one: mingled with some hardships, there had been much fun. We had seen where armed rebels had been, at any rate; and if we had not come in contact with the veritable greybacks it was no fault of ours. In addition, we had been so well treated by the people on the route, that I doubt if any man belonging to the One Hundred and Sixteenth will ever think of Pennsylvania but as a State overflowing with "apple butter." At Hanover and Hanover Junction, where, both in going and returning, long stops were made, the inhabitants flocked to the cars in droves, with pitchers, cans, crocks, and almost every other household utensil, filled with this delicious article. They did not forget to bring in addition goodly loaves of sweet bread, and in every way manifested their appreciation of our services which were yet to be performed. When, months afterward, in the lowlands of Louisiana, we heard of the fearful battle between the vast armies of Meade and Lee, on this same ground at Gettysburg, we wondered if the very spot where we had bivouaced that night of October 13th, was made holy ground by the sacrifice of loyal blood; and we felt, in a measure, better acquainted with the battle of Gettysburg than with any other in which we ourselves were not engaged.

CHAPTER IV.

Our time now, was occupied about as it had been, before our expedition into Pennsylvania, with constant drilling eight or nine hours each day. Once or twice, in order to accustom the regiment to marching with their knapsacks and equipments complete, Col. Chapin received permission to take us through the beautiful grounds of Druid Hill Park, which is said to be second only to Central Park, in New York, in beauty as well as extent. A long and dusty march to and through a portion of its winding paths, made a rest beneath the shade of its noble trees very acceptable.

A quantity of blank-cartridges were drawn by the Quartermaster, and our battalion drills were enlivened by the rattle of musketry and the *smell* of burned powder, if nothing more. We were practised in file-firing, by company, by wing, and by battalion; and although in our after use of ball-cartridges, we never found much occasion for the practice of any prescribed mode of firing, still this drill was of much benefit to us in getting our ears accustomed to the sound, and our nostrils acquainted with the smell of exploded powder. It also gave us still another lesson in obedience to orders, for woe be unto the man whose impatience would not permit him to await the command "fire." So constant was our drilling, and so firm in his demands was the Colonel, that before many days the whole eight hundred muskets would be discharged as if by one man.

A young man well versed in the mysteries of the snare drum, had been induced to accompany the regiment on its departure from Buffalo, and on our arrival in Baltimore, a large drum corps was at once organized, with which he labored most faithfully until they acquired considerable skill in handling the drumsticks. This added materially to the interest of our parades. All felt, however, that a brass band would be of great value to the regiment, and on the 18th of October one was organized. It was composed of men from the ranks who had had some experience in such matters, from which number John Martin, of Company "A," was selected as leader. The requisite instruments were obtained in Baltimore with subscriptions from officers and men of the regiment, and about a year later some additions were made to the number. It proved a very great assistance, and was fostered and cared for throughout our entire term of service.

Still more attention, if possible, was now paid to the cleanliness of the men than ever before; and soon a sort of rivalry between the companies sprung up, not only as to which should turn out the most men for dress parade, but as to which should present the finest appearance. Such rivalry could not but be beneficial, and these things are only mentioned here to give the reader a reason why we should claim a high position for the One Hundred and Sixteenth in those things which soldiers know are essential.

November 2d an order was received from Gen'l Emory, which set the whole camp in commotion; it read as follows, viz:

"I. The following regiments, having been designated, will hold themselves in readiness to march at a moment's notice, on distant service: 110th N. Y. V., Colonel D. C. Littlejohn; 114th N. Y. V., Colonel E. B. Smith; 116th N. Y. V., Colonel E. P. Chapin; 128th N. Y. V., Colonel D. S. Cowles; 38th Mass. V., Colonel S. Ingraham.

"II. The commanders of regiments will see that the arms and equipments of each man are complete, and that he has in his knapsack one pair of shoes, and a complete change of underclothes, *i. e.*, shirts, stockings and drawers."

This, indeed, was something to the point. "Distant service" meant more than a ride into Pennsylvania, and many were the conjectures as to what our destination would be. In obedience to the order, each man in the One Hundred and Sixteenth was soon supplied with the surplus clothing, and every spare moment was occupied in letting the "old folks at home" know of our orders. No doubt some who were not as "old," but just as dear, were also informed. While waiting the final order to move, private Henry W. Weeks, of Company "B," was accidentally wounded by the discharge of a pistol in the hands of a member of Company "G." It was not considered a dangerous wound, but it rendered it impossible for him to accompany the regiment, and he, with some five or six others, sick in camp, were sent to the Stewart Mansion Hospital in Baltimore.

On the morning of November 5th, orders to move at once having been received, Camp Chapin was reduced to a perfect litter of boards, poles, straw, bottles, etc., the accumulation of our short stay; and to the music of our brass band we moved down Eutaw street through some of the less pretentious streets of the city, and emerged on the wharf, which was good evidence that our extra pair of shoes would not be required immediately, the inference being that we were to go on distant service by water. The small steamers *Robert Morris* and *Baltimore* were placed at our disposal, and after some hours delay we marched on board and steamed out into the harbor, there to be transferred to the large ocean steamer *Atlantic.* When we had reached her, however, they were, for some reason, not ready to receive us, and we were forced to remain all night on board these small boats. It was a bitter cold night, and we were so crowded that hardly room could be found to stretch our tired limbs for a few hours sleep. To add to our discomfort it commenced snowing toward night, and morning found us covered with it, cold, dispirited and hungry. But the warmth of the sun, with orders to at once change our quarters to the large and commodious steamer *Atlantic*, dispelled all this, and we were soon securing, not our berths exactly, but a place to sleep on the floor of the hold.

Our good fortune in being assigned to so large and safe a ship cannot be overrated, as many of the troops were placed on board the merest apologies for ships, in the shape of small propellers, unseaworthy in every respect, and deserving the name given them by the boys, of "cracker-boxes." Four companies of the One Hundred and Fourteenth N. Y. Vols. were placed on the *Thames*, one of this class, and came as near going to the bottom, every soul of them, in the terrific gale which we encountered, as men ever did. In addition to the One hundred and Sixteenth, three companies of the One Hundred and Fourteenth N. Y. Vols. were quartered on the *Atlantic*, making about twelve hundred men, and when the immense quantities of stores for the subsistance of such a number of men, and the horses of the field and staff, with their forage, is taken into account, it will not be presumed that we had any apartments to let. For some days no accommodations in the shape of bunks were provided, but at last these were erected, and our quarters thus made much more comfortable.

It was now found that our ship was hard aground, and no efforts of her powerful engines were able to move her in the least. To lighten her, the troops were all transferred to the *Robert Morris* again, and then the ponderous wheels were set in motion with better success, for away she went, a distance of about ten miles, and then stuck fast on a bar. All efforts to again move her were unavailing, and nothing was left for us but to quietly await help. For forty-eight hours we waited as patiently as could be expected, and on the morning of the 11th no less than six steamboats came to our assistance, but their united strength, together with that of our own ship, were not equal to the task, and once more the troops were transferred to these steamers. Besides this, most of the stores were also removed, an undertaking of no mean magnitude, and which required a deal of hard work. Most heartily we labored, and our labor was rewarded, about nine o'clock A. M., November 12th, when our noble ship yielded to her fate, and left the bar behind her. After a short run of an hour or two she hove to. All day long we worked re-loading her, and at night sailed for Fortress Monroe, where we arrived the next day, November 13th.

Fortress Monroe may be a very nice place. Possibly it is a fine place to visit; but our experience, like that of Jeff. Davis, was not calculated to impress it thus upon our minds. For nearly three weeks we remained there sleeping on ship board, and spending our days in vain attempts at drilling on the sandy beach, or viewing the monster guns and other curiosities to be seen within the walls of the fort proper. O, how tired we used to get of the daily transfer from the *Atlantic* to the lighter, from that, in turn, to the shore, and at night *vice versa.*

It may have been a military necessity that the fleet should gather at this point weeks before it was intended to sail, but whether it was or not, the result of this delay was far from beneficial in more points than one. The morale of the men was fast retrograding, and worse than this, if possible, the measles broke out and made sad havoc among us; one hundred and fifty of the One Hundred and Sixteenth were left here when we finally started, nearly all sick with this disease.

After being landed from the steamer, on the 18th, we proceeded to the small village of Hampton, distant about two miles from the fort, and there received our first greenbacks, in payment for our services thus far rendered to Uncle Samuel. It was a glad day for us, as our funds were very low, and came just in time to enable us to procure some extras for our Thanksgiving dinner, that day of feasting being near at hand. Those of the officers whose finances and ideas of extortion would permit, had made arrangements with the purser to sit at the ship's table during our trip. Those not thus permitted established a separate mess, the ship's people agreeing to cook whatever should be provided. Most of the bill of fare was procured from the commissary stores, but as liberal a supply of vegetables as it was prudent to take with us, was also secured. Those who partook of the Thanksgiving dinner of this mess, will not soon forget it. The courses, though not so numerous as at first-class hotels, were sufficient for all practical purposes, and with the good feeling which followed, enlivened the day wonderfully. It may be as well to state just here, that the long delay in our departure made sad havoc with the supplies of this mess, and that ere the end of our voyage vinegar was about the only article left.

The morning of December 4th broke clear and beautiful, and brought with it orders to proceed at once to sea. This was cheering news to men housed up in such close quarters, and on every hand the "heave-a-ho!" of the sailors, as they ran up the anchors, and the cheers of the soldiers as they crowded the decks could be heard. From every mast and spar flags of all kinds and characters floated, and everything announced as best it could, that BANKS' EXPEDITION was about to sail.

At ten o'clock we steamed from the fortress, rounded Cape Henry, and when about ten miles out hove to, awaiting the arrival of the *Baltic*, which, by virtue of the presence of Gen'l Emory on board, was the flag ship. All day long we waited and watched, but not as before, for now all was new. The easy and graceful roll of our huge ship on the waves created a sensation not unpleasant. All around us lay the balance of our fleet, while the antics of the porpoises, jumping, rolling and tumbling over each other, gave us enough to engage our minds until about eight o'clock P. M., when, the *Baltic* having arrived, the fleet was divided into two lines, one led by the flag ship, the other by our own good *Atlantic*, and a flash of colored light gave the signal to go ahead.

Not a soul aboard our ship knew our destination. Col. Chapin had sealed orders, which were to be opened when off Cape Hatteras, and communicated to the captain of the vessel, and to no one else. Speculate as we would, it was to remain a secret for ten days at least, as we knew that neither would divulge it. The night was a beautiful one and many remained on deck, until quite late, watching first this thing and then that on ship board, the lights of the other vessels in our wake, as they rose and fell with the waves, or the still more wonderful phosphorescent sparkle of the water, as our monstrous wheels lashed it into fury. Tiring at last of even these new sights, the men went below to seek their first sleep on old Ocean. The night passed with nothing to mar our comfort, except it may have been the constant jar and clatter of the engine, to which we were strangers. The morning disclosed evident indications of a storm, which boded no good to weak stomachs. Most of the fleet were in sight; but as the day advanced the storm increased in fury, and when night closed in upon us, but three vessels of our line were to be seen, while that led by the *Baltic* was nowhere in sight. The recollection of that night and of the following day will never pass from the memory of any member of the One Hundred and Sixteenth. Had it not been that we were happily on board one of the staunchest crafts afloat, the recollection would be a painful one, from the fear we should have experienced; but, situated as we were, we could almost laugh in the face of old Boreas as we looked upon the boiling and seething waters around us, and felt sure of riding the storm in entire safety. Nowhere does the awful power of an Almighty hand manifest itself as in a storm at sea. Pent up within the compass of our noble ship, we could see nothing but raging billows, as far as the eye could reach in every direction. One moment we were on the crest of a wave, mountains high, and the next plunging down, down, as if to be buried beneath it, only to rise again higher than before with a feeling of relief.

With a few exceptions, every soldier on board was brought to that point where it was found impossible for him to "hold his own." Accounts were settled that had been running an indefinite period; and the digestive organs were cleansed as they had probably never been before. By those who were, fortunately, on their "sea legs," an immense deal of sport was had at the expense of the unfortunates. The woe-be gone expression on the countenance of Chaplain M——, with the painfully-anxious look of Captain W——, would have led one to suppose that both had come to that point where neither the religion of the one, nor the pleasures of the other, could afford them any relief. Much discomfort was of course experienced by the men, crowded as they were in the hold; but a constant care that the quarters were well cleansed, and that the deadlights were always open to secure good ventilation, made matters more endurable than they would otherwise have been.

This storm lasted some twenty-four hours, and when it had abated in a measure the *Baltic* appeared in sight, and not long after a signal was seen flying at her foretop; Capt. Eldridge, of our ship, soon deciphered it, and informed Col. Chapin that Gen'l Emory desired their presence on board the flag-ship. The waves were running mountains high, and it seemed like madness to attempt to reach the *Baltic* in a small boat. But the order must be obeyed. Accordingly, with great difficulty, one of the boats was lowered, and at great risk Col. Chapin and Capt. Eldridge, with six stout sailors, managed to get into it. The distance between the ships was over a mile, and with anxious hearts we watched the brave men in their perilous undertaking. They reached the *Baltic* in safety, and after a consultation returned to us, and then we pursued our course, in company with the flag-ship and two others of our fleet.

When six days out, Matthew H. Andrews, of Company "G," was taken sick with congestive chills, and lived but a few hours, notwithstanding every attention was paid him, and every effort made that was possible to save his life. At sundown of the day on which he died the body was brought on deck, and in the presence of the entire command the Chaplain read the Episcopal service for such occasions. As he pronounced the words, "we therefore commit his body to the deep," the board was slowly raised, and amid the most profound silence, the ship being stopped, it plunged into the blue waters of the sea, and all was over.

After reaching the coast of Florida, our course lay much nearer the shore than before, and the weather being delightful, we saw, dim and indistinct in the distance, what our sailor friends told us were the forests.

When we started some surmised that our destination was Wilmington, others thought it was Charleston or Mobile; but as each of these points was passed speculation ceased, and we were informed by Col. Chapin that our rendezvous would be Ship Island, where we arrived December 13th. Here we found a large fleet just about to start for New Orleans, and received orders from Gen'l Banks to unload the troops and stores, encamp on the Island, and await the return of a smaller steamer from New Orleans, it having been ascertained that our ship, with two others, could not cross the bar at the mouth of the river, on account of their drawing too much water. For the same reason the *Atlantic* was unable to get nearer than about a mile to the shore, and the next morning the men were all landed in small boats, as was also the entire cargo of commissary stores.

Ship Island is the most desolate and God-forsaken spot upon this footstool. It is situated some twelve miles from the coast of Mississippi, and is seven miles in length, varying from one-half mile to three miles in breadth. It is entirely destitute of vegetation, for the most part being simply one vast sand-bank, and is just the place to send deserters to, but hardly a suitable place for loyal soldiers. Nevertheless, it was our only resort, and, affording a change from the cramped life on shipboard to camp life once more, was hailed with pleasure by most of us. Ground was selected, and a camp laid out, which was soon covered with our tents, and presented a very familiar appearance. The whole routine of camp duties was at once resumed, and we found that our six weeks on board the *Atlantic* had made a strict attention to drilling very necessary, if we would retain our standing. Nearly two weeks were spent here, at what the boys, by common consent, called "Camp Canaan," enlivened by but one day of sport. This was Christmas. At dress parade the night before the Colonel informed the officers that he proposed, for the day, to turn over the command of the regiment entirely to the men, and instructed them to see that each Company at once elected its officers, and these in turn were to select the field officers, which were as follows, viz:

Colonel—Sergeant John H. Rohan, Company "D."
Lieut. Colonel—Sergeant Jacob C. Newton, Company "A."
Major—Corporal William Tibbetts, Company "C."

A great deal of sport was the result, as all of the officers were for the day reduced to the ranks, and were nearly all detailed for guard duty, while those not thus employed, were ordered to thoroughly police or clean up the camp, bring wood and water to cook with, etc. The object was not solely to afford amusement, but to see how well the duties which might at some future time devolve upon the men, would be performed by them. Guard mounting in the morning, and dress parade at night, were never more satisfactorily performed than on that Christmas Day; and when the time came for the officers to resume their swords, all felt that the day had been well spent.

Most of the infantry regiments composing the regular army, and some of the volunteers, were provided with dress coats and shoulder scales, which added very much to their appearance. Col. Chapin, before we left Baltimore, made a requisition for a sufficient number of these articles to supply the One Hundred and Sixteenth; and the requisition was filled, but not in time to issue them to the men before our departure. They were, therefore, carried along by the Quartermaster, and at Ship Island the regiment appeared for the first time on dress parade in their gala costume.

On the 29th, the steamer *North Star* having arrived, we proceeded to break camp, and at five o'clock P. M. left Ship Island and Camp Canaan forever, as we all trusted.

Early the next morning we entered the river by the South-west pass, and leaving the clear blue waters of the Gulf of Mexico, passed into the dirty, muddy current of the Mississippi. Forts Jackson and St. Phillip were passed about ten o'clock, and we wondered as we passed them, situated at nearly opposite points on either bank, how Farragut ever succeeded in running them. Here we caught our first sight of real Southern scenery. On either side of the river forests of beautiful magnolia, interspersed with here and there an orange grove, were constantly coming into view, while at almost regular intervals the stately mansion of the planter, surrounded with the negro quarters and immense sugar-mills, were seen. At quarantine we were boarded by a surgeon, but nothing being found which required our detention there, we proceeded on our way, and at eight o'clock P. M. anchored off the city of New Orleans.

The next morning, December 31st, Col. Chapin went ashore, reported to Maj. Gen'l Banks, and received orders to proceed some five miles above the city, to Carrollton, and report to Gen'l Emory. Returning immediately, we were soon steaming past the deserted levees and warehouses of the Crescent City, and before noon were at our camping ground, busily engaged in pitching our tents and preparing for still another home.

CHAPTER V.

The dawn of the new year eighteen hundred and sixty-three found us still hard at work—for times and seasons of all kinds receive but little attention from soldiers—and, except an occasional greeting of "a happy new year," the day passed about as others did. The camp was named, in honor of our Major, "Camp Love," and was our abode for four weeks, during which time all had permission to visit New Orleans; and as the New Orleans and Carrollton Railroad was within a hundred yards of our camp, nearly all availed themselves of the privilege. We found it a beautiful city with many points of interest, in the very best sanitary condition, clean and neat, but rebel from centre to circumference. No open insult was ever offered us, but the scowl of hate was seen on almost every countenance, indicating the inclination, if only they dared. Its business seemed to be entirely ruined. Whole blocks of stores were found tenantless, and the only trade perceptible was that carried on with the soldiers whom the citizens hated so fervently. How the people of that beautiful city must, even then, have cursed the day that saw them partakers in the great crime of rebellion.

Our month at Camp Love, like those at Baltimore, was a constant scene of drilling. From early in the morning until late in the afternoon, we were exercised in the art, and special attention was given to the minutest details of guard duty. Immediately adjoining our camp was that of the Thirty-eighth Mass. Vols., and between the two regiments a spirit of rivalry was engendered, which aided materially in insuring perfection.

Orders were received about this time giving the organization of Gen'l Banks' army. It was to be known as the Nineteenth Army Corps, and was composed of four divisions, of three brigades each, which were commanded as follows:

First Division—Brig. Gen'l Wm. H. Emory.
Second Division—Brig. Gen'l Cuvier Grover.
Third Division—Maj. Gen'l C. C. Augur.
Fourth Division—Brig. Gen'l T. W. Sherman.

These divisions were known, not by their numbers, but by the name of the general commanding—as "Emory's," "Grover's," or "Augur's" Division. The One Hundred and Sixteenth was attached at this time to the Third Brigade of Emory's Division, commanded by Col. O. P. Gooding, Thirty-first Mass. Vols., and composed, for the most part, of the troops with whom we had become somewhat acquainted, and whose colonels all ranked ours.

It soon became manifest that Col. Edward P. Chapin, of the One Hundred and Sixteenth N. Y. Vols., was just the man needed to command a brigade, and the only way in which this could be brought about was to transfer him with his regiment to some brigade where his seniority would entitle him to the command. Accordingly, on the third day of February, we were ordered to proceed to Baton Rouge, and report to Maj. Gen'l Augur. Thus we parted from all the regiments with which we had been associated in Baltimore, on Ship Island and at Carrollton; with but one of them—the One Hundred and Fourteenth—were we ever again brigaded, but with it in many subsequent places, both in victory and defeat, did we by our mutual regard make up for the separation.

The *Chee-ki-ang*, a steamer which had been engaged in the Chinese trade, was placed at our disposal, and about two o'clock P. M. of the 5th, we reached Baton Rouge. The Colonel at once reported at head-quarters, but found Gen'l Augur absent in New Orleans. We were consequently obliged to remain all night on board the wharf boat, and such of our number as could not find accommodations there were forced to take up their lodging in the street. During the night it rained very hard, which added nothing to our comfort. In the morning, Gen'l Grover, who was in command of the post during the absence of Gen'l Augur, sent a staff officer to conduct us to our camping ground, situated on what was called the clay-cut road, some little distance outside the town. He knew nothing of the disposition which Gen'l Augur desired to make of us, and as the general was expected back very soon, we were left entirely to ourselves. The ground selected for our camp was low, and, as there had been a good deal of rain, did not present a very inviting appearance. A few days' hard work, however, with pickaxe and spade, soon drained it nicely, and enabled us to make a very comfortable place of it.

On the arrival of Gen'l Augur, his division was organized. The First Brigade was composed of the One Hundred and Sixteenth N. Y. Vols., Col. E. P. Chapin; Twenty-first Maine Vols., Col. Johnson; Forty-eighth Mass. Vols., Col. Stone; and the Forty-ninth Mass.Vols., Col. Bartlett, with Col. Chapin in command. When the fact is mentioned, that these regiments with which we were brigaded were nine months regiments, nearly one half of whose term of service had already expired, the work before their Brigade Commander will be fully understood by all who ever knew anything of such short-lived enlistments. Col. Chapin well understood the task before him, and entered upon it with that energy which characterized his every movement.

As a regiment we were all proud to see him a Brigade Commander, and although it deprived us of his undivided care, we knew he would ever keep a lookout for our best interests, and see that we did not lose our high standing. In the organization of his staff he took from us Adjt. John B. Weber, and Lieuts. Robt. F. Atkins and Orton S. Clark, thus devolving upon those who remained a larger share of duty. Lieut.-Col. Robt. Cottier, by this change, became our immediate commander, and by his unbounded good nature won the respect and esteem of all.

Our position here at Baton Rouge was the most exposed of any that we had as yet occupied, being but twenty miles from Port Hudson, from which point the enemy's cavalry occasionally came to annoy our picket line. It was here that the first detail of men for picket duty was made from the One Hundred and Sixteenth; and the feelings with which we then anticipated our tour of this duty, as well as when posted on the line, can better be imagined than described. Later in our experience it was the subject of many a laugh. A stump was transformed into an enemy, intent on passing within the line. Giving no heed to the challenge, it received the contents of a musket, only to remain as dumb as before. Some unlucky quadruped, horse, cow or hog, in seeking to obtain the wherewithal to live by grazing near the line, would, perhaps, startle some sleepy sentinel and be found in the morning beyond the need of grazing. Alarms on the picket line at Baton Rouge, for some time, were very frequent, and generally were caused by something like the above; but as we became accustomed to the duty, and learned to scan closely everything within the range of vision, they became less frequent, and finally very rare indeed.

Our time was again fully occupied with drilling, and in addition to company and battalion, we were exercised twice a week at least in brigade evolutions, with occasional reviews by either the Brigade or Division Commander.

Baton Rouge is situated about one hundred and twenty miles from, and on the first bluff above, New Orleans. At the time of which we write, it contained some three thousand inhabitants; but before the war it boasted of twice that number. It is the capital of the State of Louisiana, and in the State House, which occupied a very prominent position, the ordinance of secession was passed which they imagined would sever their connection with the United States. Some two weeks before our arrival it was accidentally burned, leaving only the bare walls to mark the spot where this deed was done. Not far from the State House, and fronting the river, is the Deaf and Dumb Asylum, a large, handsome building, erected at great cost, and used then as a hospital for the army.

The streets of the city are all regularly laid out, well lined with shade trees; and graced with some fine residences. Here, however, as at New Orleans, we detected the same curl of the lip, and the same manifest hatred of both us and our cause. At the extreme northern portion of the city, stands the United States Arsenal, comprising some five or six large brick buildings, which afforded a fine place for the storage of supplies and ammunition. The bakery attached thereto afforded an abundant supply of "soft-bread," which we were very glad to receive in lieu of the "hard-tack" we had been eating so long.

Soon after the capture of New Orleans by Maj.-Gen'l Butler, he occupied Baton Rouge, with a force under command of Brig.-Gen'l Williams. On the 5th day of August, 1862, the rebel Gen'l Breckinridge appeared before it, and attempted its capture, but after a severe struggle he retreated from the field, leaving our forces the victors. Among our killed was Gen'l Williams, who fell bravely defending the old flag, in the early part of the engagement. At that time a portion of the town was destroyed by order of Gen'l Williams, the better to enable our army to defend its position, and for this a very bitter feeling was ever after manifested toward us.

During our stay here, a large fort—embracing within its limits the Arsenal—was planned and constructed, and, in honor of the hero of the battle of Baton Rouge, was called "Fort Williams."

Thus far we had seen no real service. Our time had been well occupied in preparation for efficient service whenever we should be called upon; and rumors were now floating about to the effect that Gen'l Banks was soon to advance on Port Hudson with his entire army. One very sure indication of the truth of this rumor was the reception of an order for a thorough inspection of the troops. This inspection was a very searching one, conducted by the Inspector General on Gen'l Augur's staff, who made a report of our Division to Gen'l Banks. Not long after an order was issued from the head-quarters of the Department of the Gulf, which commented very severely on the condition in which most of the troops were found, and closed as follows:

> "The General Commanding cannot close this order without first contrasting the condition of these regiments with that of the One Hundred and Sixteenth N. Y. Vols. and Thirty-eighth Mass. Vols., the zeal of whose officers, as well as men, to perfect themselves in their profession, places them far in advance, and makes them an object of emulation to all the troops in this department.
>
> "By command of MAJOR GENERAL BANKS,
>
> "RICHARD B. IRWIN,
>
> "A. A. Gen'l."

On the 8th of March orders were read on dress parade that all extra baggage was to be stored at the arsenal, including our tents, and that we were to hold ourselves in readiness to move at a moment's notice. The next day small shelter tents were issued to the regiment, and except for a very short time the following September, and while on provost duty in Washington, just previous to our return home, the One Hundred and Sixteenth never occupied anything else than these, for a shelter, during its entire term of service.

For several days troops had been arriving from New Orleans, until Baton Rouge and the country around was one vast camp, presenting a very pleasing appearance at night, with the thousand camp-fires on every side. On the 11th and 12th Gen'l Banks reviewed his army, and at four o'clock on the morning of the 14th we left our camp, took the Bayou Sara road leading to Port Hudson, and followed the advance of our army which had preceded us the day before.

We found the heat of the sun very oppressive before noon, and knapsacks, which had contained all that they could possibly be made to hold in the morning, before the sun was an hour high, were the receptacles of nothing not absolutely necessary; nevertheless, considering that it was our first march, and that all this was to have been expected, with sore feet, etc., etc., we felt that we had done very well indeed, when, at two o'clock in the afternoon, we went into bivouac, some twelve miles from Baton Rouge. The country around was levied on for such articles as our appetites called for, and we proceeded to make ourselves as comfortable as possible, in the way of care for the inner as well as the outer man.

Our bivouac was some four miles from Port Hudson, and three or four miles inland from the Mississippi river. Admiral Farragut was even then preparing to go up the river after dark, to run the rebel batteries at Port Hudson, and get above them if possible; while the army, by its presence on the land front of the enemy's works, it was hoped, would draw the fire of some of his heavy guns, and keep from the water batteries so large a number of the garrison, as to make the work of Admiral Farragut comparatively easy.

It was part of a general plan which was weeks in developing itself, and which eventuated in the capture of Port Hudson. Had its execution been as free from faults as was its inception, this rebel stronghold would not so long have defied us—but more of this in its place.

Quietly we laid ourselves down for a good night's rest, after our hard day's work, in anticipation of bloody scenes upon the morrow, when we should demand the surrender of Port Hudson, and, if need be, enforce it at the point of the bayonet. Not long, however, were we permitted to enjoy our sleep, for about ten o'clock a heavy sound, as of distant thunder, aroused us, and we heard in quick succession these sounds repeated. We were not slow in understanding that it was the rebel batteries disputing Farragut's right to ascend the river. For hours we watched, with anxious hearts and silent tongues, the progress of the fight. Our eyes followed in their upward flight the shells from our mortar boats, and saw them, with increasing velocity, descend with death and destruction where we knew the rebel camps were.

Soon after midnight the heavens began to assume a lurid light in that direction, giving sure indication that one of our fleet had been set on fire. As we strained our eyes it soon became evident that it moved down stream, the light increasing continually in brilliancy. Faster and faster it moved on, as it felt the friendly current of the noble stream bearing it away from its enemies, and nearer and nearer the fire advanced to the magazine, where thousands of pounds of powder and hundreds of shells were stored.

An aide from Gen'l Augur now informed Col. Chapin that Farragut had passed the batteries with at least two of his fleet; and ordered him to return at once with his brigade to Monticeno Bayou, and there await further orders. The One Hundred and Sixteenth was in line with but little loss of time, and just as we filed into the road the whole heavens were lit up for an instant as at noonday, and a report as of the discharge of ten thousand heavy guns deafened our ears, and all was still. The frigate ***Mississippi*** had finished its work in our navy, and was no more. The sight was grand beyond description, impressing itself upon the minds of those who witnessed it so indelibly, that the remembrance of it will never pass from their memory. As speedily as possible we retraced our steps, crossing Monticeno Bayou early on the morning of March 15th, and going into bivouac on its southerly bank. About five o'clock P. M. a very severe rain storm, accompanied with a gale of wind, opened upon us, and we found our shelter tents no protection at all. The rain poured down in torrents, soon converting our camping ground into a sheet of water, and for two hours we literally swam in the element. The storm then ceased, and by the aid of good fires we managed to dry our clothing and pass a comfortless night. The next day Gen'l Banks issued an order to the effect that the object of the expedition had been attained, and congratulating us on our success.

While in camp at Baton Rouge, and more or less intimately associating with the other regiments of our brigade, we had made in our minds an estimate of each of them, and found our estimate correct in this short campaign. The Forty-ninth Mass. Vols. was well drilled and disciplined, and we found them free from fright, when the Twenty-first Maine Vols., and Forty-eighth Mass. Vols., were only anxious to reach Baton Rouge, if not Portland and Newburyport, before they stopped. Col. Bartlett, of the Forty-ninth, was a young man but twenty-two years of age. He was a thorough soldier, who before Yorktown had lost a leg; but returning home and recovering, had raised this nine months regiment, and was now ready to risk his life once more. Col. Stone, of the Forty-eighth, was a lawyer of some distinction at home, but succeeded better with briefs than with muskets. This much by way of introduction to the following verses, relative to this campaign, written by an officer of the Forty-ninth :

THE PASSAGE OF THE MONTICENO.

Banks, of Shenandoah fame,
  By the Crescent City swore,
That Port Hudson on the river,
  Should defy his might no more.

By the Crescent City swore it,
  And sent without delay
An order through his *chief of staff*,
  To summon his array.

He summoned to him Farragut,
  And gave him orders sealed;
Then on the *Empire Parish*
  With his staff he took the *field*.

Attend ye to the story,
  Which I will now relate,
It happened in the lowlands
  Of Louisiana State.

'Twas on a cool March morning,
  When we our steeds bestrode;
And ere the day was dawning
  Struck the *Bayou Sara* road.

We crossed the Monticeno,
  By *plank bridge* and pontoon;
And halted for the *bivouac*
  Just three hours after noon.

We plucked the rails from off the fence,
  Of boards there were but few;
And spread our scanty shelter tents
  To shield us from the dew.

The air was filled with squeal of *pigs*,
  And cackle of the geese;
While stalwart oxen lost their hides,
  And simple lambs their *fleece*.

And now the night is falling,
  Soon rose the evening star,
And in the deep'ning twilight
  Gleamed camp-fires from afar.

But hark, what noise arises?
  This night we sleep no more,
For the tide of battle surges
  On Mississippi's shore.

And now an aide from Chapin,
  The driller of brigades,
An order brings to form the line
  In haste without *parade.*

Upon his own black stallion,
  Sat the gallant Brigadier,
And he called to him the Colonel,
  And he whispered in his ear,

"Our army has attacked the fort
  And been repulsed, they say ;
In haste o'ertake the Forty-eighth,
  And homeward lead the way."

The road is blocked with wagons,
  Dame Rumor flits around,
But swiftly marched the Forty-ninth
  In silence back to town.

The Forty-ninth marched swiftly,
  But swifter far than they,
Beneath their feet the Forty-eighth
  Let no grass grow that day.

Their Colonel (Stone) was ordered
  By Mr. Banks, they say,
To hold the Monticeno
  And keep the foe at bay.

This Colonel was from *Newburyport,*
  A city by the sea ;
A lawyer of repute, I ween,
  But not a warrior he.

He seemed to lose his whereabouts,
"My boys, make haste to flee;
Ye must be back to Newburyport
By dinner time," says he.

"Och, sure! bejabers, that we will!"
Responded brave O'Brien;
Then rode majestic down the line,
As fierce as any lion.

The Bayou Monticeno reached,
No foe was there discovered;
And silence was the deity
That o'er the valley hovered.

Ah! then the gallant Forty-eighth
Did mighty deeds of valor,
And courage on each countenance
Assumed the place of pallor.

And still the Colonel, homeward bent,
Their manly zeal arouses;
"Press on, brave boys, and seize and hold
Our lumber and cook-houses!"

'Twas thus for many a weary mile,
In toilsome march we find them;
Before them were their household gods,
The Forty-ninth behind them.

And now, a short half mile ahead,
The old camp greets their vision;
And each indulges sweet foretaste
Of sleep and dreams Elysian.

But look! behind a cloud of dust
Our eyes are now discerning;
It cannot be! it is, it is!
An order for returning!

The reverend Chaplain, worthy soul,
Had trotted on before;
And so he did not hear his flock,
How dreadfully they swore.

The sun was near his setting,
The clouds betokened rain;
When having reached the Bayou,
We pitched our tents again.

And now in all its terror
The elements are roaring,
And down in furious torrents
The watery flood is pouring.

O orange groves and palm trees,
O land of milk and honey,
Where zephyrs were so very soft,
And skies so bright and sunny.

We thought to spend a winter here,
Should Stanton so decree it,
Would be the thing; but on that night
We really couldn't see it.

All o'er the deeply furrowed field
The waters rose so high,
Our boys could neither make their beds
Nor keep their powder dry.

The guns with rust were covered o'er,
And many a luckless wight
Began to think his chance was slim,
If forced into a fight.

But if he dared to try his piece,
And if it chanced to go,
He had to stand at *shoulder arms*
For half a day or so.

At Bayou Monticeno,
For six long days we stayed,
To tempt the rebel soldiers
Our precincts to invade.

We gobbled up their sugar,
We licked their syrup fine;
And longed to lick the rebel
Who dared approach our line.

But only to O'Brien
  And the gallant cavaliers,
Who brought their pluck from "Rhody,"
  The enemy appears.

In vain did Mr. Dudley,
  His whole brigade deploy,
And make his grand manœuvres
  The rebels to decoy.

For as that famous army
  Aforetime marched in vain,
So Dudley did go forward
  And bravely back again.

Of all that week's adventures,
  The muse lacks words to tell;
"I never see that!" she says, with Jock,
  And sighs—"Ah! well, well, well!"

At last there came a missive,
  On dress parade 'twas read;
'Twas General Banks who sent it,
  Now what do you think it said?

"My valiant boys, take courage!
  Our object is attained,
Your cue is to be jubilant,
  For victory has been gained.

Perhaps you called it running,
  The morn you were so fleet;
But the truth is you were making
  A masterly retreat.

You see I merely wanted,
  While Farragut passed through
The gauntlet on the river,
  That you should halloo—Boo!!!

I came a week beforehand
  To Baton Rouge, you know,
And had a very grand review,
  But that was all for show.

And now, my boys, I thank ye
  For the gallant deeds ye've done;
Go back to camp and rest ye
  On the laurels ye have won.

And in the long hereafter,
  Be this your glorious boast:
We went with Banks' army
  To Port Hudson—almost!"

CHAPTER VI.

On the evening of the day following our arrival at Monticeno Bayou, the One Hundred and Sixteenth was detailed from our brigade with the One Hundred and Seventy-fourth N. Y. Vols. from the Second Brigade, and the proper complement of cavalry and artillery, with orders to proceed to Baton Rouge, where transports were in waiting to convey us up the river to Winter's Plantation, opposite from, and some three miles below, Port Hudson. From there we were to proceed, if possible, above it and communicate with Admiral Farragut.

Col. Parmalee, of the One Hundred and Seventy-fourth, by virtue of his rank, was in command of the expedition. With little delay our bivouac was broken, and after dark we set out for Baton Rouge. We arrived there in due time, embarked toward morning on a river transport, and before noon had disembarked and were marching up a road leading into a belt of woods at Winter's Plantation. The roads were in a terrible condition from the recent heavy rain, the mud in some places being knee deep; but by dint of severe labor we advanced some two miles, when we were halted, and a portion of the cavalry sent out to reconnoitre. Just what report they made to Col. Parmalee we never knew, but presumed, from the fact of our retracing our steps, that a large force of the enemy must have been seen. This presumption was strengthened after our return by an order that the troops should sleep on board the transports. Notwithstanding this, Lieut. Jones, of Company "H," a daring fellow, to gratify his love of adventure, applied that night for permission to take about twenty volunteers from the One Hundred and Sixteenth, and see what he could find in the direction of Port Hudson. Permission was given, and with a sturdy set of boys he left us early in the evening. Nothing was heard of the party until toward midnight, when the beaming face of the Lieutenant announced to those not in the "land of nod" that he *had* found something, nothing less than six prisoners, in the persons of a Captain Youngblood and five men, a rebel signal party, whom he very suddenly came upon, when about three miles out, and captured with all their signals, without the firing of a shot.

The next morning the balance of the Second Brigade arrived, and Col. Dudley, its commander, assumed command of all the forces at Winter's Plantation.

Our boys soon found, in an old store-house a short distance above where we were encamped, a large supply of prime smoking tobacco. This they were not slow in appropriating, and for months many of us were able to enjoy our pipes without calling upon the Sutler. In going to and returning from this place, we passed in plain sight of the water batteries of Port Hudson, and yet not a hostile movement had we seen; and when, the day after Col. Dudley's arrival, a company was detailed from the One Hundred and Sixteenth to escort a Lieutenant of Engineers, on Gen'l Banks' staff, to a point from which he might capture the batteries with his pencil, we could not repress a sneer. Capt. Kinney, with his company, "E," was ordered to accompany this "knight of the pencil," and obey such orders as he might give. The levee road, following the river, was the one upon which the Captain's judgment would have directed him to go, inasmuch as the levee, four feet in height, offered sure protection from both shot and shell. But, while taking this himself, the Lieutenant bravely ordered the company deployed as skirmishers, and to advance at right angles with the river. They had proceeded but a short distance when a shell came shrieking at them from across the river. For full twenty minutes the line advanced, shells dropping all around them, when the gallant young Lieutenant, having secured a safe position behind the levee, commenced his picture. Quite a number barely escaped these shells — one man, Frederick Barch, was slightly wounded, enough so to entitle him to the honor of being the first man wounded by an enemy in the One Hundred and Sixteenth.

It having been decided that no good could result from our remaining longer at Winter's Plantation, we received orders, March 22d, to return to Baton Rouge. By two o'clock in the afternoon we were all on board the *Sallie Robinson*, a government transport of the very worst Mississippi river kind. We went wheezing our way along, and, as the current was in our favor, we found ourselves alongside the wharf-boat at Baton Rouge by five o'clock. It had commenced to rain soon after our starting, and as many were forced to remain on deck with no shelter they were drenched to the skin. This did not dampen their ardor at getting back to old quarters, and ere the sun went down the One Hundred and Sixteenth occupied its old ground on the Clay-cut Road.

We found the whole of Gen'l Banks army here occupying every available spot, and extending outside the town so far as to materially increase the length of our picket-line. Orders were issued within a day or two directing the Divisions of Gen'ls Emory and Grover to proceed at once to New Orleans, while Gen'l Augur's Division was to remain at Baton Rouge. But little time was occupied in carrying it into effect, and we soon found ourselves again the only troops in town, with the exception of two regiments of colored troops, a battery of artillery and a squadron of cavalry; but with a picket-line requiring nearly one half the number of men reported for duty, to occupy. To obviate this and lessen the picket duty of the command, the troops were drawn into the town; a new line was established, with cavalry videttes on each road some distance in advance, and the One Hundred and Sixteenth prepared once again to enjoy a season of quiet.

We had seen, except at a distance, no enemy; had accomplished nothing, so far as we could see, and yet we felt more like old campaigners than when we started, two weeks before, for Port Hudson. Had we never seen any more service we should have looked back with some pride and satisfaction upon this, our second campaign. That our operations at Winter's Plantation had proved so signal a failure, we regretted; but have always thought that had Col. Parmalee advanced as soon as we landed, without being frightened by the stories of a few old negroes, and before the enemy could have suspected our intention, we should have succeeded in reaching and communicating with Admiral Farragut. As it was the One Hundred and Sixteenth had, in the persons of Lieut. Jones and his party, all the honor that attached to the affair, and we contented ourselves with it.

In the new disposition of the regiments the One Hundred and Sixteenth found itself encamped on the banks of the river, immediately in front of the Deaf and Dumb

Asylum, used, as has been stated, as a hospital. It was the most beautiful ground for a camp we had thus far had, and, were it not that almost every day some poor fellow was carried from it to his long home, would have been the most pleasant. We named it, in honor of our noble river at home, "Camp Niagara," and for two months remained there.

About the first of April, information was received that a detachment of the regiment which had been left sick at Fortress Monroe when we sailed for New Orleans, were at quarantine just below that city, unable to reach the regiment, owing to the refusal of the Surgeon to permit them to do so. Lieut. John R. Dobbins was dispatched to New Orleans with instructions to procure an order for their release, and on the third day of April he arrived at Baton Rouge with some fifty men. They had sailed from Fortress Monroe about January 1st, 1863, on board the clipper ship *Monticello*, together with detachments from many other regiments of Banks' Expedition, and made a quick trip of only eight days. They found, just before entering the Mississippi river, that a case of small pox had broken out, which, before they reached quarantine, was increased by two more, causing their detention there until the first of April—a long and tedious separation from the regiment, very far from beneficial to them.

The heat of a southern sun now began to manifest itself, and we found that drilling during the day was very debilitating. Accordingly, an hour or two in the early morning with dress parade, and another hour in the evening, was considered sufficient to keep us in good condition. Vegetation, such as there was, we found as far advanced as it would have been in our northern homes three months later, and flowers of many kinds were found in bloom. Not far from Camp Niagara, and just outside the picket line, was a magnificent magnolia grove, covering a number of acres, and from it many pure white blossoms were plucked and enclosed in letters to friends at home, as specimens of this beautiful southern flower.

Upon the lofty walls of the ruined State House a signal station had been established by Gen'l Augur. From this a fine view of the surrounding country for miles was obtained, with an extended vision both up and down the river at the expense of some tedious climbing; many, however, were found who gladly paid the price and considered themselves well rewarded. From this station, May 2d, a heavy cloud of dust was seen rising in the direction of Port Hudson, and as it approached, Gen'l Augur ordered a portion of our cavalry to reconnoitre the Bayou Sara road, upon which the force was advancing, and ascertain who and what it was. We were not left long in suspense, for in less than an hour a courier rode swiftly into town with the information that it was a large cavalry force of our own from Tennessee. None were found willing to believe this, but not much time was given for words about it, as following this courier came the advance of the column, clothed in Federal blue, and no mistake. A description of them, as they marched into Baton Rouge, covered with dust and dirt from their long ride, it would be impossible to give, nor is it a part of the record of the One Hundred and Sixteenth; suffice it to say, that the force was in command of Col. Benj. H. Grierson, and was composed of the Sixth and Seventh Illinois Cavalry. It comprised about one thousand men, who had left La Grange, Tenn., seventeen days before. They had traveled eight hundred miles, eluding the enemy almost entirely; had destroyed two railroads and property to the amount of four million dollars; had captured one thousand prisoners and over twelve hundred horses, and had now reached Baton Rouge in safety. It was one of the most brilliant raids of the war, and for it Col. Grierson was made a Brigadier General. Their arrival furnished about the only excitement of those rather dull days; but this soon lost its charm, and many expedients were resorted to to while away the time which hung so heavily on our hands. One of these was a grand vocal and instrumental concert, gotten up by some of our German singers, but participated in by some not connected with the One Hundred and Sixteenth. It was held in the Methodist Church, and drew together a large and attentive audience, who seemed highly pleased. The following was the programme :

PART FIRST.

1.—Overture, "Baton Rouge March,"—Band 50th Mass. Vols.

2.—Solo and Chorus, "Rock me to sleep, mother,"—Glee Club 116th N. Y. Vols.

3.—Cavatina, "Ernani Involani," (Verdi)—Signorina Alboni.

4.—Piano Solo, "Home, Sweet Home," (Thalberg)—Blau, 116th N. Y. Vols.

5.—Solo, "Heart Bowed Down," (Bohemian Girl—Balfe)—Sergt. Woehnert, 116th N. Y. Vols.

6.—Quartette, "The Day of the Lord," (Kreutzer)—Liedertafel, 116th N. Y. Vols.

7.—Song, "Her bright smile haunts me still,"—Signorina Alboni.

PART SECOND.

1.—"Could I hush a father's sigh," (Bohemian Girl)—Band 50th Mass. Vols.

2.—Quartette, "Faderland," (Liedertafel)—116th N. Y. Vols.

3.—Duet, "O Sponsi mi," (Rossini)—Signorina Alboni and Blau.

4.—Solo and Chorus, "Come where my love lies dreaming,"—
Glee Club 116th N. Y. Vols.
5.—Aria, (Magic Flute)—Lieut. Brunn, 116th N. Y. Vols.
6.—Mocking Bird,—Band 50th Mass. Vols.
7.—Irish Song, "Kitty Tyrell,"—Signorina Alboni.
8.—National Airs—Band 50th Mass. Vols.

It may not be amiss now to leave the One Hundred and Sixteenth quietly in Camp Niagara, and briefly note the fortunes attending Gen'l Banks in his Teche campaign.

The departure of Emory's and Grover's Divisions from Baton Rouge has been already mentioned. They proceeded to Brashier City, situated in Western Louisiana, on the Bayou Teche, from which stream the country derives its name of the "Teche." Here they found an independent brigade under the command of Brig. Gen'l Weitzel. The object to be attained was the capture of Port Hudson, and the plan of the campaign, as it finally developed itself, was to advance with the force there assembled through this Teche country to Alexandria, on the Red River; descend the Red River, cross the Mississippi, and landing at Bayou Sara, just above Port Hudson, march down upon it; while Gen'ls Augur and Sherman, with their Divisions, came up from Baton Rouge and New Orleans respectively. Uniting these forces, Gen'l Banks hoped to capture this stronghold.

On the 11th day of April, all things being in readiness, he moved with Emory's and Weitzel's commands, by land, sending Grover up the Atchafalaya River, to intercept the retreat of the enemy known to be strongly posted but twelve miles above Berwick city at Fort Bisland. Soon after they started, the crack of an occasional musket plainly indicated that the skirmishers had found an enemy, who was, however, easily driven until nightfall. The next morning a further advance was made, but it was not until late in the afternoon that the battle of Fort Bisland opened in earnest. It was a severe engagement while it lasted, but darkness entered its protest, and our forces waited the dawn of another day to renew the contest. It came in due time, and soon after daylight the attack was renewed, lasting until afternoon, when it was found that the enemy had evacuated his position, for the reason, no doubt, that Gen'l Grover had secured a position in their rear which threatened the capture of the entire garrison. No time was allowed to examine the nature of the position so unexpectedly secured, but our forces at once pushed on after the retreating rebels. Numerous stragglers were captured, but nothing was seen of the main force. A march of fifteen miles brought our army to Franklin, the largest and most important town in the Teche country. Here they found Gen'l Grover's command, which had fought the enemy at Irish Bend the day before, gaining a decisive victory. The advance was continued from day to day until May 4th, when Gen'l Banks with his victorious army entered Alexandria.

The effect of this successful march of some one hundred and seventy miles, where no federal force had ever penetrated, was most salutary upon the inhabitants, adding much to their respect for our army, and a proportionate decrease in that for the rebel army.

On the 13th the army left Alexandria, proceeding to Simmsport on the Atchafalaya River, a short distance below its junction with the Red River. On the 21st they embarked on transports and proceeded up the Atchafalaya, down the Red, and across the Mississippi to Bayou Sara, about six miles above Port Hudson, where we will leave them and return to the One Hundred and Sixteenth.

News of the success attending Gen'l Banks in his advance through Western Louisiana reached us occasionally, and as we read of the battles of Fort Bisland and Irish Bend, and of the entry of his army into Alexandria, we bit our lips and wondered why we could not have participated in them. We did not then know that this movement was but the opening of the siege of Port Hudson, in which the One Hundred and Sixteenth was destined to play as important a part as the men we envied, and that while Emory's Division could inscribe on their battle flags "Fort Bisland," and Grover's Division "Irish Bend," Augur's Division would soon be enabled to inscribe on theirs "Plain Store." Could we have foreseen it, we should have been better contented with our seemingly unfortunate lot.

On the evening of May 19th, orders were received by Col. Chapin to move his brigade early on the following morning on the Bayou Sara road, and join the Second Brigade of our Division, commanded by Col. N. A. M. Dudley, of the Thirtieth Mass. Vols., and Col. Grierson's Cavalry, then bivouaced at Merritt's Plantation, about five miles from Port Hudson. At three o'clock the next morning reveille aroused us from our slumbers, and at five o'clock we were outside the limits of Baton Rouge. That place was not seen again by any of us, except the wounded, for nearly three months. The road was very dusty, and, being shut in on either side by forests, the sun beat down upon us unmercifully. The houses and barns, and Monticeno Bayou, as we passed, wore a familiar look from our previous tramp over the same road, and we enlivened the time in conjectures as to what particular house we should pass next, or in efforts to solve the mystery of our present movement.

At two o'clock P. M. we reached Merritt's Plantation, and found the Second Brigade, with Grierson's Cavalry quietly in camp; along side of them we soon pitched our shelter tents. During the night Gen'l Augur, accompanied by his staff and escort, arrived, assumed command, and at once ordered everything in readiness for an early advance the following morning.

May 21st, so full of trial and yet of promise to the One Hundred and Sixteenth, dawned clear and beautiful. It was the crisis in the life of the regiment. Before nightfall we were, by our prowess, to be heroes, or by our cowardice a disgrace to our uniform. And now a few words in relation to our schooling for the real work of soldiers. From the time that we arrived in Baltimore, September, 1862, up to this time, our life had been one of constant labor. Hour after hour the line officers had drilled their companies in the School of the Soldier, School of the Company, and in Skirmishing. The regiment was then so thoroughly instructed in all battalion movements that company officers became almost superfluous, so well did the men understand them. Finally, as a portion of Col. Chapin's Brigade, we had received at his hands an insight into its intricate evolutions of great value to us. All this labor had not been thrown away, as was demonstrated by the readiness with which each man, from the highest in rank to the lowest, performed every duty and executed every command. We had at last become, as all good soldiers must, perfect machines, so far as our present life was concerned, and it only remained to see how we would behave under fire.

CHAPTER VII.

At six o'clock our meagre breakfast had been disposed of, and we were once more advancing in fine style in the direction of Port Hudson.

The road upon which we were marching runs from Baton Rouge to Bayou Sara, passing four miles in rear of Port Hudson, from which place another road runs, intersecting the first at a collection of two or three houses called "Plain Store" (from a store situated at the junction, and from the immediate vicinity being known as Port Hudson Plains). It was this point which Gen'l Augur was directed to reach and hold until Gen'l Banks might join him with the army, which had been operating in Western Louisiana.

Our advance was marked by nothing unusual until about ten o'clock, when our further progress was disputed by a force of the enemy, who had planted a section of artillery in our front, and seemed to say, "thus far, but no farther." A section of Battery "G" Fifth U. S. Artillery was at once unlimbered, placed in position, and for two hours or more a heavy fire was maintained. Some of the enemy's shells came unpleasantly near us, causing a duck of the head—so familiar to new hands—as they whizzed by. Their range, however, was very poor, nearly all passing over our heads and creating quite a commotion among the tree tops. A very heavy dew had fallen during the night, and as one of these shells tore through a tree under which Major Love and Captain H——— were standing, some scattering drops moistened the face of the Captain. Turning to the Major, he asked, with astonishment: "Do shells ever have water in them?" a question which but few of us could have answered from our own knowledge, but which caused the Major to laugh immoderately.

The nature of the ground gave the enemy every advantage, knowing as he did every path and road leading through the woods and fields, and fighting entirely on the defensive, he had the choice of position. It was a time of severe trial to Maj. Gen'l Augur, as, with perhaps a single exception, not one of the regiments in his Division had ever before been under fire. His anxiety must have been intense, but not a sign of it was manifested to us. He was the same cool and collected man that we had seen so often in Baton Rouge, and the fact that he was so took away half our fears.

The brigade of Col. Dudley was in advance of Col. Chapin's, and while the artillery duel was in progress the regiments of that brigade were deployed to ascertain the position of the enemy's infantry. Those of Chapin's were disposed of to support our batteries. The losses thus far had been entirely from the Second Brigade and the artillery. Not a man of our brigade had been injured. After some two hours of deafening roar of cannon, and just as Col. Chapin was directed to relieve the other brigade with his own, the firing ceased and the enemy left the field in our possession. Col. Dudley moved forward to the Port Hudson road, and proceeded to bivouac his command for the night. A section of Battery "G" Fifth U. S. Artillery was placed in this road, to support which Col. Chapin was directed to send the Forty-eighth Mass. Vols. After seeing this regiment on its way to the designated point, he proceeded to bivouac his three remaining regiments some distance below Plain Store on the Bayou Sara road. The One Hundred and Sixteenth and Forty-ninth Mass. Vols. filed to the right into an open field, while the Twenty-first Me. Vols. turned to the left. The command to "stack arms" had hardly been given, when from the direction of the battery the Forty-eighth Mass. were supporting, we heard again the report of artillery. All preparations for a bivouac were at once suspended, and, standing to our arms, we wondered what was the trouble.

One of Col. Dudley's staff officers now rode up to Col. Chapin, and directed him to send the One Hundred and Sixteenth to the front at once. The Colonel looked at him for a moment, and quietly inquired by whose direction he brought the order. "By command of *Gen'l* Dudley," was the reply, and off he rode. Turning to Adjt. Weber, the Colonel directed him to inform *Col.* Dudley that he was not aware that Gen'l Augur was either dead, or had turned over the command of his Division to him; and that until such was the fact, he should not obey any of his orders. It was well that he did so, for hardly had the Adjutant left the Colonel, before Captain Shaw, of Gen'l Augur's staff, ordered him to send to the General two of his best regiments. Accordingly, the One Hundred and Sixteenth and Forty-ninth Mass. were moved across the road into the field on the left, and followed a wagon path which intersected the Port Hudson road about where our battery was in position supported by the Forty-eighth Mass. We had advanced but a short distance on this path when we were startled by a heavy discharge of musketry immediately in our front, and simultaneously a disorganized body of panic-stricken men burst into the ranks of the Forty-ninth Mass., throwing that regiment into confusion. It was a trying moment for the One Hundred and Sixteenth; a confused mass of terror-stricken men rushing past us, flying from danger the magnitude of which we did not know. We were hemmed in on either side by a dense wood, hearing the "zip" of bullets and the whistling of shells, and knowing nothing of our situation. All this was sufficient to try the nerve and mettle of a veteran regiment, much more those of a new one engaged in its first fight. Now the benefit of our laborious attention to duty, like bread cast upon the waters, returned to us. As the voice of Maj. Love called out "stand fast," every man obeyed, and like a rock we stood until the rabble was past. Then with firm step we obeyed the command "forward march." Advancing but a short distance we were met by Gen'l Augur, who directed Maj. Love to halt his regiment and form line. The command was no sooner executed than from our rear a heavy volley of musketry was poured into us. As no time was allowed for changing front in the prescribed manner, we were simply "faced about," thus bringing the rear rank in front and forcing us to fight the battle which followed—to use a military term—by "inversion." Without delay we proceeded to return the fire of the enemy.

Some twenty or thirty rounds had been discharged, when Gen'l Augur, who was near, enquired of Maj. Love if his regiment would stand a charge. The Major replied, "The One Hundred and Sixteenth will do anything you order them to." "You have my order then, sir," said the General. Riding down the front of the regiment, exposed to the fire of his own inexperienced men as well as that of the enemy, Major Love informed the commandant of each company of the General's order, then rode back to the centre of the line, and taking off his old hat waved us on, leading us about twenty paces in advance. The yell which now broke from our throats and echoed through the woods, had in it that which the enemy must have felt to their finger tips. They knew what was coming and "stood not upon the order of their going, but went at once," retreating across an open field and into another belt of woods, where, making another stand, we were halted and again commenced to return their fire. But a very few rounds of ammunition were discharged, however, when Gen'l Augur, who had followed our movement, ordered us to charge a second time, which was as successful as the first, utterly routing the rebels, and ending the battle of Plain Store.

To secure the fruits of this victory, Companies "C," Capt. Tuttle, and "H," Lieut. Jones, were sent out to scour the woods, and soon after brought in some seventy prisoners. These prisoners were loud in their protestations of love for the old flag, and being for the most part of French origin, expressed their loyalty by crying "*Vive la Republic.*"

Thus ended the battle of Plain Store in which the only real fighting had been done by the One Hundred and Sixteenth, and which was a glorious victory. It gave to us what was of more value than millions of money would have been, the prestige of victory in our first encounter with an enemy. The character of a regiment is always settled by its first engagement. Our loss was thirteen killed and forty-four wounded. Among the latter was Lieut. Charles Boruski, of Company "E," who survived but a short time. Carefully our dead were collected, and with saddened hearts we placed them in as pleasant a spot as could be found, and

"We left them alone in their glory."

The regiment which broke in so shameful a manner and created such disorder in the Forty-ninth Mass., was the Forty-eighth Mass., Col. Stone. On the first approach of the enemy they left the section of artillery which they were to support, and scattered like sheep. It is but just to say, however, that two companies, under Lieut. Col. O'Brien, did not join in the rout, but remained at their post until reinforced.

Col. Bartlett of the Forty-ninth, by the exercise of wonderful control over his men, soon brought order out of confusion, and stood ready to assist the One Hundred and Sixteenth should help be required.

Col. Chapin, by his position as commandant of the First Brigade, was of necessity deprived of leading his regiment in this its first fight; but he was at all points where his presence was required. One of his staff-officers, Lieut. Tucker, had a leg shot away by a shell during the engagement. The same shell striking the ground immediately in front of the Colonel's horse, caused the animal to throw up his head, striking the Colonel on the nose, but doing no harm further than causing a severe bruise.

After the fighting was all over, and it had been ascertained beyond a peradventure that the rebels had retired within their fortifications, Gen'l Augur rode up to Col. Chapin, and said: "I congratulate you, Colonel, on the decided victory we have gained to-day, especially as to your regiment, the One Hundred and Sixteenth, am I mainly indebted for it. They have most gallantly driven Miles' Legion, who claim never to have been driven before." After he had ridden away, the Colonel said to those around him, while his face lighted up with a smile: "That hour's work more than repays me for all the care and anxiety the regiment has cost me."

To Maj. Geo. M. Love were we indebted for the success of that day. To his almost unexampled gallantry in leading the charge in person, was due the victory of the One Hundred and Sixteenth at Plain Store.

The next two days were spent in quietly awaiting the arrival of Gen'l Banks from Bayou Sara, and of Gen'l T. W. Sherman from New Orleans, that together we might invest Port Hudson, and in the name of our common country demand its surrender. These forces having arrived, at six o'clock on the morning of the 24th we left the spot so memorable to us, and taking the direct road leading into Port Hudson had ere nightfall made connections with the troops on our right and left, within less than a mile of the fortifications. Then commenced a work which lasted us for six long weeks, and was attended with more hardships than we had ever dreamed could befall us.

That the Mississippi River affords many points where the rebels could plant batteries and impede navigation no one at all acquainted with its course will dispute. Any one who has traveled along the noble stream will acknowledge that, of the many places of this kind to be found on its banks, none were more favorable than Port Hudson. Situated in a bend of the river, some two miles in extent, and on a bluff nearly one hundred feet above high water mark, it was on the river front perfectly impregnable. A large tract of table land, containing more than one thousand acres, extends back from the river something over a mile, at which distance it breaks off into very rough and broken land, covered with forests and cut up with numerous ravines. Here it was that the rebels had constructed their line of earth-works, extending seven miles from the river below to the river above the village. The works themselves were not as strong as they might have been, or as they would have been had not so much reliance been placed upon the natural defences of the position which it was presumed would add at least one-half to their strength. Every thing possible was done to aid even these natural defences. Ravines, by which an enemy might approach the works, were filled with huge rocks and trees, while for a distance of a thousand yards in front of the fortifications the woods had been all cut down and the trees left in every conceivable position, making what is termed a "slashing." It was a difficult task to get through this "slashing" even when alone, and with no enemy to endanger your life.

On the evening of May 24th, as has been stated, the different Divisions composing Gen'l Banks' army had formed a continuous line, the flanks touching the river above and below the doomed place, and we had it invested. On the extreme right was Gen'l Emory's Division, on the right centre Gen'l Grover's, on the left centre Gen'l Augur's, and on the extreme left Gen'l T. W. Sherman's, with Col. Grierson's Cavalry to protect the rear. The whole force with which the siege of Port Hudson was commenced was twenty thousand men, distributed over a line at least eight miles long. The base of supplies was Springfield Landing, some four miles below Port Hudson on the river.

Early on the morning of the 25th, Col. Chapin directed Company "B," Capt. Barnard, and Company "G," Capt. Sizer, sent out as skirmishers on his brigade front. They were deployed and advanced to the edge of the woods in our front, where they remained all day. A pleasant spot within supporting distance of them was selected, where the rest of us remained, getting used to the roar of artillery which every hour increased. A council of war was held during the day by Gen'l Banks, in which all the General Officers participated, and at which it was determined to at once assault the works. But two of the Generals dissented from this determination—Gen'l Augur and Gen'l Weitzel—whose better judgment was, in the fatal result of that assault, recorded, as it were, in blood.

In accordance with this determination, Col. Chapin received orders calling for volunteers from his brigade, as follows:- one field officer, four captains, six lieutenants, and two hundred enlisted men, the whole to constitute a storming party to precede his brigade in the assault. Fifty of this number were to carry "fascines" (a bundle of branches five or six feet in length), which were to be thrown into the ditch immediately in front of the works, to enable those who followed them to cross it without difficulty.

The following named officers and men of the One Hundred and Sixteenth volunteered for this terrible duty: Maj. George M. Love; Captains John Higgins, Richard C. Kinney, and Charles F. Wadsworth. Lieutenants Jas. S. McGowan, Wilson H. Grey, Warren T. Ferris, Wm. J. Morgan, and John R. Dobbins. Sergeants Rollin C. Hubbard, Jno. L. Carmer, Harry H. Enders, John Hopps, John G. Dayton, Chas. B. Adams, and H. W. Wahley.

Corporals—Authur F. Smith, Wm. H. Rose, George Townsend, Lewis Filbert, Charles Wall, Jethro Bale, Joshua D. Baker, C. Smith, Augustus Cadugan, Addison Cole, John Miller, Horace A. Paxton.

Privates—John H. Dingman, Charles E. Paine, John Farrell, Isaac Colvin, Wm. H. Sawdy, Wallace Calkins, Jehial Woodard, Jacob Deiffenbach, John Voll, Michael Bund, C. Fisher, F. Hildebrand, Wm. Bump, P. Foster, F. Hellreigle, Jno. Gethiker, F. Caldwell, Chas. Chittenden, James P. Tabor, E. C. Bacon, Lloyd Rice, Jas. H. Weingarden, Donald McGilvary, Thos. Griffiths, Christian Weller, Wm. B. McMichael, David Crosby, Theodore B. Norris, John Bump, Wm. Martin, Daniel H. Hubert, Payson Morrow, James Cameron, Jacob Zumstein, Curtis Rowan, James F. Ryther, James Maloney, Theodore Robinson, Wm. B. Lathrop, John Dorner, John Wilson, Henry Myers, David Weissinger, Henry W. Eno, Chas. Bramiller and Milton Hill.

The whole regiment were busily engaged the next day in preparing the "fascines," and making such other preparations as were possible for the coming assault.

Col. Chapin felt the necessity of becoming as well acquainted with the ground over which his brigade must pass ere they reached the fortifications as was possible. Upon the extreme right of our whole line he was informed there was a signal station, from which a splendid view of the whole of the enemy's works and the grounds intervening was to be had. He lost no time in climbing to its summit, and on his return was so well satisfied with his examination that he confidently predicted our success. He did not take into consideration the fact, that from so great a distance he was unable distinctly to see the impediments which had been thrown in our way; but from the fact that to him it seemed a level plain, thought that it was so. Alas, before forty-eight hours had passed, he found his brigade inextricably fixed in one mass of fallen trees, and at the mercy of the foe.

CHAPTER VIII.

THE morning of May 27th dawned upon us as others had done before, and gave no token of what was in store for us.

Col. Chapin was astir bright and early, and ordered Companies "B" and "G" again deployed as skirmishers, the first upon the left of the road leading into Port Hudson, and the latter upon the right. They were directed to advance to the outer edge of the slashing, there to remain until the grand assault, when they were to push on and getting as near the works as possible, act as sharp-shooters, and prevent the rebels from making use of their heavy guns. Having seen that the order was obeyed in its first part, he turned his attention to Holcomb's Second Vermont Battery, attached to his brigade, which he handled with great skill, training some of the pieces with his own hands and sending the shells so much to the annoyance of the enemy as to elicit a sharp response at almost every discharge.

About noon the whole brigade was moved forward into the woods, immediately in rear of the line held by Companies "B" and "G" of the One Hundred and Sixteenth. An hour was spent in getting the brigade line properly formed, and organizing the storming party from which so much was expected. Many more than the required number had volunteered from the brigade, and the field officer chosen was Lieut. Col. James O'Brian, of the Forty-eighth Mass., as brave and gallant a man as ever wore a leaf; full of Irish fire, and well adapted to lead the stormers in their perilous undertaking. The wisdom of the choice was made sadly manifest when his lifeless body was found the next day as near the coveted works as flesh and blood could get. From the One Hundred and Sixteenth Lieut. William J. Morgan was selected to command its portion of the party, and when all the necessary preparations had been made, Col. Chapin advanced to the storming party and after a few words to them as a body, addressed the men of the One Hundred and Sixteenth as follows: "Men of the One Hundred and Sixteenth, you must do your whole duty to-day. Remember that you do not go unsupported. My brigade will follow close on your heels. Do your duty and we will drink Mississippi water to-night." Then turning to Lieut. Col. O'Brian he said, pointing to the rebel flag which could just be seen through the trees, "Colonel, I want you to notice the man who takes down that flag, and give me his name." O'Brian smiled as he replied, "Colonel, I have designs on that flag myself, and if I secure it will you promise to strike a blow for my country if ever it attempts to gain its liberty?" With a grasp of the hand he answered, "If I am able to wield a sword, I will."

Every thing was now in readiness, and yet the moment had not come. As we waited a painful silence crept over us; but few words were spoken by any one, and those few were in whispers. They were awfully solemn moments, such as only those who have experienced them can appreciate. Home, with all its endearing memories rose before us, and the dear face of a father, mother or wife, would present itself, causing more than one eye to grow dim with moisture, and yet no one could detect a faltering look; all seemed, and all were, calm and determined, ready to do and die should God so ordain. During these few moments, Col. Chapin, with some three or four other officers, mounted a large tree which had been blown over and lodged. From this the Colonel swept with his field-glass the ground in our front, and as he looked exclaimed, "My God!" evidently comprehending at that moment the impossibility of our succeeding. At this moment the Second Vermont Battery, Capt. Holcomb, was run up the road leading into Port Hudson as far as possible, and opened a terrific fire upon the works. It was hoped that this would drive the enemy from their artillery, and give us a better chance to reach the fortifications; but the distance was too great, and it proved only a signal to the rebels that they might expect an attack from that point. This cannonading was continued for about ten minutes, and as it ceased, "forward," rang out the clear voice of Chapin, who, placing himself by the side of Col. O'Brian, led us out of the woods. With a deafening yell the One Hundred and Sixteenth essayed to repeat its glorious charge at Plain Store; but no sooner were we out of the woods and in view, than a perfect hail storm of solid shot, shell, grape and cannister, and bullets, was opened upon us; and as we found our way impeded by the dense slashing, our line of battle soon lost its precision, at length disappeared entirely, and we were a disorganized mass, each man seeking shelter behind some friendly log or stump. From behind these we were enabled to return the fire of the rebels, and with such directness that we soon silenced all his heavy guns, and were only annoyed by bullets. After leading Col. O'Brian and his storming party out of the woods, and directing him as to the course he should take, Col. Chapin gave his attention to his brigade, urging on the men with alternate cheers and threats. Conspicuous by his dress coat, and also by a white Panama hat which he wore, he was, no doubt, singled out as the commanding officer by some rebel sharpshooter. He was first wounded in the knee, which did not, however, disable him, and almost immediately shot through the brain, the ball entering just under the eye and passing out of the back of the head, killing him instantly. This was in the early part of the engagement, and leaving the brigade without a commander to direct its movements, each one pursued the course which to him seemed best.

While lying here and wondering if we were not to be reinforced, and thus enabled to rise from our shelters and make one more attempt to gain the prize, we saw the beautiful folds of our spangled banner emerge from the woods. It was the Second La. Vols. (white), Col. C. J. Paine, of Dudley's Brigade, and a noble sight it was to see them bravely advance to our assistance; but it was of no avail, they were forced to seek shelter, as we had done, from the leaden hail. Soon after this our hopes were once more revived, as away on our left we heard the lusty cheers of Sherman's Division. Occasional glimpses of their line could be obtained as they advanced in splendid style, but ere the works were reached they were forced, like us, to give up the attempt.

Toward sundown a flag of truce was displayed by some of Gen'l Grover's troops, who had charged before we did, and almost instantly every rebel gun was silenced. The flag of truce was unauthorized by Gen'l Banks, or by any general officer, but was the freak of some badly demoralized man; however, we were not slow in taking advantage of it, and before it was ascertained that it was unauthorized most of us were back within the woods. All of the wounded and some of the dead were brought back with us, among whom was the body of our lamented Colonel. Not many men would have been missed, and his untimely death as sincerely mourned by those not relatives, as was Col. Chapin; and as many a sun-burned, powder-begrimmed man looked upon those features so mangled, he would turn away and shed bitter tears that the man he had learned to love was cold in death, and that the voice it had been his pleasure to obey was hushed forever. Of those who mourned his loss that night, Gen'l Augur, our Division Commander, was one; and as Adjt. Weber applied for permission to proceed at once to New Orleans with the body, he replied, "God bless the dear fellow; yes, of course, you can go." An escort was provided, and before the morning of May 28th dawned the body was at the old head-quarters in Baton Rouge. Without any delay transportation was secured, and it was conveyed to New Orleans. Here it was properly embalmed, placed in a metallic case, and, fortunately, Capt. Eldridge, with whom our trip from Fortress Monroe was made, was found. During our four weeks stay on board his ship, the *Atlantic*, he had become very much attached to Col. Chapin, and was pained to learn that his course was so soon ended. He was now Captain of the steamer *Fulton*, just about to start for New York, and to his care Adjt. Weber gave the remains, together with the faithful Tim Flannigan and the horse presented to the Colonel in Buffalo.

That night of May 27th, with its terrible memories, will never be forgotten by the men of the One Hundred and Sixteenth. One by one, as fast as found, our brave comrades were brought in, some few slightly, many very badly wounded, until our loss was found to be one hundred and one enlisted men killed and wounded, besides Col. Chapin killed, and Maj. Love, Lieuts. Grey, Jones and Morgan, wounded. Maj. Love's wound was a severe one, the ball entering just under the shoulder blade, and lodging. It made it necessary for him to leave us, and with all the wounded who could be moved he went to Baton Rouge. Lieut. Jones was a very great sufferer from his wound, and from the first all hopes of his recovery were given up. He lingered some two days in great agony, and was at last freed from suffering by death.

Sad, indeed, were our faces as we gathered round bivouac fires that night. The work we had hoped to accomplish that day was still unperformed, and as we heard the groans and entreaties of the wounded, not far from us, we could but think that the next trial made would see some of us in a like condition. Besides all these sad reflections, our Colonel was dead, our Major was severely wounded, and Lieut. Col. Cottier had, ere we left Baton Rouge, tendered his resignation, and now an order was received from Gen'l Banks accepting it. Thus we were deprived of all our field officers, and we expecting, we knew not how soon, to make a second assault upon the besieged place. Truly it was a sad time for the One Hundred and Sixteenth.

We parted with Lieut. Col. Cottier with unfeigned regret. He had endeared himself to all by his genial good nature, which nothing could in the least disturb. We had found him with us at Plain Store, and in the fatal assault of the 27th, doing his utmost to give us victory. He was without an enemy in the regiment, and all wished him well as he left us.

Capt. John Higgins, of Company "D," and Capt. John M. Sizer, of Company "G," were appointed by Gen'l Augur acting field officers, and they were subsequently commissioned and mustered into the service as Lieutenant Colonel and Major respectively.

The next day Col. Johnson, of the Twenty-first Me. Vols., being the senior colonel in the brigade, assumed command, but retained it only until the following day, when, by order of Gen'l Augur, the Second La. Vols. (white), raised in New Orleans by Gen'l Butler, was transferred from the Second Brigade to ours, and its Colonel, Charles J. Paine, by virtue of his seniority, relieved him. Col. Paine was a Massachusetts man, a splendid soldier in every particular, a rigid disciplinarian, and we soon found in him a worthy successor to Chapin. He remained in command until the following August, when he went North, and was subsequently made a Brigadier General and Brevet Major General of Volunteers, serving again under Gen'l Butler in the Army of the James.

It was now determined that our only hope of success was in laying siege to the place, and unless it surrendered, destroy their artillery and thus make a second assault less disastrous, if not successful. Accordingly large numbers of the heaviest siege guns were brought into requisition, and the troops kept constantly employed at night in erecting earthworks for them. In addition to this, one company each day was sent out as sharpshooters, to within three or four hundred yards of the enemy's works. This duty was extremely hazardous, and fully as fatiguing as that of digging earthworks, as will be seen by the following extract from a letter of one of the officers, detailing a day's experience with his company on the advanced line: "The weather was intensely hot, and the water we had to drink was warm, and unpalatable, being obtained from a swamp. To lie all day on a field under a burning sun, or a shower of rain, your only amusement watching the enemy, and firing an occasional shot, which was sure to bring a dozen in reply, compelled to satisfy thirst with swamp water, and hunger with a piece of salt meat and a few hard tack, is certainly a situation to which the term luxurious cannot be naturally applied."

The work of erecting batteries was completed on the morning of June 12th, and at 12 o'clock noon on that day, every piece of artillery, both from our land batteries and from the gunboats on the river, was opened on the doomed place. For nearly an hour was that terrific cannonade continued, and then Gen'l Banks, by flag of truce, demanded the immediate surrender of the place. The soldierly reply of the rebel Gen'l Gardner was, that his duty was to defend, not to surrender.

The following night, June 13th, the One Hundred and Sixteenth was ordered to the support of Holcomb's Battery, nicely posted in earthworks, within four hundred yards of the fortifications. About two hours before daybreak, June 14th, we were moved to the left some distance, and with the other regiments of our brigade, directed to deploy five companies as skirmishers, holding the remaining five in reserve. These skirmishers were to creep as near to the works as was possible, and at a given signal, were to open a heavy fire on the enemy, while all the artillery followed suit. The object of this movement was to lead the enemy to suppose that we in the centre were the attacking force, and while he bent all his energies to defend this point, the real attack was to be made on the right and left, where it was hoped no men, or but very few, would be found to resist.

Our orders were obeyed to the very letter, and after two or three hours the five companies in reserve were also deployed and joined the skirmish line. Our artillery had by this time dismantled all the heavy guns of the rebels, and we found it a much easier day's work than that of May 27th, owing to the fact, that only muskets were used against us, and also that our two weeks experience had been of great value to us. All day, and until nightfall, we remained here under the broiling heat of a summer sun, and were then withdrawn.

In this engagement the One Hundred and Sixteenth lost one officer and four enlisted men killed, and twenty-three wounded. The officer killed was Lieut. Timothy Linahan, a brave little fellow, who did honor to the One Hundredth N. Y. Vols. from which he graduated. This list was much smaller than the one we had mourned three weeks before, but still sufficiently large as to again depress our spirits, and lead us to question if our commander-in-chief knew aught of his profession.

On our left the forces under Gen'l Dwight attempted the capture of what was termed the "citadel," situated just on the brink of a deep ravine, the strongest point in the whole line of defences, and the possession of which was the ambition of the said Dwight. He failed, however, to realize his hopes, getting his troops into such a position under the guns of this work, that they could neither advance or retire, and quietly remained there all day.

The assault on the right, although gallantly made, and sustained with brave determination throughout the entire day, was unsuccessful, so far as gaining an entrance was concerned; but our line was advanced in some places, to within fifty yards of the rebel works, an advantage patent to all eyes, and which enabled us to mine their works subsequently with greater ease than would have been the case had we been three hundred yards distant.

Col. E. B. Smith, of the One Hundred and Fourteenth N. Y. Vols., fell in this attack mortally wounded, and survived but a few hours, while Lieut. Col. Rodman, of the Thirty-eighth Mass. Vols., was killed. On the 27th of May, the same day upon which we lost our dearly loved Chapin, Col. D. S. Cowles, of the One Hundred and Twenty-eighth N. Y. Vols., was also killed; so that in these two assaults on Port Hudson, these four regiments who were brigaded together at Baltimore, who came upon Banks' Expedition together, and whose history had been more or less intimately connected, were now, by the fortunes of war, deprived of their commanders, and thus enabled to sympathize with each other in their sorrow, and mourn each other's loss.

CHAPTER IX.

Upon the right, where Gen'l Grover's troops had effected so close a lodgment, extensive preparations were now made to mine the works of the enemy. Day and night without any cessation men were kept at work, until they had drifted in so far that the sound of the rebels inside their fortifications could be distinctly heard nearly over head; but as all this does not immediately concern the One Hundred and Sixteenth, it must not be enlarged upon; suffice it to say, that ere the mine was exploded, Port Hudson was surrendered, and many lives no doubt were saved.

Our brigade was now very much reduced in numbers by the long lists of killed and wounded, and by sickness, of which, from exposure, there was considerable, especially in the Twenty-first Me. Vols., and Forty-eighth Mass. Vols. Upon our front were three batteries, one of which—Holcomb's Second Vermont—was advanced well up to the enemy's works. One half at least of the command was required to support these batteries, while with the remaining half we had to cover our entire front, a mile at least, with sharpshooters by day, and pickets by night. From this it may be presumed that our duties were laborious in the extreme; seven-eighths of our time was spent either in the rifle pits, supporting these batteries, or on the advanced line of sharpshooters and pickets. This latter duty, although it may seem strange to the reader, was always preferred, as there we were enabled to choose our positions, and from behind some log, watch, as intently as a cat does a mouse, the first "Johnnie" who dared to show so much as his top-knot. This was seldom our good fortune, for our few weeks at Port Hudson had made excellent marksmen of most of us, which fact the rebels had learned, and to save their precious heads, used sand-bags for a protection. Two of these were placed upon the parapet, with a slight interval between, and then one was put upon the two, covering the opening and forming a loop-hole, from which they could watch us in security, while our only hope was to send our compliments through these small holes. This was no easy task, but there was excitement about it, and very few were found who did not prefer it to the support of the batteries. There we were forced to crowd into a narrow pit, some two feet deep, and jammed and wedged together, sore from bruises, thirsty and hungry, but above all, dirty beyond anything our friends at home would have believed, and beyond our ability to prevent, we lay under a hot June sun during the long hours of the day.

During these days the time of some of the nine months regiments expired, and much dissatisfaction was manifested that Gen'l Banks did not at once discharge them and send them home; but except in two instances no open mutiny was indulged in. These two regiments were the Fourth and Forty-eighth Mass. Vols. The former was attached to Grover's Division, and from a lack of ability or willingness on the part of their brigade commander, they were allowed to go to such lengths, that the whole regiment were put in arrest by Gen'l Banks and confined at his head-quarters until a court-martial finally sent a good portion of them to the penitentiary at Baton Rouge.

The latter had the honor of belonging to our brigade,

and the use of stern measures by Col. Paine, the brigade commander, saved them the open disgrace they so richly deserved. It was on one of the nights soon after their time had expired, according to their figuring, that the Forty-eighth was directed to proceed to Holcomb's Battery and relieve the One Hundred and Sixteenth, who had been on duty there for twenty-four hours. Col. Paine was informed that one company had held a meeting shortly after the receipt of this order, and solemnly resolved that they would do no more duty; but he hardly thought that men who had been under the command of Col. Chapin and himself would *dare* to attempt the carrying out of such a resolution. Not long after, however, word was brought that Col. Stone had, to his disgrace, left his bivouac with but nine companies, and that the mutineers were there congratulating themselves that the assertion of their rights was so successful. Sending an aide with instructions to bring the company to his quarters at once, he dispatched another to his own regiment, the Second La. Vols. (white), with an order for Capt. H——, with his company, to report at the same place, and waited their coming.

In about half an hour the gallant sons of Massachusetts marched up with a determined look, which seemed to say, "We have taken a stand upon our rights, sir, which you cannot force us to retract." They were formed immediately in front of the Colonel's tent, and just then Capt. H——, with his company, arrived. They were formed in rear of the mutineers, and when quiet had been secured, Col. Paine ordered Capt. H—— to cause his company, whose pieces were already loaded, to come to a "ready," and if any man in the other company attempted to leave, to shoot him down. A perceptible change was seen to pass over the faces of the mutineers at this unexpected mode of treatment. Calling up each man, he inquired his name and rank, and then demanded if he *had* refused to do duty, and if he *still* refused. From the record made upon the spot, but three of the entire company were found who had the courage to answer the last question in the affirmative. These three were placed under guard, and the rest of the company proceeded, without a murmur, to join their regiment in the rifle pits, and this was the last of the mutiny of the Forty-eighth Mass. Vols.

The sap on Grover's front was every day gaining ground, and it was presumed that when finished and exploded, a breach would be made in the enemy's works sufficient to enable our army to enter at once. However, to prevent any failure, it was deemed best to organize one storming party for the whole command, to be composed of volunteers from each regiment. These were to be collected in a body and officered and drilled as a regiment in the peculiar duties expected of them.

On the 24th of June an order was received calling for these volunteers; and although the bitter experience of our two unsuccessful assaults it was feared would prevent any response, yet twenty-four brave boys were found in the One Hundred and Sixteenth who were willing to offer themselves once more for this perilous undertaking. Their names were as follows: Frank Bentley, Isaac Colvin, Philip Linebits, Daniel Covensparrow, Andrew Cook, Charles Fisher, F. Hildebrand, H. Daniels, John M. McComber, Christian Grawi, Francis Oberfill, Frederick Niewardie, James Gallagher, Thomas Maloney, Cornelius Fitzpatrick, Theodore Hansel, Frederick Weber, Samuel Whitmore, William Martin, Fred Jost, Jacob Zumstein, Henry Favre, Jacob Tschole and Albert D. Prescott. They left us and joined the other volunteers, who were organized into two battalions under the command of Col. Birge, of the Thirteenth Conn. Vols. They remained there until after the surrender of Port Hudson, an occurrence which prevented the necessity of another assault, and doubtless saved most of their lives.

Amid all our trials there were occasional occurrences which served to enliven our dreary hours of duty, and afforded us many a hearty laugh. Upon the staff of Col. Paine was Lieut. R——, of the gallant Forty-eighth Mass. Vols., who acted as Commissary of Subsistence, and from the nature of his duties was not expected to establish for himself much of a reputation for bravery, nor was it necessary that he should gain a name for the opposite; but in spite of himself he did, and many were the practical jokes perpetrated at his expense. Brigade head-quarters was established in the edge of a piece of woods, through which a road ran, terminating about half a mile distant at the lower battery, which it was part of our duty to support. Every night after dark, a regiment marched through this road to relieve the one posted there the night before, and it was customary for one of the staff officers to accompany it. A plan had been matured by Lieut. A——, of the staff, to give Lieut. R——, the Commissary, a good scare, having first secured the countenance of the Colonel, who enjoyed a good joke in its place as well as any one. Accordingly, by direction of the Colonel, he informed R—— that it would be his duty, just at dusk, to conduct the relieving regiment through this road to the lower battery; and to prevent the possibility of his returning by any other route, or of his not coming back at once, Lieut. P——, also of the staff, accompanied him. Mounting their horses they were soon on the way. Lieuts. A——, W—— and C——, enveloping themselves in some old mosquito bars, that they might, in the dusk of the evening, resemble as closely as possible our greyback enemies, and arming themselves with muskets, proceeded some distance down the road, ensconced themselves behind some large trees, and waited the return of R—— and P——. In a short time the sound of their horses' feet was heard as they rode leisurely back, and soon their forms appeared. Allowing them to get nearly past, the concealed "Johnnies" rushed out and demanded their immediate surrender. R—— was upon the point of acceding to the demand, when P——, who was in the secret, urged his horse forward at a gallop, calling to R—— to come on, which he was not slow in doing, riding off at full speed amid the click of two or three musket locks. Thinking that the ruse had worked splendidly, the lieutenants proceeded back to head-quarters, entering at intervals to escape detection. Here they found R—— in a high state of excitement, his eyes protruding and his hair almost on end, recounting to the Colonel how he and Lieut. P—— had been nearly taken prisoners by the rebels. To the question of the Colonel as to how many there were, he replied, that there could not have been less than a dozen. It was manifest that the joke could be extended, and all soon began to show evident signs of fear. A reconnoisance was at once proposed, and mounting their horses, they all started once more down the road, R—— gradually falling behind and not venturing very far from head-quarters. Pretending to see something alarming, those in advance wheeled their steeds and rushed back, only to find R—— there before them, and with exultant look, demanding if they thought him a fool. Several times this performance was repeated, each time to the increased excitement of poor R——. At last, wearied with exertion, the whole staff assembled around the Colonel and gravely discussed the matter. One proposed that the brigade be turned out and a thorough examination of the woods be entered upon; another, that Gen'l Banks be at once informed that a force of the enemy had broken through our line, and were now prowling about our camps. The Colonel at last expressed himself as of the opinion that it would not be safe to go to sleep with these fellows in such close proximity, and with only the head-quarter's guard to care for the horses, equipments, etc. He therefore directed Lieut. P—— to remain on duty until midnight, then to call Lieut. R——, who was to remain in charge until daybreak, at which time Lieut. C—— would relieve him. Completely exhausted, R—— announced that if he was to go on duty at midnight, he should at once retire; after which the restrained mirth of the company burst forth, and after a hearty laugh at poor R——'s expense, all turned in except P——, who allowed that he was going to see the thing out. Sitting down, he occupied an hour or so in letter writing, and then before midnight armed himself with a musket and proceeded to rouse R——. He found him sleeping very soundly, but after repeated efforts at last awoke him, and told him that it was the Colonel's order that he should shoulder the musket and walk a certain beat which he pointed out to him, carrying his gun either at a "support," or a "right shoulder shift," and consoling him with the thought that he was to have the best part of the night left him. Without a moment's pause, from that time until daybreak, he walked his beat as faithfully as ever soldier did. Of course the story circulated throughout the whole brigade, but all were careful to keep the secret from the redoubtable lieutenant, who told it himself with great gusto, to the infinite delight of all.

Some months after, and just as Col. Paine was about leaving for the North, he told R—— the whole story, who took it all in good part, but avowed his determination, ere he left, to get even with the staff.

Our glorious Fourth of July was well kept by the entire command, national salutes being fired at daybreak, noon and sundown, different only from those fired at our homes in the number of guns used; a difference so marked, that none of us ever have since heard the like.

Two days later the glad news of the surrender of Vicksburg to Gen'l Grant enabled us for the first time in many days to exercise our lungs, which opportunity was embraced with a hearty good will. Our lusty cheers were no doubt divined by the besieged garrison, but many inquiries like this—"I say, Yank, what are you'ns cheering for," were yelled at us; and when they were informed that Grant had captured Vicksburg, with Pemberton and his entire army, some would not believe it, while many evinced no surprise.

That night two companies of the One Hundred and Sixteenth under command of Capt. Kinney, occupied the advanced post at Holcomb's Battery, and between twelve and one o'clock, a bugle from within the works was heard to sound the call, "cease firing." Immediately thereafter, a party of horsemen were seen advancing carrying a lantern elevated on a pole. They were halted and duly challenged by Capt. Kinney, who was informed that they had a dispatch for Gen'l Banks from Gen'l Gardner, and requested that it be forwarded at once. It was sent to Col. Paine, who directed Lieut. Clark, of the One Hundred and Sixteenth, serving on his staff, to proceed to Gen'l Banks' head-quarters, some two miles in the rear, and deliver it. It read in substance as follows: "I am informed that Gen'l Pemberton has surrendered Vicksburg to Gen'l Grant. If the report is true, I have to request a cessation of hostilities, with a view to an agreement of terms for the surrender of Port Hudson." In reply, Gen'l Banks transmitted a copy of Grant's dispatch to him announcing the surrender, and utterly refused a cessation of hostilities, demanding an unconditional surrender. On the reception of this reply, which was delivered by Brig. Gen'l Stone, Gen'l Gardner at once surrendered the post and garrison. Three commissioners from each side were occupied during the whole of July 8th, in making the exact terms of capitulation, during which time the rebels freely visited our works and were visited in return by us, hobnobbing in as friendly a manner as though nothing like enmity had ever existed between us. Terrible were the stories they told us of hunger appeased with mule meat, and freely were they supplied by us with hard tack and coffee, which they devoured so greedily as to leave no doubt in our minds of the truth of the stories. In return, they gave us of their very limited supply of corn cakes which we found exceedingly palatable, after weeks spent in munching Uncle Sam's hard tack. Canteens were exchanged, and many mementoes of the siege of Port Hudson were secured by us. All this friendly intercourse was the result of mutual respect. We could not but admire the endurance and pluck manifested so often by these men we were now conversing with, even if that endurance was in a mistaken cause; nor could they but admit that our assaults upon their works had exhibited many daring deeds of valor, and from being deadly enemies seeking each other's lives, we were now on as friendly terms as was possible under the circumstances.

We found the men tired and sick of the war, ignorant almost to a man of exactly what they were fighting for, and swearing that they would never more bear arms for Jeff. Davis' Confederacy. As a general thing the officers paraded their grey uniforms and stood aloof, or when drawn into conversation, manifested a surly desire to renew the conflict so soon as they were able.

By the terms of capitulation, the whole force of Gen'l Gardner, except the general officers, were to be paroled, the officers retaining their side arms, and the formal surrender was to take place the next morning at nine o'clock. But a portion of our troops were to take possession at that time, and each Division Commander was directed to select two of his best regiments for this purpose. Gen'l Augur selected from his Division the One Hundred and Sixteenth, and Second La. Vols. (white), a compliment of no mean value. Accordingly, on the morning of July 9th, 1863, the One Hundred and Sixteenth marched up the road they had so long watched, drew near to the fortifications which had twice been almost within their reach, and finally entered the place which for six long weeks they had sought for. That it was a proud and happy hour the reader need not be told. Upon the right, the post of honor, leading the occupying force, was the storming party under command of Col. Birge, a fitting position for men who had expected with their bayonets to force a way for those who now followed them so quietly. Filing to the right, we marched to the level plateau, near the bank of the river, our flags flying and drums beating. Here we found the whole rebel force drawn up in line of battle, and when directly in front of them we were halted and faced to the front. Gen'l Gardner now rode up to Gen'l Stone, Chief of Gen'l Banks' staff, and in a few brief words surrendered the forces and fortifications of Port Hudson, at the same time presenting his sword in token of his defeat. The sword was received, but immediately returned, with complimentary remarks on the gallant defence made. Turning to his little army, Gen'l Gardner gave the command, "ground arms," and over six thousand conquered rebels bowed before their conquerors, as they laid their guns upon the ground. Upon the flagstaff, near by, the glorious old stars and stripes floated out in the breeze, amid the shouts of thousands of voices, and the thunders of saluting guns. All these proclaimed that Port Hudson was ours, and that we had completed the severing of the Southern Confederacy and opened the Mississippi.

Port Hudson is a very small place, numbering about a dozen houses, and except as a rebel military post and the history of its siege and capture, probably never would have been heard of outside of its immediate vicinity. We counted much upon an examination of the fortifications, which the days we were to spend there resting after our hard work were to afford us the opportunity of doing; but ere the sun went down that day, the One Hundred and Sixteenth was marched on board the steamer *Gen'l Banks*, and proceeded to Donaldsonville, some sixty miles below.

At Port Hudson we parted with our Division Commander, Maj. Gen'l Augur. As the ranking officer under Gen'l Banks, he was entitled to better treatment than he received during the siege; but from some cause the opinions of much younger men, greatly his inferiors, were allowed to have more weight than his. He stoutly opposed the assault of May 27th, so disastrous in its results, and afterwards was treated in so formal a manner by those at army head-quarters, that he deemed it best to withdraw as soon as possible from the department. His health breaking down before we entered Port Hudson, he sought and obtained a leave of absence, went North, and was assigned to duty as commandant of the defences of Washington.

We had thought very much of him at Baton Rouge, where his kindly features seemed to speak of a warm heart; but when at Plain Store he showed himself so well able to handle his command in the hour of danger, and at Port Hudson evinced so much care for us, with such unfeigned sympathy in our hardships and losses, we almost worshipped him, and every man felt when he knew of his departure, that we had lost a dear friend. That he thought something of the One Hundred and Sixteenth was manifested on more than one occasion, and when nearly two years later we found ourselves, by the shiftings of a soldier's life, in the vicinity of Washington, he learned of it, and through his influence we were assigned to duty in his command, as a portion of the provost guard of our nation's capital.

CHAPTER X.

The siege of Port Hudson enabled Gen'l Dick Taylor, commanding the rebel forces west of the Mississippi, and who had been so badly beaten by Gen'l Banks on his advance to Alexandria, to succeed in collecting his scattered army. In hopes of drawing Gen'l Banks away from Port Hudson, he had, at two or three points on the river bank between Baton Rouge and New Orleans, erected batteries, and thus laid an embargo upon the use of the river. Finding that this did not have the desired effect, he next threatened New Orleans, and presenting himself with an army of ten or twelve thousand men before Fort Butler, at Donaldsonville, the junction of the Bayou La Fourche with the Mississippi, demanded its surrender. The fort was garrisoned by two hundred and twenty-five men, under the command of Major D. D. Bullen, of the Twenty-eighth Me. Vols., who refused to capitulate. An attack was at once made by the rebels, but the position was most gallantly defended, the enemy losing, in prisoners alone, almost as many men as composed the garrison, besides a large number killed and wounded. It was to attend to this force of rebels that a portion of Gen'l Banks' army at Port Hudson was so hurriedly embarked, among which was the One Hundred and Sixteenth.

At eight o'clock on the morning of July 10th we arrived at Donaldsonville, where we found the enemy's picket line, and every preparation made by them to renew the attack upon the fort. A strong picket line was at once thrown out, before which that of the enemy fell back, and, except some skirmishing, nothing transpired for two or three days.

Donaldsonville was at one time the capital of Louisiana, and was now the county seat of Ascension Parish. Before the desolation of war it had boasted its thousands of inhabitants, and had been a beautiful city, the abode of elegance and refinement, as was evidenced by several fine churches and public buildings which had escaped the destruction visited upon the place by Admiral Farragut, for outrages on his fleet; now, however, it had a deserted look, and its inhabitants could be counted by hundreds.

On the 13th, Dudley's Brigade of Augur's Division, upon the north bank of the Bayou La Fourche, and Morgan's brigade of Grover's Division, upon the south bank, were moved forward, and meeting with some considerable resistance, our brigade was ordered to the support of Dudley. We advanced about a mile and a half, and there went into bivouac an hour before noon. There being no indications of an engagement, preparations for our mid-day meal proceeded with more than the usual promise of a good dinner, as we were encamped on a large plantation, whose owner, either willingly or unwillingly, furnished a supply the like of which had not been seen by us for many weeks. Fresh pork and beef, chickens and geese, and wherever a remarkably good caterer was found, sweet potatoes and cabbages, invited us to a meal fit, in our eyes, to set before a king. Some were fortunate enough to dine early, but most were either, while anxiously waiting its cooking, or engaged in the merits of the case, aroused by the rattle of musketry in our front, and ere the precious viands were devoured we were ordered into line, and hurriedly moved to the front.

The road upon which we advanced ran parallel to the bayou, and following it some little distance, meeting at almost every step wounded men from Dudley's Brigade, we filed to the right into another road running at right angles with the other. The One Hundred and Sixteenth being on the left of the brigade, its left rested on the Bayou road, where a section of the First Maine Battery was in position. We found on either side of the road we occupied a deep ditch, into one of which we were ordered. This afforded us good protection from the fire of the enemy, who were now driving Dudley's Brigade slowly back. The behavior of this brigade was excellent. Coming back in line of battle, they were halted, faced about, and firing a volley, would continue the retreat, loading their pieces as they did so. The One Hundred and Sixty-first N. Y. Vols., Lieut. Col. Kinsey, was in our immediate front, and behaved most gallantly. Passing through our line they formed some distance in our rear, and the advancing rebels called our attention.

Some eight hundred yards in our front was a large house, with its negro quarters and barns. As the rebel line came into view from behind these houses, a few scattering shots greeted them from such of our boys as could not restrain the desire to unload their pieces; but nearly all, in obedience to instructions, held their fire. Almost breathlessly we watched the advancing line. It was, indeed, a beautiful sight, for never were men better handled than were these rebels.

Our line it will be remembered was in a ditch, immediately in front of which was a fence, and as a consequence we were almost entirely hidden from view, so that the rebels were advancing to a reception they had but little idea of. Col. Paine, our brigade commander, watched the approach of the enemy with a practised eye; and when the moment came and his order was given, we poured a volley into them before which their line melted as though it had been wax, and those not killed or wounded, sought the protection of the adjacent houses.

In the meantime the section of the First Maine Battery, already mentioned as in position on the Bayou road, was receiving from across the bayou a fire which showed plainly that our forces on that side had fallen back, enabling the rebels to get upon our flank, and using the levee for protection would very soon make it impossible for us to hold our line. Several battery horses were killed, and the lieutenant in command found that the remaining horses, with nearly all his men, had left him, taking with them one of the guns. It would not do to leave the other gun to be captured, and the fire from across the bayou was every moment becoming sharper. In this dilemma, Capt. Tuttle, of the One Hundred and Sixteenth, whose company, "C," was on the left of the regiment, came to the lieutenant's assistance with a portion of his men. Amid a perfect hailstorm of bullets they seized the piece and dragged it in safety to the rear; but hardly had they commenced the perilous undertaking before a ball entered poor Tuttle's head, and he fell dead, another offering from the One Hundred and Sixteenth.

After his repulse, the enemy made use of the houses, and from windows and other openings soon made our position very uncomfortable, especially as we could seldom see enough of them to return the compliment, while they were enabled from their elevated positions to make almost every shot tell. Besides this, the increasing fire from across the bayou, to which we could not reply, contributed very largely to our annoyance, and made us long for either an order to advance or retire.

Gen'l Weitzel, in command of all our forces at Donaldsonville, soon ascertained that Col. Morgan with his brigade, on the opposite side of the bayou, had retreated, thus exposing our flank, and directed Col. Paine to fall back, which we did in good order.

Immediately after leaving our position we entered a corn field of immense growth, the stalks being between six and seven feet in heighth; and when it is remembered that we were in Louisiana, and that it was the 13th day of July, none will dispute the assertion that it was hot in that corn field. Suffocating would be a better term, for it really seemed as if the air was directly from the burning fiery furnace mentioned by the Prophet Daniel. Many poor fellows found it impossible to keep up, and dropped down, only to be captured by the rebels, who advanced as soon as we fell back. Passing through this corn field we reached the Bayou road and returned to the vicinity of Fort Butler. Thus ended the battle of "Cox's Plantation." It was a repulse, the discredit of which could not attach to the One Hundred and Sixteenth, or Paine's Brigade. We had fought well, defended our position with a heavy loss to the enemy long after Col. Morgan retreated, and only retired when ordered to do so. Where the dishonor did rest can be told when it is known that Col. Morgan was at once put in arrest by Gen'l Weitzel, court-martialed and dismissed the service. The loss of the One Hundred and Sixteenth was, in killed, one officer and four men; wounded, one officer and twenty-two men; missing, prisoners, twenty-one men. Total, two officers and forty-seven men.

Gen'l Dick Taylor did not deem it prudent even after our repulse to renew the attack, but remaining a day or two left the vicinity, learning, no doubt, that his efforts to draw Gen'l Banks from Port Hudson had failed. His victories at Brashier City and other points, where he had captured some hundreds of prisoners and a large amount of stores, were barren, in view of the grand results at Port Hudson.

His troops were loth to believe that Port Hudson had fallen, as the following incident will show. Among our wounded left upon the field was a soldier fast losing consciousness, to whom a rebel general came bringing a surgeon with him. The surgeon examined him and told him there was no hope of his recovery and that he must die. The general then asked him, in view of the fact that he was so soon to appear before his Maker, to tell him whether Port Hudson had really been captured by Gen'l Banks or not.

Our stay at Donaldsonville was protracted until August 1st. We managed to make ourselves in a measure comfortable, but found that to keep cool in Louisiana during this season of the year was entirely out of the question. Nothing has been said thus far of the health of the One Hundred and Sixteenth, owing to the fact that, excepting a few cases of diseases consequent upon the prolonged seige at Port Hudson, but very few had been really sick; and even now, with the intense heat of a July sun pouring down upon us, not many were on the sick list. One great cause of this was the fact already mentioned, that but very few men were accepted by Surgeon Hutchins in Buffalo who were not able to endure hardships. Another was, that we had arrived at New Orleans in just the right season, mid-winter, to enable us to become acclimated before the heated term set in.

While here at Donaldsonville, Col. Paine, in whom we had all come to have great confidence, received a leave of absence and left us for the North. Major Geo. M. Love, who had received a commission as Colonel of the One Hundred and Sixteenth, having almost recovered from the wound received at Port Hudson, assumed command of the brigade.

At ten o'clock, August 1st, the One Hundred and Sixteenth broke up its bivouac at Donaldsonville, went on board the government transport *Excelsior*, and at six o'clock that afternoon tied up to the wharf boat at Baton Rouge. Without much time being lost we found ourselves back in Camp Niagara, after an absence of only two months, but which from the scenes we had passed through seemed like two years.

Here we found sick and wounded comrades who had left us during the siege of Port Hudson, and around many a camp fire we rehearsed the events which had transpired after they left us.

Two weeks were spent here, and then the One Hundred and Sixteenth was ordered to garrison Fort Williams, where we found a good camping ground and better accommodations than ever before.

The time of the nine months regiments, of which there were three in our brigade, was now about expiring. The Twenty-first Me. Vols. did not leave Port Hudson with us, its time being so nearly expired that it was deemed best to leave them there for the few days they had to remain, rather than transport them down the river, and now the Forty-eighth and Forty-ninth Mass. Vols. were ordered to proceed home by the way of Cairo.

The loss of so many regiments made a reorganization of the Nineteenth Corps necessary, and we were announced as a part of the First Brigade, First Division, composed of the Thirtieth Mass. Vols., One Hundred and Sixteenth, One Hundred and Sixty-first, and One Hundred and Seventy-fourth N. Y. Vols., and Second La. Vols. (white). Col. Dudley, of the Thirtieth Mass., being the senior colonel, was to be its commander; but strange to say, there was a scarcity of general officers, and he was accordingly placed in temporary command of the division, leaving Col. Love, for the time being, brigade commander.

The flag which the good citizens of Buffalo had presented to us when we left for the seat of war had suffered terribly. At Plain Store no rebel bullet had dared to enter its sacred folds, but at Port Hudson it received many such marks, besides being torn almost to shreds by a charge of cannister. The fact being made known to Captain D. P. Dobbins, he procured another more beautiful if possible than the first, and while in camp at Fort Williams it was received, and in the name of the donor presented to the regiment in a speech by Col. Love. At the request of Capt. Dobbins the old one was returned to him for safe keeping, and has since been deposited by him in the rooms of the Buffalo Historical Society.

Orders were received on the 12th of August detailing Lieut. Col. Higgins, Capt. Carpenter, Lieut. Clark, and six enlisted men, to proceed North for the purpose of bringing to the regiment such conscripts as should be assigned to it. With many messages to friends at home from those less fortunate than themselves, they left us.

CHAPTER XI.

It was on May 1st, 1863, that an order was issued by direction of Maj. Gen'l Banks, commanding the Department of the Gulf, proposing the organization of a Corps d'Armee of colored troops, to be designated as the Corps d'Afrique. It was to consist ultimately of eighteen regiments, representing all arms,—infantry, cavalry and artillery, organized in three divisions of three brigades each. The regiments were at first to be limited to five hundred men, a limit based upon the opinion that the valor of the soldier is rather acquired than natural, and that with a race so unaccustomed to military service as the slave of the South, much more depended on the immediate influence of officers upon individual members than with those that have acquired more or less of warlike habits and spirit by centuries of contest. It was also used as an argument in favor of this limit, that the average of white regiments was less than that number, entirely overlooking the fact that the average of the white regiments, although not exceeding that number, yet represented the substance of a full regiment of one thousand men; and subsequent experience proved the fallacy of this limitation, for when the chaff was separated from the grain nothing but skeleton regiments remained. The regiments were to consist of ten companies, each having the following minimum organization: 1 captain, 1 first lieutenant, 1 second lieutenant, 1 first sergeant, 4 sergeants, 4 corporals, 2 buglers, and 40 privates. The regimental organization was to be the same as that fixed by law for an infantry

6*

regiment. Previous to this and during Gen'l Butler's administration of the affairs of the department, four regiments of colored troops were organized and known as the Louisiana Native Guards; but the people were not fully prepared for the admission of colored troops, and the subject required delicate handling, so delicate, indeed, as to seriously impair the efficiency of these regiments, and it was not until these regiments were incorporated into the Corps d'Afrique that they manifested any degree of soldierly qualities. Brig. Gen'l Daniel Ullmann had also begun the organization of a brigade of five regiments, and these with Col. Hodge's regiment of engineers were likewise transferred and formed part of the "Corps d'Afrique." The recruiting for the corps was regulated by a commission appointed by the commanding general to whom all questions concerning the enrollment, recruiting, etc., were referred, subject to the proper approval from head-quarters. Subsequently this authority was transferred to a superintendent, and when conscription became the order of the day in our Northern States, the benefits of this system were likewise applied to the newly made freedmen of the South. The entire corps was placed under the command of Brig. Gen'l Geo. L. Andrews, formerly chief of Gen'l Banks' staff, a graduate of West Point, and a soldier of eminent ability. To his untiring energy and perseverance is due a great part of the credit, which in spite of all obstacles and underhanded machinations the Corps d'Afrique earned the right to claim, and it was with sincere regret that the officers of the corps parted with their general, when sickness caused him to seek a healthier climate.

Shortly after the battle of Cox's Plantation, Adjt.

Jno. B. Weber, then serving on the brigade staff, was selected to organize a regiment for the Corps d'Afrique, and immediately entered upon his new duties, establishing his head-quarters at Baton Rouge. Numerous were the applications sent in to him by the officers and men of the One Hundred and Sixteenth for positions in his regiment, and as Col. Love had very kindly permitted him to select such as he desired from among the applicants, and as he was well acquainted with their military qualifications, it is fair to presume that it was an able representation from the veterans of the One Hundred and Sixteenth. There were thirteen of our boys altogether who obtained positions in this regiment, and as it was in this manner intimately connected with us, we give it a place in this record as part of our history. The following is a list of these persons with their former and subsequent rank:

Colonel—Jno. B. Weber, late Adjutant.
Lieut. Colonel—Robt. F. Atkins, late Captain.
Adjutant—Richard M. Hair, late Sergeant Major.
Quartermaster—J. L. Claghorn, late Commissary Sergeant.
Captain—Philip J. Weber, late Second Lieutenant.
" Oscar F. Tiffany, late Second Lieutenant.
" Jno. W. Tuttle, late Sergeant.
" Rollin C. Hubbard, late Sergeant.
1st Lieutenant—Jno. L. Carmer, late Sergeant.
" " Willard S. Berry, late Sergeant.
2d Lieutenant—Charles Faul, late Corporal.
Sergeant Major—Geo. S. Grimes, late Private.
Quartermaster Sergeant—Geo. L. Ebbs, late Private.

Recruiting operations for the new regiment were carried on briskly and with energy, and was only once seriously interrupted by an order issued by Adjt. Gen'l Lorenzo Thomas, who, although sent from Washington to assist and facilitate enlistments, yet it seems was prevailed upon by the "chivalry" to narrow down the field of our operations. In spite of this, however, the regiment gradually approached completion, and on the 19th day of September, 1863, a commission was issued to Adjt. Jno. B. Weber, and on the 8th day of October he was formerly mustered into service at Port Hudson (the regiment having previously been ordered to report there) as Colonel of the Eighteenth Regiment Corps d'Afrique, which designation was subsequently changed in General Orders to that of the Eighty-ninth Regiment U. S. Colored Infantry. Col. Weber was on the same day placed in command of the Second Brigade, Second Division, which command he held until the consolidation of his regiment, except at short intervals while detailed for court-martial service. Drilling was now the order of the day, and much hard work in that line was got over with for about two weeks. From that time forward fatigue duty, which meant throwing up fortifications, was a task to which the colored troops at Port Hudson were subjected for about six months. In spite of these disadvantages and the deterioration of discipline which inevitably follows such constant and uninterrupted fatigue duty, yet guard-mounting and dress parades showed visible signs of improvement, and for excellence in guard duty the regiment was several times specially and publicly complimented by orders from post head-quarters. The cleanliness of the camp and its sanitary condition was also often the subject of favorable comment in the report of the post officer of the day.

Nothing of special interest occurred to vary the monotony of every day camp life, until some time in March, when the preparatory orders for the celebrated but ill-fated Red River campaign were received, designating Col. Weber's brigade as part of the colored troops to participate in the movement. Then came the usual hurry and bustle incident to preparations for active service, followed by countermand orders (as far as concerned the Second Brigade), which are, as a general thing, quite as usual. The place of the Second Brigade was filled by that of another belonging to the Corps d'Afrique, and it was ordered that the entire strength of the regiments composing the former brigade, with the bare exeception of ten men to a company, should be transferred to those regiments selected for active service. These ten men per company were left to the choice of their respective commanders, and were to be considered a nucleus whereupon to build new and complete organizations. These selections were the source of many anxieties both on the part of the officers and men, for many of these newly-made freedmen had become sincerely attached to their officers. They regarded this transfer, as it was called, as only another method of changing masters, and that they were freemen was considered on their part an open question. In return for this transfer of men, the Second Brigade was promised by Gen'l Banks a full complement of one thousand men per regiment, this being held out as an inducement by the powers that *were*, to submit quietly to an operation from which every soldier knows there lies no appeal. "Experience has proved"—thus argued this famous order—"that wherever our armies entered upon new fields or territories not previously despoiled by the ravages of war, contrabands innumerable flocked to our standard and returned with us to our strongholds, and it was not doubted but what a sufficient number of men could be procured to not only fill up the Second Brigade, Second Division, but every other regiment of the Corps d'Afrique to the full maximum of one thousand men." But the best of plans often go amiss, and he of "masterly retreat" fame found that experience had likewise taught the rebels a lesson, and nearly all of the able-bodied negro males were run into the interior upon the first approach of our armies, and consequently Gen'l Banks came back with a less number of blacks than he had when he started. This was a sad blow to the officers of the skeleton brigade, numbering now about four hundred enlisted men, for upon the Red River campaign depended their only hopes for the completion of their organization, the country in the possession of our forces having previously been drained of nearly every able-bodied negro available for military service. It was a settled opinion among the officers of the brigade, that they could not long remain in this condition, for the injustice to the Government of keeping in service officers for four complete regiments to regulate the affairs of scarcely a battalion was manifest to the most casual observer. These opinions soon found vent in rumors of consolidation, and about the middle of June, 1864, a private communication from an officer of Gen'l Banks' staff reached Col. Weber, that orders for consolidation had been issued from department head-quarters, whereupon he tendered his resignation as Colonel of the Eighty-ninth, which was accepted June 26th, 1864. The anticipated orders were duly received at regimental head-quarters three or four days after, and the officers were all honorably discharged, with the exception of those who preferred remaining in the service with some other regiments. A few, after enjoying a short visit among their friends at the North returned to Louisiana, and again entered the service.

Thus ended the existence of the Eighty-ninth Regiment U. S. Colored Infantry, and, for reasons previously stated, we give it a place in our record on account of the former intimate connection of its officers with our own One Hundred and Sixteenth.

CHAPTER XII.

Our quiet life in Fort Williams was destined to be of short duration. Premonitory symptoms of a move were constantly becoming stronger, until, on the 27th day of August, orders were received to report at once to New Orleans. Our comfortable tents were turned over to the post quartermaster with every thing not essentially necessary on a campaign, and soon the One Hundred and Sixteenth were on board a transport on their way to New Orleans. On our arrival there Col. Love was directed to embark his whole brigade, consisting of five regiments, on board the clipper ship *Alexandria*, a large and beautiful craft. Upon examination, however, he found it impossible to crowd more than two regiments on her and accordingly reported the fact to Gen'l Weitzel, who succeeded Gen'l Augur in command of our division. An inspection of the fleet was ordered, and Col. Love with two other officers made a thorough examination of every vessel. They reported an entire lack of accommodations, the result of which was that more ships were at once chartered, and the One Hundred and Sixteenth with the Second La. Vols. (white) were not very uncomfortably situated on board the *Alexandria*.

Maj. Gen'l W. B. Franklin, about this time was assigned to the command of the Nineteenth Corps, and of this expedition, which was to proceed to Sabine Pass, upon the coast of Texas, and capturing the forts there situated establish a base of supplies and march inland.

When everything was on board and ammunition and

supplies had been stored away in the hold, we made fast to a steam tug and started down the river. A rather tedious sail of about twelve hours brought us to the mouth of the river, where we found a large number of vessels all at anchor, and loaded, as the *Alexandria* was, with troops.

Early on the morning of Sunday, the 6th of September, signals were seen flying from the flag-ship upon which Gen'l Franklin had established himself, and the usual bustle of raising anchors and putting to sea, with the cheers of the men, made a very animated scene.

Four gunboats, ten ocean steamers and sailing vessels, with a half dozen river steamers, comprised this formidable expedition, which was to sweep from the coast of Texas every vestige of rebellion. The man who secured the vessels upon which the troops were now setting out on the treacherous waters of the Gulf, should have been dismissed the service in disgrace, and it is not beyond question but that all who had a share in its organization should have received the same fate. One of the steamers was minus a wheel and was making the trip under great disadvantages, while most of our artillery with their horses were on board river steamers, about as fit for service in the Gulf as egg shells would have been, and ere the return of the fleet, some of these deposited their burdens in deep water.

Our noble ship under a press of canvass sailed majestically over the waters, doing about as well, so far as we could see, as those propelled by steam. Our trip from Fortress Monroe on board the large steamer *Atlantic* was for a portion of the time most delightful, but for real pleasure we found a sailing craft much superior to a steamer. All was still, no clatter of engines or splash of monstrous wheels, but easily and gracefully we seemed to be borne along by nothing; and to add to our enjoyment we found the captain of the ship a noble-hearted specimen of the American sailor, ever anxious to make our stay with him a pleasant one.

Toward night, on the 7th, we reached the designated point, and were told that the long sandy beach was Texas, and that Sabine Pass was before us. Nothing occurred that night to prevent our enjoying a good sound sleep, and we awoke on the morning of September 8th to find it a clear, beautiful day, and with every indication of an attack being made upon the fort.

The *Clifton*, one of our gunboats, ran in and opened her guns during the forenoon, but elicited no response, and returned to her consorts. Some of the troops were transferred from the large vessels in which they arrived, to smaller ones, but the One Hundred and Sixteenth were undisturbed throughout the day and had a fine view of all the operations.

About two o'clock P. M. there was a general movement of the gunboats, and two transports loaded with troops, toward the works. Three of the gunboats passed well in toward the inlet, leaving the others to guard the transports. They opened a heavy fire upon the forts, which, however, made no reply until one of them defiantly turned her bow up the channel; then the enemy opened upon them, and with such good effect that when the smoke cleared away two of the gunboats the *Sachem* and *Clifton*, were seen entirely disabled and flying white flags in token of surrender, while the third slowly returned towards the fleet. Before darkness had closed in on the scene, we observed two rebel steamers come down the inlet and tow the lost gunboats out of our sight, and this was the finale of the Sabine Pass expedition.

Months afterward we learned that this fort mounted but three guns and was garrisoned by but fifty men. Comment is unnecessary.

During that night Gen'l Franklin directed the fleet to return to New Orleans, and when we turned out the next morning we found our ship already under way. Had the wind been favorable we should have made a quick run back to the mouth of the river, but we found a strong head wind opposing us, the sea was very rough and every hour becoming more so. Besides all this our rations were nearly used up, and the supply of fresh water on ship-board almost exhausted. Short rations had been experienced before and we had been days with nothing to eat, but never in our previous service had we been deprived of water. Now, however, the water casks were empty and we two hundred miles from where we could get a supply. To add to our trouble, the captain of the tug having our ship in tow found that his fuel was nearly exhausted, and leaving us to work our way to the Mississippi, he steamed away and was soon out of sight. The Second La. (white), the regiment on board with us, were a class of men entirely different from the One Hundred and Sixteenth, and discipline was at a very low stage among them. They threatened open mutiny, and for a short time things on board the *Alexandria* looked dark indeed. However, by the use of stern measures they were controlled, and in hopes of getting assistance to enable us to reach the river as soon as possible, a flag of distress was hoisted. Seeing this, one of the gunboats bore down upon us to ascertain the cause. The captain upon learning our condition inhumanly refused to aid us; but upon Col. Love threatening to report him so soon as we arrived at New Orleans, he came alongside and with much difficulty a line was attached to our ship and in due time we arrived safely at the mouth of the Mississippi. Crossing the bar, we remained but a short time and were then towed up the river to Algiers, opposite New Orleans, on the 13th of September. Algiers is really a portion of New Orleans, although known by another name, and was before the war a place of considerable business importance, there being extensive iron works then in operation there; but now it was, indeed, one of the waste places of the earth.

Three days were spent here, during which time we saw fresh evidences of another campaign. A railroad running from Algiers to Brashier city was employed night and day in transporting troops, and the necessary supplies and ammunition for them, to the latter place, which was evidence enough that we would soon proceed there. On the 16th our expectations were realized. The One Hundred and Sixteenth were placed on board a train of cars, and in less than twelve hours we found ourselves in this *city* of perhaps a hundred inhabitants. Upon every side of us, as we left the cars, were camps, showing plainly that a large force was concentrating here, and we soon learned that all considered it an army to march overland into Texas. We learned, too, that besides our own Nineteenth Corps, another, the Thirteenth, was here, composed almost entirely of Western men which had been sent into the Department of the Gulf soon after the capture of Vicksburg and Port Hudson. Our corps was composed mainly of Eastern troops, and we soon found it impossible to live in peace with these western men, as they were constantly telling of their prowess, and what *they* would now do in this department if we paper collar soldiers would only let them alone. They were almost destitute of discipline, wore whatever dress they pleased, be it a uniform or not, and considered whatever they could "gobble" as theirs by inalienable right. Many hard words ended in harder blows, as we allowed that we knew a thing or two perhaps as well as they, and when only a few weeks later Gen'l Burbridge with a whole division of this Thirteenth Corps was surprised and badly defeated, we did not lose the opportunity of retaliating in kind.

The next day we crossed Berwick Bay and remained until the 20th instant, awaiting the slow process of crossing the entire army. When this had been accomplished we again started, made a short march of but five miles and went into bivouac. A good night's rest enabled us to rise prepared for a forward movement, but the day passed and still we lay in camp. The same thing was repeated for five successive days, when bright and early on the morning of the 26th of September, we broke camp and took up our line of march. Pattersonville was soon passed and then Fort Bisland, where a portion of our corps had some months before achieved a victory; nine very long miles were scored ere we went into quarters for the night.

Until October 3d we remained here, and it seemed very much as though our generals were unable to tell just how, or when, or where to move. On the morning of the 3d, stringent orders against the pillaging of the country through which we passed having been issued by Gen'l Franklin, we at last got a final start.

We had heard very much of this Teche country, as it

was called, from the Bayou Teche, which waters this whole section of country, and as this was our first visit we were pleased to find that the stories of its beauty had not been exaggerated. It was, indeed, the garden of Louisiana, a rich farming country, which even after the ravages of contending armies was good to look upon. During the day we passed through Franklin, one of the largest and most flourishing towns in the State, and a short distance beyond it went into bivouac.

Early the next morning we moved on again, cutting across Irish Bend to avoid a long detour, and after a toilsome march of twelve miles again went into camp for the night. The following day enabled us to add twelve miles to our march, and to bivouac opposite the wreck of the gunboat *Hart*, which completely obstructed the navigation of the Bayou. Two days the army remained here, while the cavalry and the One Hundred and Sixteenth were sent out eight miles to ascertain all that was possible of the enemy. None was found, however, and we remained there forty-eight hours, when the army joined us. Before daybreak on the morning of the 8th, we were again in motion, and about daylight passed through a collection of houses called New Iberia. The day was very warm, but notwithstanding the heat we marched sixteen miles and bivouaced on a large plain, equal in extent to some of our western prairies. We were now nearing Vermillion Bayou, across which lay our line of march, and where, it was rumored, the enemy had erected strong fortifications; and as we started on the morning of the 9th, every one expected a fight at this point. After marching some ten miles we came within sight of the bayou, and by direction of Gen'l Weitzel the One Hundred and Sixteenth was ordered forward as skirmishers; the right wing was deployed, the left held in reserve, and at the command we moved cautiously forward. The ground over which we advanced was a level plain unobstructed by any trees, and our line nearly a mile in length was a sight worth seeing. We found no difficulty in reaching the bayou, and leaving the line Col. Love rode back to Gen'l Weitzel and reported the fact. He directed three volleys to be fired across the stream, and if no response was received to cross. The volleys were fired, and receiving no reply, a detachment of our boys soon managed to erect a sort of bridge from the burned timbers of the bridge destroyed by the enemy, and the One Hundred and Sixteenth was the only regiment that crossed that night.

We had suffered severely for water for two days, our only supply being found in large buffalo holes. These holes are a sort of pond, in most cases perfectly round, no streams issue from or empty into them, and yet they are seldom dry; the water is, of course, stagnant and unfit for drinking purposes. From these we were forced to procure our supply of water, and the cool water of Vermillion Bayou that night was, indeed, a God-send. Most of the next day was consumed in erecting a new bridge, and when this was completed so as to be used, the army crossed the bayou, but marched only a mile or two beyond and went into bivouac.

October 11th we marched fourteen miles to a small and exceedingly dirty stream, appropriately named Carrion Crow Bayou, and were glad to find that Gen'l Franklin had ordered a five days' rest. On our approach to this bayou the same duty was required of the One Hundred and Sixteenth; and, deployed as at Vermillion Bayou, we found more difficulty in driving the enemy, but finally succeeded in doing so, and after a while were relieved by a portion of the Thirteenth Corps.

Nine days we remained at Carrion Crow Bayou, during which time the enemy made a reconnoisance in force. After the hurry and bustle of getting into line ready to receive them, we had nothing to do but retire to our quarters again, they not deeming it advisable to risk an engagement. Among the field officers of the different regiments and the general staff officers there were some very fine horses, and as the weather was delightful, much time was whiled away and a great deal of sport enjoyed in racing. The contagion spread to the negro servants, and many a young African showed his speed to crowds of idle soldiers.

Many inquiries were made as to what had become of our advance into Texas, but none were found able to understand our movements or account for the delay. We had, however, been soldiering long enough to let the morrow take care of itself, and therefore were content.

At last, on the morning of October 21st, we once more broke up our camp and moved forward, the Thirteenth Corps in advance. They met with some little opposition from the rebels under Gen'l Green, but easily drove them. Before noon we reached Opelousas, but before entering the town turned to the right, and after a short time went into bivouac on the banks of a small but pleasant stream, called Bayou Barri-croquet, having marched seventeen miles. Our stay here was extended to ten days, and as it rained almost constantly it was far from being pleasant. In addition to the rain, great difficulty was experienced in supplying the army with rations, and consequently our bill of fare was reduced to the lowest possible limit. Whether all this induced the abandonment of the Texas campaign, or whether other causes, not so apparent, made it impracticable we did not know. One or both did, however, cause it to be given up, and on the 1st day of November we commenced to fall back, marching that day to our old camp at Carrion Crow Bayou. On the 2d, the march was continued to Vermillionville, near the bayou of the same name. The Thirteenth Corps was for some reason detained, but started some time during the day. One of its divisions, commanded by Gen'l Burbridge, encamped some distance from the balance of the corps at Bayou Grand Coteau, and, isolated as they were, the rebels surprised them, and coming from all directions, had but little difficulty in making sad havoc among them. The fight was a bloody one while it lasted, the enemy leaving a large number of dead when he retired, as he did at once, and our forces losing over five hundred in killed, wounded and prisoners. After reaching Vermillionville, we lost no time in preparing for a good night's rest, which we were permitted to enjoy only until midnight, when a report of the surprise of Gen'l Burbridge having reached us, the Nineteenth Corps was aroused and put in motion for the scene of the engagement. The distance was nearly, if not quite, fifteen miles, and it was traveled in less than five hours, which in consideration of the darkness was rather good time. We found no enemy, but saw the evidences of his bloody work in numerous hospitals, where surgeons were busy attending to the wants of the wounded. The whole day was employed in burying the dead and making preparations for removing the wounded. After a somewhat anxious night in anticipation of the return of the rebels, we moved at daybreak on the 4th back to Vermillionville, arriving there before night and occupying our old camp.

Gen'l Weitzel announced to the troops the welcome intelligence that we were to remain here some days, and we soon made our quarters quite comfortable. Horse racing was again the order of the day, and exciting trots, and even hurdle races, were of almost daily occurrence. The rains had ceased, and ten days of most delightful weather was enjoyed, with just enough duty to perform to keep us in trim.

. On the 11th, a reconnoisance, composed of our cavalry, ran upon a superior force of the enemy near Carrion Crow Bayou, and were forced to beat a hasty retreat. The enemy followed them almost into our camps and then, satisfied, withdrew, while we were set at work forthwith erecting earthworks. A strong line cutting across lawns and hedges, through dooryards and fields, soon gave us a secure position, which, however, was never used, as on the 16th we once more re-commenced our retrograde movement. Camp Pratt, an old rebel camp of instruction, afforded us a resting place that night. The day following we passed through New Iberia, and went into camp some two miles below the town, where we were directed to prepare to remain all winter.

Every available habitation not occupied was demolished to provide the necessary materials for huts and fire places, and before forty-eight hours passed over our heads we were most comfortably situated.

New Iberia is situated on the Bayou Teche, upon which stream a line of transports was plying before many days between it and Brashier city, bringing us our supplies. On the 20th of December, we were glad to welcome Lieut. Col. Higgins and Lieut. Clark who had been North after conscripts, but returned with none of our friends to swell the ranks of the One Hundred and Sixteenth. To our inquiries as to the whereabouts of Capt. Carpenter and the six men who went on this duty with them, we were informed that they were still at Elmira, N. Y., and might, if more successful, bring some conscripts when they returned.

CHAPTER XIII.

THE new year of eighteen hundred and sixty-four found the One Hundred and Sixteenth still at New Iberia. Although in a southern climate where we cold-blooded Northerners had been wont to think such a thing as a cold winter, if any winter at all, was entirely out of the question, we found as we greeted one another with a "Happy New Year, sir," that overcoats and gloves were far from being unseasonable. We thought of the happy scenes which we knew so well were being enacted at home, and could not help wishing that not many more such days should pass and find us absent members of the family circle; and the thought which at once followed, that our wishes were echoed there, was by no means the least pleasant one that crossed our minds that day.

Rumors of a move to Franklin for winter quarters was all that interrupted the monotony of camp life, and even this interruption was hardly noticed. The weather grew perceptibly colder, and indications of a storm of snow somewhat surprised us. On the night of the 5th, these rumors were confirmed by orders to move at eight o'clock the next morning. As we turned in, everything indicated a snow storm. A certain peculiar appearance of the skies, so often noticed before such storms, was to be seen, and if anything further was needed, the piercing cold of a stiff north-easter added its voice; and when we turned out bright and early the next morning, all doubts disappeared, for it had snowed, and that, too, to the depth of an inch and a half. It was cold and most certainly uncomfortable, but after all it seemed like a good old friend whose absence had been long mourned, and whose unexpected return, although surprising, was none the less pleasing.

But what had all this to do with moving? An early breakfast was hastily eaten, our tents were struck, the wagons loaded, and the hundred and one things performed which are always necessary when an army moves. At last, and before the designated hour—eight o'clock—arrived, we were ready for our march. Delay at such a time when all are waiting for the sound of the bugle to move is annoying, but we had experienced it before and did not worry ourselves much on account of it. At last an orderly reached Col. Love's quarters with a countermand, and unloading our wagons we prepared to pass another night at New Iberia. Before we slept that night, the same orders to move at eight o'clock the next morning were received, and the morning proving clear and beautiful we got off at last.

The roads were frozen hard when we started, but the heat of the sun with the tramp of an army over them, took the frost out and rendered them one vast bed of mud, which made our progress very slow and toilsome. Especially was this the case with the artillery, the heavy wheels of the guns sinking into the mud up to the axle, and miring some of the horses so that it became necessary to shoot them to prevent their falling into the hands of the enemy. All day we toiled along, and making ten miles, bivouaced for the night in an old sugar house.

The next day we again marched ten miles, encamping for the night at Harding's plantation. An early start the following morning, January 9th, enabled us to reach Franklin, the end of our journey, for the present at least, at eleven o'clock. The troops were distributed about town, our brigade being assigned camping ground a short distance outside of the village on the Bayou road.

Although it was supposed that room enough had been given for the comfort of the different regiments, it was soon found that they were too much crowded either for comfort or health, and to add to our discomfort a cold rain set in, continuing for three days, and the consequence was a perfect sea of mud.

As soon as the rain ceased and the mud dried up sufficiently to permit of a change, the One Hundred and Sixteenth was moved about half a mile nearer town to a beautiful piece of green sward. It was the selection of Gen'l Emory, who had been assigned to the command of our division, Gen'l Weitzel having left us at New Iberia to return to his home at the North. He enjoined upon us the necessity of harming nothing, and expressed the hope that we would ornament it and make as pleasant a camp of it as possible.

It was fortunate that our regiment secured so beautiful a situation, both for their pleasure and reputation, as the improvements and embellishments we soon made added much to the fair name we had already acquired; and as the camp was visited almost daily by gentlemen and ladies, residents of Franklin, and by fellow soldiers from other regiments, we attained considerable notoriety as a model regiment for cleanliness. In addition to this it made our soldier home a pleasant one, and, no doubt, every officer and man who enjoyed the winter there, will look back to his stay in Franklin as the pleasantest part of his experience as a soldier.

The regiment at this time was under the command of

Lieut. Col. John Higgins, and to his good taste with that of the line officers, was due the credit of "Camp Emory," a name which was at once given it, in honor of our old general.

Major Sizer and Surgeon Hutchins, whom we always delighted to honor, were soon after our arrival at Franklin, detached as Acting Assistant Inspector General and Medical Director, respectively, on Gen'l Emory's staff, and the regiment thus lost their valuable services.

Camp Emory merits a more extended description. Its situation has already been spoken of as most delightful. It was a fine piece of green sward, perfectly level, and with just enough trees to shade it, but not to mar its beauty or interfere with the laying out of the camp in proper shape. Each company street was laid out, nicely graded and ditched, and building huts and covering them with our shelter tents, our camp soon assumed the appearance of a little village. From each hut a rude chimney was raised, and the smoke to be seen issuing therefrom told of a good comfortable fire within, which bade defiance to all Jack Frost's assaults.

But it was the ornaments erected by the different companies which gave notoriety to the camp and attracted many visitors, and a hurried description of them must be given.

Company "B," on the right, made quite an alarming display of very heavy guns, which, however, on close inspection proved to be "quakers," and they were, therefore, very peaceful in their disposition. Company "G" had erected a tower, or castle of sods, which would in the spring have presented a beautiful appearance, when the grass was grown on its surface; also, an arch across the street with the name "Glen Gowen," in nicely cut letters. A monitor built after the most approved model, with revolving turret, mounting four guns all complete, graced the street of Company "E." It was duly christened "Faugh-a-Ballagh," which being interpreted means, "Lave the way." To Company "I" must be given the palm for getting up what certainly attracted the most attention, and what was most appropriate to our calling. It was a miniature earthwork, eight feet square, mounting four guns, which, however, like Company "B's," were entirely harmless. It was perfect in all its appurtenances, having a ditch, sallyport, and curtain complete, and reflected much credit on the engineering skill displayed by the company. Companies "D," "K," "F," "A," "H," and "C," each displayed their taste in some manner, all making, as before mentioned, one of the handsomest camps ever seen.

Louisiana forests abound in a kind of moss with which most of these ornaments were covered, which, no doubt, greatly enhanced their beauty. Rustic seats were scattered about the grounds, affording what soldiers are not apt to have. One of the trees was transformed into a sort of tower, with winding stairs, from which a good, although not very extended, view of the different camps and village was obtained. It was really a delightful spot, and merited the distinction it received.

The following description of Camp Emory is taken from the record of the One Hundred and Fourteenth N. Y. Vols.:

"The camp of the One Hundred and Sixteenth New York was a place of especial resort, being regarded as one of the greatest curiosities in the army. Situated in a very romantic spot, its inmates had, with a great amount of pains and pride, enhanced the natural beauty of the location. By the use of moss and evergreens, they constructed arbors, bowers and arches, resembling architecture of every kind. Their grounds were laid out with exquisite taste. Flower beds, miniature forts and monitors, rustic seats and shrubbery, every where met the delighted eye. In the evening, when the camp was lit up by fires the effect was perfectly enchanting, reminding one of the fabled scenes of oriental magnificence."

Our stay in Franklin extended over a period of about two months, from the 9th of January until the 15th of March, and our time was employed in making our habitations comfortable, and in drilling by company, battalion and brigade, with an occasional review. We found Franklin a very pleasant place, its inhabitants as agreeable as could be expected, and we were well pleased with our winter's stay there. The weather was very fine most of the time, which, no doubt, added much to our comfort.

On the 19th of February a reorganization of the troops was made preparatory to the spring campaign, and in it the One Hundred and Sixteenth was transferred to the Third Brigade, First Division, Col. Lew Benedict commanding. The change, however, was unpalatable to our officers, and their desire for a return to the old First Brigade, with which we had for so long a time been connected, was gratified soon after the 1st of March. Brig. Gen'l Dwight, in the turnabout just mentioned, was assigned to the command of the First Brigade; but as he was on some duty in New Orleans, Col. Love retained command. While we remained at Camp Emory, great exertions were made by the officers to make our dress parades a feature, and they were very successful. The bayonet exercise was taken up and thoroughly studied by them; the companies were then drilled for hours in single movements and combinations, and finally the whole regiment was exercised in it. Long before our departure, our evening parades were visited by many citizens and officers of other regiments. Upon one occasion, Gen'ls Franklin and Emory were among the spectators, and when the parade was dismissed, both expressed themselves as very much gratified, Gen'l Franklin remarking that he had never seen it equalled. When it is remembered that he was a graduate of West Point the compliment will be better appreciated.

About the middle of February, after we had got things settled very nicely, and were really enjoying the expenditure of time and labor we had made in getting thus settled, unmistakable evidences of a move were plainly perceptible. Leaves of absence and furloughs were returned with that never to be forgotten "disapproved," disfiguring them. All extra baggage was ordered stored in New Orleans. Inspections for the purpose of seeing how the men were provided with clothing were had, all of which told us that before long our comfortable quarters must be given up and we start once more roughing it. The camp must give place to the bivouac, and our comparative peace and quiet to the dread realities of war.

It would have surprised our friends at home, and it might have even shocked some of the more staid and sober ones, could they have witnessed the eagerness with which most of us prepared to leave so beautiful a resort as our Camp Emory. To have heard the cheers which greeted the final order to "fall in," on the 15th of March, would have been evidence of something but little short of madness; but, dear friends, remember that your soldier boy is not his own master. He is subject in a great measure to the views and whims of others. To a certain extent he comes and goes, not at his own will, but at the bidding of another. He rises in the morning, not as you do, when you please, but when reveille is beaten; and in all well regulated camps his light is extinguished when a higher power says it shall be. This is the reason he cheers at the order to leave his snug shanty.

Time had worked sad changes in our ranks. The eighteen months service which we had rendered to our country had witnessed the death of Col. Chapin, Captains Tuttle and James Ayer, Lieutenants Boruski, Jones, Linnahan and Cottier. Scores of our comrades had passed to their final home, while quite a number had been discharged by reason of disability contracted in the line of duty.

From a complete complement of officers we were reduced to barely enough to perform the necessary duties, and inasmuch as most of these had risen from the ranks, it may be well to give the roster of the One Hundred and Sixteenth when we started on the Red River campaign:

FIELD AND STAFF.

Colonel—GEO. M. LOVE, commanding First Brigade.
Lieut.-Colonel—JOHN HIGGINS.
Major—JOHN M. SIZER, detached on division staff.
Adjutant—JNO. C. NIAL.
Surgeon—C. B. HUTCHINS, detached on division staff.
1*st Asst. Surg.*—JNO. COVENTRY.
2*d Asst. Surg.*—M. E. SHAW.
Quartermaster—ALEX. GOSLIN, detached on brigade staff.

COMPANY OFFICERS.

Company A—Lieut. Orton S. Clark, detached on brigade staff.
Lieut. Jacob C. Newton.
Company B—Capt. Wilson H. Gray.

Company C—Lieut. Henry A. C. Swartz.
Company D—Capt. E. Wm. Seymour,
Lieut. Geo. W. Miller, acting regimental qr.-master.
Company E—Capt. Richard C. Kinney.
Company F—Lieut. Charles F. Crary.
Company G—Lieut. John H. Rohan.
Company H—Lieut. John G. Woehnert.
Company I—Lieut. Wm. J. Morgan.
Company K—Capt. Warren T. Ferris,
Lieut. Geo. H. Shepard.

CHAPTER XIV.

At eight o'clock on the morning of March 15th, 1864, the One Hundred and Sixteenth started upon what will always be known as the Red River campaign. The day was a delightful one, the air cool and bracing, and taking the cut-off road cutting across the neck of Irish Bend, headed in the old direction of New Iberia.

A large force of cavalry and mounted infantry had been organized in New Orleans, during the winter, and now arrived from there under command of Gen'l A. L. Lee. Two very small divisions of the Thirteenth Corps under Gen'l T. E. G. Ransom, also joined us, and these with our division of the Nineteenth Corps, commanded by Gen'l Emory, composed the force which under Gen'l Franklin, was to proceed to Alexandria, one hundred and seventy miles distant on the Red River.

A march of fourteen miles after so long a season of quiet, told severely on our pedal extremities, and enabled us to relish our evening meal, and enjoy our night's sleep more than usual. March 16th we started at seven o'clock A. M., and made about sixteen miles, going into bivouac at Camp Pratt, some four miles beyond New Iberia. March 17th, started again at seven A. M., and reached Vermillion Bayou, a distance of fifteen miles, about two o'clock P. M. A good night's rest enabled us to get off on the 18th at six A. M., and that day we traversed twenty-one miles, encamping at Bayou Grand Coteau, where, the fall before, Gen'l Burbridge, of the Thirteenth Corps, was surprised by the rebels and badly cut up, causing our brigade a night march of fifteen miles to support him. On the 19th we moved at six A. M., making sixteen miles, and going into bivouac at Little Washington. During the day it rained, but not enough to cause us much inconvenience. March 20th was Sunday, a day of rest indeed to us, which all heartily enjoyed after our five days' march. Near us was the Bayou Courtableau, which furnished us a good opportunity for bathing, and was improved by all.

March 21st, at six A. M., we were once more on the move, and more rain having fallen during the night, we found the roads heavy and marching rather more difficult; however, we scored a good eighteen miles, and rested for the night on the upper Bayou Boeuf. It rained hard all night, and made our marching the next day still more difficult. March 22d, six o'clock found our column again in motion, and toward night we entered Holmesville, having made fifteen miles over terribly muddy roads. March 23d the sun rose clear and beautiful, and soon warmed us into new life. At seven o'clock A. M. we moved from Holmesville, and made over fifteen miles with more comfort than on the preceding day, encamping at Cheeneyville, the pleasantest village we had seen since leaving Franklin. March 24th we moved again at six o'clock A. M., with a clear, cold, bracing air, which was, however, a great help; and in consequence we made a splendid march of eighteen miles, bivouacing on the plantation of Governor Wells. As we reached our stopping place, the windows of heaven seemed to be opened, and a thunder storm, accompanied by a perfect gale of wind, burst upon us with great fury, and although it abated somewhat, continued a good portion of the night. Notwithstanding the storm, and the consequent bad condition of the roads, we were off at seven o'clock the next morning, and before night entered Alexandria, a distance of fourteen miles.

We had now traversed about a hundred and seventy miles through a magnificent country, seen many large and costly sugar houses on plantations of unheard of dimensions, upon nearly all of which vast fields extended, without an obstruction, as far as the eye could reach, containing hundreds of acres.

We had passed through the towns of New Iberia, Vermillionville, Opelousas, Little Washington, Holmesville, and Cheeneyville; but none of them are worthy of mention, being for the most part a small collection of houses, and to all appearance entirely destitute of male inhabitants.

As our army advanced, the planters collected all their able-bodied negroes and drove them into Texas for safety, leaving only the aged and very young to greet the "Yanks." The expressions of joy with which these poor ignorant beings received us were wonderful, and must have rendered any reliance their owners had placed on their fidelity of little value.

No resistance had been made to our advance, thus far, into the heart of the trans-Mississippi department, by the rebels. Gen'l Dick Taylor fell back as we advanced, burning every building on our route which contained any cotton, fearing, no doubt, that it might fall into our hands, a proceeding not at all pleasing to the owners, and which must have been damaging to his cause.

We found Alexandria a city of considerable size, and which in time of peace must have been busy with the hum of trade; but now war, with its desolations, had almost ruined it. Its streets were deserted; its stores and public buildings shut up; while the private dwellings were closed as if to exclude even the breath of the hated Yankee. It is situated on the southern bank of the Red River, about seventy miles from its mouth.

At this point we met a force of some ten thousand men, consisting of portions of the Sixteenth and Seventeenth Corps, under command of Brig. Gen'l A. J. Smith, and a fleet of gunboats under Admiral Porter.

The command of Gen'l Smith had been sent down the Mississippi from Vicksburg, and, landing at Simsport, on the Atchafalaya river, had, in conjunction with the fleet of Admiral Porter, attacked Fort de Russey, a rebel post of great strength on the Red River, some fifty miles from its mouth, and after a short but decisive struggle, captured it with its entire garrison.

Gen'l Banks and Gen'l Dwight, our brigade commander, also joined us here, having made the trip from New Orleans by the river. Gen'l Dwight at once assumed command of the brigade, relieving Col. Love, who returned to the One Hundred and Sixteenth. Many regrets were expressed that he could not remain in command of the brigade, as he had shown himself worthy of the position.

Two days were spent at Alexandria, during which time the paymaster with his greenbacks made his welcome appearance, and replenished our scanty supply of the needful.

There was now concentrated at this point an army of about forty thousand men, as follows: The cavalry under the command of Gen'l Lee, numbering about eight thousand, and which formed the advance. Two divisions of the Thirteenth Corps commanded by Gen'l Ransom, numbering some eight thousand. The Sixteenth and Seventeenth Corps under Gen'l Smith, ten thousand strong; and the Nineteenth Corps commanded by Gen'l Franklin, of about ten thousand men. Besides these there were two or three brigades connected in some manner with the fleet.

Shreveport was our destination, and real success could not be expected without the aid of the gunboats, and their co-operation depended entirely on the depth of water to be found in the river. Some two miles above Alexandria are the falls, or more properly speaking, the rapids; and unless there was a sufficient depth of water here the fleet could not pass to the help of the army, nor could transports reach us with supplies.

Some difficulty was experienced in getting the larger vessels of the fleet above the rapids, but at last all were over, and we were ready for a forward movement.

The cavalry and the Thirteenth Corps departed by the road, while the command of Gen'l Smith embarked on transports and ascended the river.

Gen'l Grover's Division of the Nineteenth Corps was left at Alexandria, and on the morning of March 28th, our division (Emory's), left its bivouac, feeling quite refreshed by the two days' rest. A heavy rain the night before had reduced the road to one bed of mud; but, nevertheless, at night we had left Alexandria eighteen miles in the rear, and found ourselves on the Bayou Rapides, near the famous piney woods. The next day we entered them, and for two days plodded on through their seemingly interminable length, making only about sixteen miles, owing to burned bridges which had to be repaired.

We were now traversing a section of country where

the rebels had held undisputed sway. No force of ours had ever penetrated thus far, and Yankees were indeed a curiosity, not only to the blacks, but to such of the whites as were to be seen. We found the country very different from the southern portion of the State, being much more rolling, and for the first time since our advent to the Department of the Gulf we saw stones.

On the 31st we crossed Cane River, which is simply the old bed of the Red River, where years ago it used to run; but for some good reason, no doubt, it forsook its old channel and opened for itself a new one. By this a very large bend was avoided and its course shortened by some miles. The new channel and the old form an island of large extent, upon which is the village of Cloutierville, a small and wasted looking place, work upon which seemed to have been stopped centuries before.

The crossing was effected upon a pontoon bridge, and we found ourselves "out of the wilderness," in what we were informed was the most productive cotton growing land in the State. Here, again, we saw the tracks of our retreating enemy. Every little way the black and smouldering ruins of gin-houses were seen, in which large quantities of cotton had been stored, but which had all been destroyed, rather than that it should fall into our hands.

This day's march was perhaps the most fatiguing the One Hundred and Sixteenth had thus far accomplished. It was eleven o'clock ere our wagon train had crossed the pontoon, and before six o'clock that night we had counted twenty-one miles in the face of a strong wind, which blew the dust in clouds about our heads, and filled our eyes with Louisiana soil. The march was resumed again early the following morning, April 1st.

Soon after starting we re-crossed Cane River and were again obliged to wait until nearly noon for our trains to safely cross the bridge. This, too, was a windy, dusty day, and with blistering feet we marched some eighteen miles, and went into bivouac near a cotton-gin, which, by some mistake, had escaped the torch of Dick Taylor. It was found to contain a goodly supply of cotton, and that night we each enjoyed a good soft bed, more costly than we had ever before occupied. When we left in the morning the ground was covered with a fleecy coat, worth, probably, half a million of dollars.

A short march of seven miles on the morning of the 2d, and we entered the substantial and ancient town of Natchitoches (pronounced Nac-a-tosh), with colors flying and bands playing, and going about a mile beyond the town, we went into bivouac. Natchitoches is the oldest place in the State, a fact well attested by the style of architecture which predominated. When the Red River flowed past its wharves its commerce was very extensive, but now that its channel was some miles distant, Natchitoches seemed to have become simply a resort for wealthy citizens, able to live at their ease. Many of the residences were almost regal in their splendor, while the court-house, a convent and a cathedral, were all imposing edifices. Among the inhabitants, most of whom were French, there seemed less of that antipathy which we had always seen manifested in other places, and the women, we were foolish enough to think, showed evident signs of pleasure at our arrival. All this impressed us very favorably with Natchitoches, and all this a few days later was explained as only their joy that we were being so easily led on to certain defeat. We remained here three days to rest and recuperate our wasted energies, and very acceptable days they were.

On the 6th of April, before daybreak, our line was formed, and to the enlivening strains of music we started once more, and scored fifteen good miles ere we slept that night at Double Bridges. April 7th we moved about seven o'clock A. M., and during the day passed a rebel camp of instruction, consisting of quite a number of buildings, over which was the name "Camp Beauregard." No orders were given to destroy, but the name soon disappeared, as did also a good portion of the buildings. A march of twenty miles enabled us to rest our weary limbs at Pleasant Hill, from which our cavalry advance had that morning driven the enemy after a short struggle, and which was made memorable two days after by a severe battle. Quietly we slumbered on the very spot which to some was so soon to be their last resting place.

Early on the morning of the eighth, we left our bivouac, cheered by the intelligence that we were to march but eight miles that day, as it was Gen'l Franklin's intention to march the Thirteenth and Nineteenth Corps but a short distance that day, to enable Gen'l Smith in our rear, to close up to within supporting distance.

The point was reached before noon, and filing to the right into an open field, we stacked arms and prepared to bivouac.

Up to this time not one of us had fired a shot at an enemy. The cavalry, since leaving Alexandria, had met with some opposition, but until they reached Pleasant Hill, no real, determined resistance had been made to their advance. At the place where we were encamped a stubborn fight had taken place that morning, but it was the conviction of nearly all that the enemy could not resist our army, and were destined to retreat into Texas, making, perhaps, a final stand at Shreveport. There were those who thought that greater caution should be exercised by Gen'l Banks in keeping his command more compact, and not permitting miles to intervene between the different corps. Had this been done, the terrible disaster that soon followed might have been prevented; but he, no doubt, was as sanguine as any of us, that Dick Taylor would not dare to risk an engagement with his army.

CHAPTER XV.

When we first arrived at the eight mile point mentioned in the previous chapter, distant canonading could be heard, which soon became more frequent, and seemed to be more distinct, as if our forces were being driven back. But our ears had become so accustomed to this sound that we gave but little heed to it, until an aide from brigade head-quarters ordered Col. Love to cease preparations for a bivouac as we were to move at once to the front, where our troops were heavily engaged with the enemy.

The cavalry under Gen'l Lee, after driving the enemy from Pleasant Hill, had pushed on after him, and, as has been stated, when eight miles from there, or where we were going into bivouac, had had another engagement, and remained there over night. Early on the morning of the 8th, they proceeded on their way, but, until within four miles of Mansfield, found but little difficulty in driving the enemy before them. Just at this point the road runs through a dense wood emerging into a large prairie miles in extent. With very little caution Gen'l Lee permitted his wagon train to follow the column so closely that when he reached this open field the train was within the wood. Here a large body of the enemy was found, who opened upon them so unexpectedly, and with such fury, as to make the holding of their position impossible. A short resistance was made, but all to no purpose; the rebels enveloped their flanks, doubled up the line, and forced them to retreat in great disorder. The road being blocked up by the wagon train, and it being impossible to turn the crazy mules and frantic drivers, Nimb's Sixth Mass. and the Chicago Mercantile Batteries, together with the supply train, were captured. Word was at once sent to Gen'l Franklin, and the Thirteenth Corps, who were between us and the cavalry, were hurried forward to a point where the cavalry had been collected and were trying to hold the rebels in check. But there was little use in a division of cavalry seven or eight thousand strong, and about five thousand infantry, trying to drive back an army of twenty-five or thirty thousand. And now the folly of keeping the different corps so far apart was made fearfully manifest. Had our army been kept well in hand the result of that day's fighting would have been a decided victory. But it was not. Eight miles from where they were needed the Nineteenth Corps lay in bivouac, while, disgraceful as is the fact, not to them, but to some one, the Sixteenth Corps was sixteen miles away at Pleasant Hill, beyond even the sound of the guns, which were dealing death and destruction to those engaged.

On the reception of the order to move to the front, Gen'l Emory at once mounted his horse, and with as little delay as possible we were on the way. As we advanced the sound of the battle waxed louder and nearer, while demoralized camp followers, black by nature, but almost white from fear, skulking infantry soldiers by twos, and cavalry by squads, passed us.

Our brigade was in the advance, led by the One Hundred and Sixty-first N. Y. Vols. The One Hundred and Sixteenth followed next, and as we neared Sabine Cross roads, where Gen'l Emory had decided to form his division, he ordered the band of our regiment to strike up a lively air. The effect was inspiriting not only on us, but upon the stragglers who now came pouring back in large numbers and utter confusion.

As we reached this cross road the One Hundred and Sixty-first was sent still further down the main road to engage the attention of the rebels, while the balance of the division were formed in line. The First Brigade was posted on the right of the road, and the other two on the left. By the sending out of the One Hundred and Sixty-first, the One Hundred and Sixteenth found itself on the extreme right of the line and behind a rail fence.

As we halted, came to a front, and awaited the coming of the enemy with our pieces at a "ready," we had a few moments in which to examine our position. Immediately in our front was a large open field, in the centre of which was a hollow, the ground rising some distance beyond and receding into a heavy piece of woods which extended well around to our right.

Down in this hollow, entirely hid from our sight, the One Hundred and Sixty-first, with the fragments of the Thirteenth Corps, were vainly attempting to stay the onward rush of the victorious rebels, and here the One Hundred and Sixty-first lost nearly one hundred men in less than ten minutes, a noble offering from one of the best regiments in the service. Flesh and blood could not, however, withstand the onset of such vastly superior numbers, and ere our line was fully formed, the brave fellows, such as were left of them, fell back slowly within our line. Pressing them closely and with exultant yells came the enemy. "Steady, men," was the whispered command of our officers; "wait until they are almost upon us," and we did wait. No line ever held its fire better. Occasionally some nervous fellow would let off his piece, but not a sound, a whisper, or a breath hardly was heard, until the dirty uniforms of the rebels were within a few paces, and then our whole line poured into them such a volley as they had not received before that day, to say the least. They were amazed, and in great confusion reeled back out of sight, and that was the last determined attack on our front that night. Not long after this a line was seen to emerge from the woods on our right, and advance on our flank. No troops could be spared from the front, and the five right companies of the One Hundred and Sixteenth were swung back to the rear, and as the force was not large, we drove them back very easily. Thus far our corps had been victorious; it had repulsed the enemy most decidedly, and saved the wagon train and artillery of the Thirteenth Corps. But our eight or ten thousand muskets could not hope to resist another attack of the whole rebel force in our front, and darkness was now our ally. Satisfied with their success, and it being too dark to undertake another attack, the enemy divided the spoils among themselves, and with jest and song which we could distinctly hear, whiled away the night.

A strong picket line was thrown out along our front, to prevent surprise, and completely exhausted, hungry and dispirited, we sat down to think. Would we remain here until morning, or would we fall back? Where was Gen'l Smith with the Sixteenth Corps, and why was he not here? These and many other queries arose in our minds only to remain unanswered.

It was a terribly cold night, and with nothing to keep us warm, we shivered, gnawed our scanty supply of hard tack, and listened to the sounds of jollity and mirth which came to our ears from our victorious neighbors, the "Johnnies." The wagon train they had captured was freighted rather heavily with liquor, and, judging from the noise and their known love for the article, it had suffered severely.

Until midnight we remained there, when covering the retreat of the army, the First Division of the Nineteenth Corps quietly and slowly retraced its steps to Pleasant Hill, sixteen miles in our rear. At this point Gen'l Smith, with ten thousand fresh men, would receive us, and it became a matter of the greatest importance to reach there before daylight, as that would reveal our retreat, and we thought the enemy's success that day would certainly lead them to follow us.

When it is remembered that we had marched from Pleasant Hill that morning, been severely engaged, and were now anxiously retracing our steps; that we had been unable to get anything more than a few dry hard tack to eat all day, and that the night being very cold we had become benumbed, it will not be doubted that we were tired and sore, or that we hailed with delight the sight of the rise of ground known as Pleasant Hill, which greeted our vision about seven o'clock on the 9th of April.

Just as we arrived there, a whooping and yelling, with the rattling and banging of two or three army wagons, gave unmistakable evidence of trouble in the rear. We were at once formed on the crest of the hill, a section of artillery placed in position to command the road, and hardly knowing or caring what was the trouble, we dropped down in our places. It proved to be the cavalry advance of the enemy, who were careful not to come too near. Col. Gooding's brigade of cavalry had been guarding the ammunition train the day before, and consequently was not engaged at Sabine Cross Roads. They were now deployed to prevent surprise, and shortly after we were relieved by a portion of the Sixteenth Corps. Going some distance to the rear, we sought the rest so much needed.

We were more than pleased with Gen'l Franklin, as the gallantry he displayed on the field proved him to be a brave and efficient officer. During the fight he was wounded, but remained in the saddle until every indication of a renewal of the fight that night had disappeared.

Gen'l Emory, too, was equal to the occasion, and evinced great care of his troops.

Owing to the impossibility of getting ambulances to the front in time, it was decided to leave all our wounded on the field, and surgeons, with such medical supplies as were at hand, were left with them. It seemed hard thus to leave those whom the fortunes of war had disabled, but as the salvation of the army depended on the celerity of our retreat back to Pleasant Hill, we were forced to depart without them.

The force now at Gen'l Banks' disposal with which to fight the enemy (for there could be no doubt of his offering us battle), were our own division numbering perhaps seven thousand men, and the Sixteenth Corps of about ten thousand, with Gooding's brigade of cavalry, the Thirteenth Corps and the balance of the cavalry being so completely scattered and demoralized, as to be worse than useless. In all we numbered some eighteen thousand muskets, and with this number we must fight an army nearly a third larger, and which was flushed with the victory of the previous day. All this was canvassed by us as we drank our coffee, smoked our pipes, and listened to the continual crack of muskets on the skirmish line, and every one of us nerved himself for spending some portion of that 9th day of April in scenes of carnage.

The day was a beautiful one. Every thing in nature seemed employed in the performance of the duty imposed by its Creator, except man, created in the image of his Maker, and he was only intent on the taking of his fellow-being's life. It hardly seemed possible that so much beauty in nature was so soon to see the fierce passions of men engaged in bitter strife, but ere the sun had set its light was dimmed by the smoke of battle, and the stars looked down upon the bleeding bodies of hundreds of noble boys who had given their lives for their country.

Almost the entire day was spent in arranging lines of battle; we to defend our position, and the rebels to rout us again if possible.

In the disposition of the troops our division was placed on the right, our brigade on the right of the division, the second in the centre, and the third on the left, with one brigade of the Sixteenth Corps as a support; another from the Sixteenth Corps was posted in *echelon* on the left of our Third Brigade, while the balance were held in reserve well to the left of our main line.

The One Hundred and Sixteenth again found itself on the extreme right of the line, its right resting on a deep ravine, with nothing but its own brave hearts and ready hands to prevent their flank being turned should the enemy repeat his adventure of the day before.

Just before the ball was opened in earnest, Gen'l

Dwight, our brigade commander, deemed it necessary to move the One Hundred and Sixteenth somewhat, not, however, materially altering our position. After the change had been effected, we found immediately in front of us a rude fortification of rails, thrown up probably by our dismounted cavalry in their fight at this place on our advance a few days before. Col. Love at once saw the advantage to be gained by making use of it, and ordered us to "lie down," but the order had no sooner been given by him than the *brave* Dwight, ever careless of his men as he was careful of himself, ordered us to "stand up," intimating that cowards only sought shelter. Not having the fear of a brigadier general before his eyes, the Colonel repeated his command, which was obeyed. To this fact may be attributed the small loss of the One Hundred and Sixteenth in the sanguinary battle of Pleasant Hill.

About four o'clock in the afternoon, there was a lull in the firing of the skirmishers, but we were prepared from this to expect the general attack. Our expectations were realized, for soon our skirmishers were driven in, and a determined attempt made to force our portion of the line back; but they counted without their host, for instead of driving us back, we forced them to retire. Five different times they charged upon our brigade and in every instance were handsomely repulsed. As has been stated, our flank was protected by a deep ravine, but this did not deter the enemy from making an attack from that point as well as the front, and the *zipping* of bullets from that direction showed plainly the new danger. Again, the right wing was swung round, and Gen'l Emory ordering up the Second Brigade, we held the position.

Another advance was now made in our front, and at the same time the whole rebel line moved forward, extending far to the left of our Third Brigade. It was a sight worth seeing—that long line of butternut uniforms—advancing slowly at first, and then, as if gathering momemtum, faster and faster, until with a yell they charged upon, and entirely enveloping the Third Brigade, swept it along as if it were but chaff, all unmindful of the reserve, quietly awaiting their coming.

Restraining their impatience, the sun-browned veterans of the West waited until the force of this charge was spent, and then, led by Gen'ls Smith and Mower, they gave the rebels one volley and then went for them with the bayonet. This unexpected movement threw the victors into utter confusion, and fleeing now themselves they were closely followed for more than a mile. In the meantime we had held our position and were only made aware of our victory on the left by hearing what we knew were Yankee cheers, and the fire in our front slackening, we responded with three times three, and with a genuine Buffalo tiger.

Darkness now closed in on the scene, and quietly we lay on our arms, not as the night before, disheartened, but happy, and awaited orders.

A fact should be mentioned here which gladdened every heart in the One Hundred and Sixteenth, as it concerned one whom we highly esteemed. Gen'l Emory with his staff remained near the right of his division until the advance on the left, and then leaving us to care for that portion of the line, went to the Third Brigade. Col. Lew Benedict, its commander, was killed almost at the first fire, and a panic seemed imminent in consequence; seeing which, Maj. Sizer, of the One Hundred and Sixteenth, Inspector General on Emory's staff, by the exhibition of just such gallantry as Maj. Love had shown in our first fight, rallied the brigade and saved it from disgrace.

A most decided victory had been gained; the disgrace of the night before had been wiped out, and a desire to follow the retreating enemy at once, or at least in the morning, was uppermost in all our hearts. But our haversacks were empty, and hungry stomachs demanded rations. What could we do without them, and they were miles in the rear hastening back to Grand Ecore? We might, and it seemed to us should, have remained upon the field long enough to at least care for the dead and wounded, and claim a victory; but it was otherwise decided, and the strange occurrence happened of the defeated flying in one direction, and the victors in the other.

We remained in this position until one o'clock the next morning, listening to the terrible cries and groans of the wounded in our front, which were heart-rending in the extreme; and then leaving some surgeons provided with supplies, to care for the wounded, we turned our backs on Pleasant Hill, and took up our line of march for Grand Ecore.

The casualties of the One Hundred and Sixteenth in these two engagements were light, compared with all previous ones. At Sabine Cross Roads there were—killed, two; wounded, nineteen; missing, one. At Pleasant Hill—killed, two; wounded, ten; among whom were Lieuts. Jacob C. Newton, and John H. Rohan, both slightly, however.

About noon on the 10th, we halted at Yellow Bayou, a small dirty stream, which refreshed us amazingly, nevertheless, as water had been very scarce for the last two days, and dropping down, we were soon enjoying the first sound sleep we had been able to get in seventy-two hours. Three days and nights we had spent in either marching, fighting or watching, and that, too, on little else than dry hard tack, and a very short allowance of that. But, although hungry, we needed rest more than food, and this we enjoyed until the next morning, when we awoke ready to devour any thing in the shape of rations, and found our wants well supplied. After appeasing our appetites we again started, and a dusty march of eighteen miles brought us to Grand Ecore.

CHAPTER XVI.

Grand Ecore stands in the same relative position to Natchitoches that Charlotte does to Rochester, being about four miles distant on the Red River, and the port of entry for Natchitoches. Here we remained ten days, during which time the place was fortified on a grand scale, working parties having constant employment for four or five days in this laborious undertaking. Here, too, we found the most of our fleet. Many of the gun-boats and some of the transports had been unable to ascend the river any further, and had remained here; while some which had been able to proceed to Barry's Landing, nearly opposite Sabine Cross Roads, found it difficult to get back to Grand Ecore. One of the gun-boats was for this reason abandoned and blown up, after having defeated, with one or two others, a force of some twelve hundred rebels, who attempted to disable them with artillery planted on a bluff, near a small town called Compti. Gen'l Green, the commander of this rebel force was killed, and their loss was very heavy in both killed and wounded.

The next day after our arrival at Grand Ecore, the following order was received, and read to the assembled regiment:

"Head-quarters 1st Division 19th Army Corps,
Grand Ecore, La., April 12th, 1864.

"General Orders No. 13.

"The General Commanding thinks it due to the officers and soldiers of this division, to express to them his high appreciation of their gallantry and efficient services, in checking the advance of the enemy on the evening of the 8th inst., and aiding in his defeat on the 9th.

"By command of BRIG. GEN'L EMORY.

"DUNCAN S. WALKER,

"A. A. Gen'l."

Frequent flags of truce were received during our stay at Grand Ecore, and it was rumored that one of them bore a message to Gen'l Banks from Dick Taylor, saying, that among the property captured was a large stock of paper collars; that his men had baked them, boiled them, fried them and stewed them, and found them of no use, and he would like to exchange them for hard bread. Whether such a message was ever received we did not know of a certainty, but it was a standing joke whenever we met any of the cavalry.

About this time Gen'l Dwight, for whom the One Hundred and Sixteenth had no great respect, was relieved from command of the First Brigade, and assigned to duty as Chief-of-staff to Gen'l Banks. Col. Geo. L. Beal, of the Twenty-ninth Maine Vols., afterwards a brigadier general, assumed command of the brigade, and after our advent into the Shenandoah Valley, took from us Capt. Richard C. Kinney, as one of his staff.

On the 21st, orders were received to be ready to move at four o'clock that afternoon, but owing to some cause hour after hour passed, and still we remained near our broken camp, waiting the final order. Darkness came on, and still we remained, the tediousness of the delay being enlivened by the burning of a large storehouse, fired accidentally. It took fire, was gradually enveloped in flames, and burned almost to ashes ere we left Grand Ecore at two o'clock on the morning of the 22d.

Forty-five miles distant, at Monet's Bluff, was the only crossing of Cane River where it was possible to cross our wagon train and artillery. The gaining of this point before the rebels could plant their batteries upon the opposite side, and dispute our progress, was of the utmost importance. Had we known that such a forced march was before us, our hearts would have failed us, but unconscious of it, we cheerily shouldered our muskets and started.

During the night the marching was comparatively easy, but when the sun was well up the next day, and poured its rays down upon us, many were forced to fall out and take things more leisurely. The order of march was, in the advance the Nineteenth Corps, followed by the Thirteenth, while the Sixteenth brought up the rear. Continual cannonading in the rear showed plainly that Gen'l Smith was being annoyed by the enemy who had pursued us.

About eleven o'clock the heat of the sun became so oppressive, and the men so fatigued, that a halt was ordered for a couple of hours. This enabled us to get some rest, and the stragglers to overtake the column, and a refreshing cup of coffee put us in fair condition to respond, about one o'clock, to the command forward again. Hour after hour we followed the course of Cane River, darkness came on and still we pressed on, until it seemed to us that all humanity had faded from the hearts of our generals. Midnight found us wearily picking our way along the dusty road.

It was a terrible march, trying to the utmost the endurance of every man. Scores were unable to keep up, and with an utter disregard of life, they fell out of the column unable to move further. One man belonging to the One Hundred and Fourteenth N. Y. Vols. dropped dead on that march from exhaustion.

At last, at one o'clock on the morning of the 23d, we halted, and dropped down in our tracks, and it is no exaggeration to say, that the whole army were almost instantly asleep. Some there were who were denied this, namely, those who must, however wearied, go on picket. From the One Hundred and Sixteenth, Company "H" was detailed for this duty, but to say that they performed the duty willingly would be a stretch of the truth.

This was the most fatiguing march the One Hundred and Sixteenth ever made, being a distance of over forty-five miles in eighteen hours. Those who were able to keep up and stack arms with the regiment that night could lay claim to remarkable powers of endurance, and the number was not very small; while those who were forced to fall out could excuse themselves on account of the unusual speed maintained, as well as the number of miles traversed.

The object of our making such a forced march as has been mentioned, was to secure the crossing of Cane River at Monet's Bluff; but it was a fruitless task, our advance finding on their arrival that the rebels occupied it in strong force, and disputed it so stubbornly as to leave no doubt that we would have to fight for its possession in the morning.

Soundly we slept the few remaining hours of that night, and by five o'clock A. M., April 23d, were aroused, and getting a hasty meal, we moved toward the crossing, some two miles distant. The cavalry skirmishers soon became engaged with those of the rebels on our side of the river, who fell back slowly, but finally reached a point where our cavalry found it impossible to dislodge them. From a battery of seven guns, planted immediately in the road on the opposite bank, shells began to visit us with a sort of admonishing sound, very persuasive in tone, but which we had not the power to heed, as just then Gen'l Emory sent an aide for Col. Love, and directed him to deploy the One Hundred and Sixteenth, holding two companies in reserve, and thoroughly skirmish the woods between our present position and the crossing, where the rebel skirmishers were supposed to be.

A very short time sufficed to deploy the regiment, and entering the woods we soon lost sight of every thing, and cautiously moved forward. We had not proceeded far before we found the ground covered with water, growing gradually deeper as we advanced, until it was up to our waists, all the time the whistling shells from the enemy's battery tore through the trees, scattering the limbs all about us, and making our position far from enviable. Had their range been better many lives would have been lost; but their elevation was too great, their shells bursting high above our heads and to our rear. We moved thus nearly to the outer edge of the woods, but found no enemy; and assembling on the right group, we returned to the brigade. Here we learned that the Thirteenth Corps, with the Third Brigade of our corps, had proceeded above the crossing some three miles, with orders to ford the stream at that point, and attack the enemy in flank and rear, which seemed our only hope.

We found our brigade about where we had entered the woods, and joining the line we awaited the movements of this flanking column. Four or five hours were spent there listening to the cannonading in our front, the shells from which came unpleasantly near, and to that in our rear, which soon after we returned, began to grow more frequent.

The lines in Tennyson's "Charge of the Light Brigade," fitly expresses our condition:

> "Cannon to right of them,
> Cannon to left of them;
> Cannon in front of them .
> Volleyed and thundered."

All this told of a severe engagement with the enemy by Gen'l Smith, and all felt that our situation was indeed critical. The enemy having interposed a barrier at Monet's Bluff, which he thought we would be unable to remove, had doubtless hurried the most of his forces to the rear, in hopes to crush that, and thus capture our immense wagon train, our artillery, and the fleet of gunboats, which he knew could not get below the rapids at Alexandria, and perhaps our entire army. But he missed his calculation, and found that in weakening his forces in our front, he made our flanking column successful, without being able to inflict much harm in the rear; Gen'l Smith beating him back at every point, and capturing some prisoners, instead of suffering defeat.

But what gloomy hours those were! Never before had we been so completely at the mercy of the rebels. Surrounded on every side, it seemed impossible for us to extricate ourselves, and the capture of almost everything pertaining to our army was expected by most of us.

Some of us laid our plans when the last moment had come, and it became a question of being either captured or shifting for ourselves, to make for the Red River, distant about eight miles, cross it, and try to reach Vicksburg. While lying here indulging these gloomy forebodings, Captain Closson, of the Fifth U. S. Artillery,

Chief-of-artillery on the corps staff, passed into the woods with five guns, two twenty-pound Parrotts, and three three-inch rifles. They were to be placed in position as near the opposing guns as could be, and when the flanking column attacked, they were to open.

To support these guns from which so much was expected, the One Hundred and Sixteenth was selected, and advancing by a dry path, we this time escaped a drenching. The position selected was an excellent one, just within the outer edge of the woods, that the enemy might not detect us, but not so far but that they were in plain sight to us.

We found here, also, the Second N. Y. Veteran Cavalry, Col. Chrysler, dismounted, and deployed as skirmishers, and many of our number joined them on the skirmish line.

Word was soon received that the flanking column had made their attack, and then our battery opened with perfect range, the first shell exploding right in the midst of the rebels, killing four mules and disabling the battery forge. They replied with great vigor at once, and for a few minutes it was a warm spot, the shells plowing up the ground on every side. During the hottest of the engagement the officer in command of our battery became confident that the enemy were about to charge upon his guns, and to repulse this attack the One Hundred and Sixteenth was ordered forward some little distance. To rise amid the screeching shells was no pleasant duty, but at the command every man arose and advanced to the designated spot. At last, finding that our flanking column was in their rear, the rebels "limbered up" and retreated.

The way was now clear, and Gen'l Emory, riding up,

said: "Men of the One Hundred and Sixteenth, I know I can depend on you; I know you always stand up to the rack. I want that opposite bank occupied." We answered him with hearty cheers, and jumping into the shallow stream we were very soon in line, where, fifteen minutes before, the rebel battery stood, and the crossing was in our possession. As the other regiments of our brigade passed us, Gen'l Emory directed them to give three cheers for the One Hundred and Sixteenth, as the regiment which first occupied the position held by the rebels.

Our loss in this engagement was but one man wounded. The severe fighting had been done by the flanking column, the loss in our Third Brigade being very heavy, among whom was its commander, Col. Fessenden, who was so severely wounded as to necessitate the amputation of a leg.

Immediately a pontoon bridge was laid, and after a good rest we once more moved on, halting about midnight, and, spreading our blankets, slept soundly till morning.

At six o'clock A. M. we started again to tramp through the immense piney woods. Henderson's Hill was our destination that night; but about noon it became evident that we were literally lost, and while anxious aides and orderlies from the generals sought the right way, we enjoyed ourselves joking about it.

At length, finding it impossible to discover the right road, or considering it probable that the one we were following would, sooner or later, terminate near Henderson's Hill, the bugle sounded the forward, and pressing on we at last emerged from the woods, near the Bayou Jean-de-jean. Crossing this we bivouaced at nightfall at Henderson's Hill, having marched about fifteen miles.

We enjoyed a quiet night, undisturbed by the enemy, and moved at six o'clock on the morning of April 25th. Under a burning sun and amid clouds of dust, we marched eighteen miles, reaching Alexandria about three o'clock P. M., and going into camp two miles above the town on the banks of the Red River. Here we lay for a number of days, during which time we learned from officers of the gunboats which lay near us, that the water was so low that none of the fleet could pass the rapids, and their curses of the Red River campaign were loud and deep.

From this information we surmised that our troubles were not yet over, which surmise was strengthened on the evening of the 28th, by orders to move at once into a new position in front of the town, the commanding general being satisfied that the enemy contemplated an attack that night. All night we lay on our arms, but nothing more than a scattering fire between the pickets disturbed our slumbers, and the morning revealed the fact that the enemy had departed.

A new disposition of the troops was now made, in which the First Brigade found itself on the banks of the Bayou Rapides, near the same ground occupied by us when we advanced. A line of fortifications was thrown up almost enclosing Alexandria, and occupied at many points with artillery.

All our supplies had thus far reached us by the Red River, our mails had been received quite regularly by the same route; but now the enemy seemed to turn his attention to putting a stop to this means of communication. Every day the navigation of the river became more perilous, and finally, on the fifth day of May, it was effectually sealed; and the army was cut off entirely from the outside world. A position was secured in a bend of the river by the rebels, where they erected a battery, supported by quite a large force, and no doubt were confident that our fleet was now certain of capture. But they were to be disappointed by the ingenuity of a despised Yankee.

The situation was a trying one for the whole army. There really did not seem now any chance to save the millions of money, represented by the splendid fleet of gunboats, lying above the rapids utterly unable to pass the narrow and rocky channel.

One man, however, had hopes that by the use of proper means they might be saved, and that was Lieut. Col. Bailey, of the Fourth Wisconsin Cavalry, on the staff of Gen'l Franklin.

He submitted to Gen'l Banks a plan for constructing a wing dam at the rapids, which he was confident would raise the water sufficiently, at and above the rapids, to float the vessels, and pass them through an opening between the wings. To most of us it seemed a work of folly, but its feasibility was manifest to those in authority, and work was accordingly commenced at once.

The One Hundred and Sixteenth was ordered to proceed to the northern bank of the river, and commence work on that wing. On the 5th of May the order was obeyed, and we found ourselves engaged in felling trees in the forests close at hand, hauling them to the river, and with great exposure to life and health, getting them into position. An immense amount of stone was quarried, some distance above the dam, and floated down to the desired position. All this was very fatiguing, especially as a portion of us were constantly employed up to our necks in water. But as almost every hour saw the water rising, which gave token that our labor was not in vain, we persevered for eleven days, and then had the satisfaction of seeing all the fleet pass the rapids and float in deep water below.

Engaged with us, on the north bank of the river, were the Twenty-ninth Maine Vols., and three Western regiments, while upon the other bank the work was performed almost entirely by Negro troops. In Gen'l Bank's report of this undertaking, much credit is given to the troops who worked so faithfully, and all the regiments except the One Hundred and Sixteenth are mentioned. Why an exception should have been made of us we are unable to state, but inasmuch as Gen'l Dwight, our old brigade commander, was his Chief-of-staff, and doubtless drew up the report, the members of the regiment are not at a loss to account for the omission.

Admiral Porter makes the following mention of the work in his report:

"The work was commenced by running out from the left bank of the river, a tree dam, made of the bodies of very large trees, brush brick and stone, cross-tied with other heavy timbers, and strengthened in every way which ingenuity could devise. This was run out about three hundred feet into the river. Four large coal barges were then filled with brick, and sunk at the end of it. From the right bank, cribs filled with stone were built out to meet the barges, all of which was successfully accomplished, notwithstanding there was a current running of nine miles an hour, which threatened to sweep every thing before it. It will take too much time to enter into the details of this truly wonderful work. Suffice it to say, that the dam had nearly reached completion, in eight days working time, and the water had risen sufficiently on the upper falls to allow the Fort Hindman, Osage and Neosho, to get down and be ready to pass the dam. In another day it would have been high enough to enable all the other vessels to pass the upper falls. Unfortunately, on the morning of the ninth day, the pressure of water became so great that it swept away two of the barges which swung round in below the dam on one side. Seeing the unfortunate accident, I jumped on my horse and rode up to where the upper vessels were anchored, and ordered the Lexington to pass the upper falls, if possible, and immediately attempt to go through the dam. The Lexington succeeded in getting over the upper falls just in time, the water rapidly falling, as she was passing over. She then steered directly for the opening in the dam, through which the water was rushing so furiously, that it seemed as if nothing but destruction awaited her. Thousands of beating hearts looked on, anxious for the result. She entered the gap with a full head of steam on, pitched down the roaring torrent, made two or three spasmodic rolls, hung for a moment on the rocks below, was then swept into deep water by the current, and rounded to safely into the bank. Thirty thousand voices rose in one deafening cheer, and universal joy seemed to pervade the face of every man present. The Neosho followed next, all her hatches battened down, and every precaution taken against accident. She did not fare as well as the Lexington, her pilot having become frightened as he approached the abyss, and stopped her engine when I particularly ordered a full head of steam to be carried.

"The result was that for a moment her hull disappeared from sight under water. Every one thought she was lost. She rose, however, swept along over the rocks with the current, and fortunately escaped with only one hole in her bottom, which was stopped in the course of an hour.

"The Hindman and Osage, both came through beautifully, without touching a thing, and I thought if I was only fortunate enough to get my large vessels as well over the falls, my fleet would once more do good service on the Mississippi.

"The accident to the dam, instead of disheartening Col. Bailey, only induced him to renew his exertions after he had seen the success of getting four vessels through.

"The noble-hearted soldiers, seeing their labor of the last eight days swept away in a moment, cheerfully went to work to repair the damages, being confident now that all the gunboats would finally be brought over. These men had been working, eight days and nights, up to their necks in water, in the broiling sun, cutting trees, wheeling bricks, and yet nothing but good humor prevailed among them.

"On the whole it was fortunate the dam was carried away, as the two barges that were swept away from the centre, swung round against some rocks on the left, and made a fine cushion for the vessels, and prevented them, as it afterward appeared, from running on certain destruction.

"The force of water and the current being too great to construct a continuous dam of six hundred feet across the river, in so short a time, Col. Bailey determined to leave a gap of fifty-five feet in the dam, and build a series of wing dams on the upper falls. This was accomplished in three days, and on the 11th the Mound City, Carondelet and Pittsburg, came over the upper falls, a good deal of labor having been expended in hauling them through, the channel being very crooked and scarcely wide enough for them.

"Next day the Ozark, Louisville, Chillicothe and two tugs succeeded in passing the upper falls. Immediately afterward the Mound City, Carondelet and Pittsburg, started in succession to pass the dam, all the hatches battened down, and every precaution taken to prevent accident. The passage of these vessels was a most beautiful sight, only to be realized when seen. They passed over without any accident, excepting the unshipping of one or two rudders. This was witnessed by all the troops, and the vessels were heartily cheered as they passed over. Next morning at ten o'clock, the Louisville, Chillicothe, Ozark and two tugs, passed over without any accident except the loss of one man, who was swept off the deck of one of the tugs."

CHAPTER XVII.

On the evening of May 12th, after all the fleet had safely passed the dam, the One Hundred and Sixteenth left its position on the north bank of the river and crossed to Alexandria, expecting to march from there at once.

Owing to some cause we remained in the streets all night, in constant expectation of the orders to move.

We were now made acquainted with the fact, that our connection with the old First Brigade had ceased, and that we were a portion of the Third Brigade. Col. Love, by order of Gen'l Emory, assumed command of the brigade, which consisted of the One Hundred and Sixteenth, One Hundred and Sixty-second, One Hundred and Sixty-fifth, and One Hundred and Seventy-third N. Y. Vols., and the Thirtieth Me. Vols.

All regretted the change, as the old First was our home, and we had formed many attachments which were hard to sever. We hoped it would prove only a temporary transfer, and so it proved.

There were now two roads by which we could reach the Mississippi. One followed the course of the Red River, by which the distance was about seventy-five miles, and the other was the one upon which we had advanced so proudly only a month before. Our experience told us that this was a good one hundred and seventy miles, and when at nine o'clock A. M., May 13th, we found the column heading in the direction of the former, we stepped off to the music of our band with light hearts.

Shortly after leaving Alexandria, we saw immense

clouds of smoke rolling up from the city, which we were afterward informed was the town itself. It was set on fire by the carelessness of some of the men connected with our army, but the rebel authorities claimed it was fired by order of Gen'l Banks. A large portion of the place was left in ruins by this disastrous occurrence.

The weather was becoming intensely hot, and as the roads were very dusty, we suffered a great deal; but, nevertheless, marched an average of fifteen miles a day on the 13th, 14th and 15th. We passed the points upon the river bank where the enemy had erected his batteries and blockaded the river, but ere we reached these points he took good care to leave, and we had only a sight of the nest, the bird having flown.

On the 16th, we left the course of the river, passed through Marksville, a small village, and came out on an immense plain, very much resembling our western prairies, except in extent. Here we found the rebels in position to dispute our further progress. At every commanding point they had posted artillery, which kept up a lively cannonading until noon, our own responding. Our whole army, except a portion of the Sixteenth Corps under Gen'l Smith, was disposed to invite an attack, and every effort possible was made to induce them to attack us, or failing in this, to engage their attention until Gen'l Smith could gain their rear.

The sight which now opened to our view was imposing beyond anything we had ever seen. Thus far in the battles in which the One Hundred and Sixteenth had been engaged, our view had been limited to our own immediate front. But now on this clear, beautiful morning, on Mansura plains, thousands of acres in extent, we could see our whole army—the bayonets of the infantry, the sabres of the cavalry, and the polished guns of the artillery, glittering in the sunlight. Away upon the right, a portion of Smith's corps could be seen moving to the rear of the enemy, while all along the line the evolutions of the different divisions and brigades were plainly visible.

The battle of Mansura was almost entirely an artillery engagement, and seldom in the history of the war has there been a sharper one.

Notwithstanding our efforts to bring on an engagement, they refused to give us battle, and as soon as they found that a force was attempting to flank them, they took advantage of their knowledge of the country, and limbering up their artillery, escaped by some unknown path.

All obstructions to our retreat being now removed, we proceeded on our way, reaching Simmsport, on the Atchafalaya river, about three o'clock on the afternoon of the 17th.

The day after our arrival at Simmsport, the following order was received:

"HEAD-QUARTERS NINETEENTH ARMY CORPS,
SIMMSPORT, LA., May 18, 1864.

"SPECIAL ORDERS, No. 48.

"Soldiers of the 1st and 2d Divisions Nineteenth Army Corps. It is my duty to express to you my high appreciation of your uniform good conduct throughout the late eventful campaign. This duty is rendered more imperative by the false reports of your operations, which have met you at this point. On the 8th of April, at the first notice that our troops in the front were engaged, the 1st Division, the only troops of the Nineteenth Army Corps then present, marched in double-quick time seven miles to the front, formed line of battle under the enemy's fire, checked him and drove him back, under circumstances the most trying that could befall troops. The whole advance composed of eight or ten thousand troops, were thrown back upon you in utter disorder and confusion, pell-mell with the enemy. You formed line of battle under the enemy's fire, and amidst the frightful disorder, with the regularity of forming for parade. You drove the enemy from before you and held the ground until ordered to fall back.

"The next day at Pleasant Hill, you of the 1st Division bore the brunt of the enemy's fierce attack, and only one brigade, that on the left, gave way, because it was unsupported; but it soon rallied, and joined in the final charge, which drove the enemy from the field. On the 23d, at Cane River, you, supported by the Thirteenth Corps, found the enemy strongly fortified to dispute the crossing of the river. Led by the 3d Brigade of the 1st Division, you turned his flank, and at the point of the bayonet drove him from the hill he occupied. At Alexandria you contributed your labor by day and night, for seventeen days, under the engineering skill of Lieut. Col. Bailey, to the great work which relieved the fleet from its perilous situation above the falls, restoring it to the country.

"This is in brief a summary of your services, for the last two months, and I know when it becomes known to the country, the judgment will be, that you at least have done your duty faithfully.

"By command of BRIG. GEN'L W. H. EMORY,

"DUNCAN S. WALKER,

"A. A. Gen'l."

The fleet of transports when they had reached the mouth of the Atchafalaya on their way down the Red River, altered their course, and descending it to Simmsport, we found them, when we arrived there, awaiting us. They were all river steamers, and getting alongside each other, with their stems up stream, they formed a bridge which answered the purpose nicely.

All our large wagon train and artillery had to be run over by hand. Hour after hour we worked until at last every army wagon, gun, caisson, forge, mule, horse and man, were across the stream, and in a very short time the bridge had dissolved into distinct bodies, which ascending the Atchafalaya, were soon at the mouth of the Red River. Gen'l Smith here embarked his Sixteenth Corps upon them and returned to Vicksburg.

On the 21st of May, 1864, the first anniversary of our fight at Plain Store, we reached the good old Mississippi, and greeted it with as rousing a cheer as was ever given, and went into camp on its bank at Morgansia. Thus ended the Red River campaign, the great failure of the war; a failure which it seemed might have been foreseen.

The object was the capture of Shreeveport, five hundred miles within the enemy's country, to occupy which would have required the constant care of the entire army; while the Red River, notoriously treacherous, must be relied on as a means of supplying the army. And what real injury would its capture and occupation by us work to the rebellion? Severed in twain by the Mississippi, was it not our best policy to let that portion west of the river quietly enjoy the pleasure of belonging to the Confederacy? That the campaign need not have ended so disastrously is certain, had the commanding general been competent to handle so large an army, or grasp so comprehensive a plan.

At Port Hudson, a year before, we had been again and again defeated from a like cause. Instead of seeing that a determined attack upon that stronghold was *simultaneously* made along our entire front, he simply ordered an attack, and that, too, before a thorough examination of the ground was made. As a natural result, the troops upon the extreme right attacked in the morning, on the right centre some time after, on the left centre still later, and on the left late in the afternoon. At each of these threatened points the rebels brought all their force to bear, and drove the assailants back, whipping us in detail. Again, the front occupied by our brigade, and over which we attempted to pass, was covered by a dense slashing; while upon our right was an open field, over which it would have been a comparatively easy task to pass, with good promise of success; yet no troops ever essayed to assault that point.

And now the same policy, or lack of policy, was repeated. Instead of keeping the different corps of his army within supporting distance, from seven to sixteen miles were allowed to intervene between them, making defeat, whenever the rebels should offer battle, as certain as that he lived, and would one day die.

It will not avail Gen'l Banks to place the responsibility of defeat upon his subordinate generals. To him would have belonged the credit of success, and to him as justly must attach the disgrace of failure. He was supreme in the Department of the Gulf, and if Gen'l Smith, with the Sixteenth Corps, as he alleges (and as is true), was simply loaned to him, and would not obey his orders, he should have been *made* to obey them or suffer the consequences.

Whatever may be said of our generals, the soldiers had well performed their part. They marched nearly six hundred miles, fought four decisive battles, built innumerable bridges and fortifications, as well as the wonderful dam at Alexandria.

Never did men work harder, better, or with more determination, and never were men less repaid for their exertions.

If at Sabine Cross Roads they were defeated, the responsibility of that defeat does not rest with them. If at Pleasant Hill they won a victory and then turned their backs upon the enemy while he was fleeing from them, leaving the dead unburied, and the wounded to die or suffer agony worse than death, they are neither cowards for turning their backs upon this victory, or heartless wretches for thus leaving their comrades uncared for. The generals may be amenable to these charges, but the soldiers are not.

CHAPTER XVIII.

Upon our arrival at Morgansia, orders were received conveying the gratifying intelligence that this would be, for the present at least, our permanent camp; and with a hearty good will we entered upon the work of making it as comfortable as possible.

The adjacent forests offered abundant material for the construction of shady arbors, and in a few days the whole camp was covered with a leafy bower, most refreshing as a shield from the overpowering heat of the sun.

No duties, except such as were indispensable, were demanded of us, and lazily we perspired the weary days through.

When we arrived here a very large mail, which had been accumulating for weeks, was received, and with the newspapers from New Orleans, gave us the first information of the movements of the world we had received for a long time. About this time, too, we learned that a new military division had been created, of which the Department of the Gulf was a part. Maj. Gen'l E. R. S. Canby was announced as its commander, to whom Gen'l Banks was to report. This very materially curtailed the power of the hero of the Red River campaign, and gave him abundant leisure to "cultivate the social element" in New Orleans.

Orders were promulgated much faster now than they could be read and comprehended. One of these constituted the Nineteenth Corps a sort of marine corps, and instructed us to hold ourselves in readiness to move upon transports either up or down the river, wherever the rebels, encouraged by their recent victories, should attempt to obstruct the navigation of the stream.

We were, however, never required for this duty, and after a few days spent in camp, we regained our wonted powers, and began to long for active service again.

The effect of the intense heat soon began to manifest itself in those regiments which joined us just before our late campaign, in constant deaths. Many times in a day the bodies of some poor boys were carried to their last resting-place from these regiments, while the One Hundred and Sixteenth enjoyed complete immunity from disease. It really seemed as if our constitutions had been hardened into adamant.

As the memorable anniversaries of Plain Store, our first fight, and the two fatal assaults upon Port Hudson, of May 27th and June 14th, reached us, our minds wandered back to those scenes so fresh in our memories, as to make it difficult to realize that twelve long months had passed since we participated in them.

Mingled feelings of satisfaction at the glorious memory of the first, and of sadness at the terrible remembrance of the latter, filled our hearts, and nerved us for the proper discharge of all the duties still in store for us.

While here at Morgansia, the almost forgotten forms of Capt. Carpenter and the five enlisted men who had been North after conscripts, made their appearance. Although absent on this duty nearly a year, they returned, as they went, alone. We had hoped to have the pleasure of initiating some of our friends into the mysteries of soldiering when this party returned, but were doomed to disappointment, their mission having been entirely fruitless.

On the 20th day of June, a re-organization of the troops in the department was made, by which we retained our corps and division designations, but in which the Thirteenth Corps was disbanded and merged in the Nineteenth.

In this re-organization the One Hundred and Sixteenth was transferred back to the old First Brigade, much to the satisfaction of all, and Col. Love resumed command.

All these orders, with a something which an old soldier seems to snuff in the very air, looked very like a movement of some kind. Speculation was rife as to what it would be, and where it would land us. Mobile was the favored point, and nine-tenths of us had about concluded that this must be the objective point, when, on the first day of July, orders were received to be ready at a moment's notice to move on board transports to New Orleans.

All the necessary arrangements to comply with the order were speedily made, and by noon of the 2d the One Hundred and Sixteenth was on board the steamer *Col. Cowles.* At three o'clock that afternoon we cast off our lines, and for the last time swung into the current of the Mississippi. Although we had been nearly two years in the Department of the Gulf, and had lain for two months in the rear of Port Hudson, participating in the seige, we had had but an indifferent view of it. Now, however, as we approached it from above, we saw how wonderfully nature had provided there for the sealing up of the river. A short stop was made there, and then we again proceeded on our way, passing Baton Rouge—which had a very familiar look, from our long stay there—before dark. Other familiar places were passed, until darkness made it impossible to distinguish them, and then we turned in, to find ourselves at six o'clock the next morning tied up to the levee of New Orleans.

All around us were troops, and still they kept arriving from Morgansia. Some were disembarked and quartered in the deserted warehouses and cotton-gins which line the levee; while others, among which was the One Hundred and Sixteenth, remained all day on board the steamers.

The next day was the anniversary of our nation's birth, the Fourth of July. In the morning we marched ashore, and, except such as took French leave and wandered about the city, we celebrated the day in the dust and dirt of the levee. There was some attempt at a proper celebration of the glorious day, but except that part performed by the military, under the direction of Gen'l Banks, there was an entire lack of enthusiasm, consequent upon the rebel element forming so large a portion of the inhabitants.

About ten o'clock that night orders were received from Gen'l Emory, directing the One Hundred and Sixteenth, Ninetieth N. Y. Vols. and Thirtieth Mass. Vols., to proceed on board the steamer *Mississippi* with all possible dispatch. The whole night was wasted in vain attempts to obey the orders of any number of self-constituted commanders, but, by four o'clock on the morning of the 5th of July the designated regiments were all on board awaiting the arrival of Gen'l Emory. At five o'clock, the General having arrived, we cast off our lines and were steaming down the river, leaving New Orleans for the last time.

The *Mississippi* was a large, new and very staunch craft, and although terribly crowded, we congratulated ourselves on our good fortune in being again assigned to one of the best vessels in the fleet.

At two o'clock that afternoon we reached the bar at the mouth of the river, and, as seemed to be our luck, grounded. All the efforts of our powerful engine were unavailing, and hard aground we remained all night, and the next day and night. On the morning of the 7th the steamer *Creole* passed us without difficulty, and the old General, who had fumed and walked the deck in great impatience at our misfortune, because of his desire to reach our destination as soon as any of his troops, transferred himself to her. Word had been sent to New Orleans of our being unable to proceed, and within an hour of the time the General left us, two steam tugs arrived, and before the *Creole* was out of sight we got off the bar.

Our pilot left us when some ten miles out, and the sealed orders being opened we were astounded with the intelligence that we were bound for Fortress Monroe.

Before noon that day we had run fifty-two miles, and during the next twenty-four hours made two hundred and forty-nine miles; and on the 9th, two hundred and thirty.

Our experience now, unlike that on our previous trip, was most delightful. The sun shone most beautifully, the only drawback to our comfort being the intense heat.

A sad occurrence happened on the evening of July 5th, which sent a thrill of horror to every heart. It was the loss overboard of private John Thurber, of Company "F," who persisted, against the direct orders of the officers of the ship, in sleeping upon some portion of the vessel very much exposed. The nights were uncomfortably warm, and crowded as the men were, it became almost impossible to get any sleep in the hold. Many of the men were in the habit of sleeping on deck, and some were constantly getting into some boxes alongside the rail, from which position the least motion of the ship would precipitate them into the sea. They were warned of the danger of occupying these places, but all to no purpose; and on the evening of the 8th young Thurber laid himself down here for his night's rest; before midnight he rolled off the rail, and his cries for help soon brought many to see what was the trouble. The ship was immediately stopped, a small boat lowered, and every effort made to rescue him, but the darkness prevented their finding him; and after diligent search we steamed on our course, leaving another of our number in the depths of the Atlantic.

Almost a dead calm prevailed on the 10th, but three hundred miles were scored, with nothing unusual transpiring. The next day two hundred and thirty-eight miles were shown on the captain's log book, and as many of us looked at these figures, we could not but think how much easier it was for us to traverse that number of miles in our then condition, than even one-tenth of the distance without the aid of steam.

At five o'clock A. M., July 12th, we doubled Cape Hatteras, by noon had run two hundred and seventy-one miles, and at five o'clock P. M. reached Fortress Monroe, a distance of sixty miles more.

Here we heard startling rumors, which our being at once ordered to proceed to Washington seemed to make authentic. The rebel Gen'l Early, we were told, was advancing through Maryland, and was even then supposed to be near the national capital demanding its surrender; and this, too, when there were hardly a handful of troops there. A portion of the Sixth Corps we were informed had but just left the fortress, having been sent up from before Petersburg.

But with all this alarming intelligence a kind Providence did not fail to give us one item of a different character. This was the glad news that the rebel pirate *Alabama* had, in a fair fight, been defeated and sunk by the *Kearsarge.*

Receiving orders, as has been stated, to proceed with all possible dispatch to Washington, the wheels of our good steamer had hardly ceased their revolutions ere they were put again in motion, her stem turned up stream, and we were sailing up the beautiful Potomac.

Upon one side lay the sacred soil of Virginia, and on the other that of Maryland. Our eyes fairly danced as we saw fields of golden grain and waving meadows of grass, so much more like our northern farms than the lowlands of Louisiana. Here and there the surface was broken by beautiful hills, the like of which had been almost unknown where we had spent nearly two years.

As we neared Mount Vernon, where rests the ashes of the "Father of his country," the ship's bell commenced a solemn tolling, which was continued until we were some distance above it. This dear spot to every one who calls himself an American, with Fort Washington nearly opposite, demanded our attention, and were sights none of the One Hundred and Sixteenth ever expected to see as soldiers.

On the afternoon of July 13th we reached the wharf, and were at once disembarked, having been nearly nine days in making the run from the mouth of the Mississippi. While we lay upon the dock waiting orders to move, a carriage drove up, in which were two gentlemen, who evidently were very glad to notice our arrival. It did not need a second look to tell us that one of them was President Lincoln, and he very soon made us acquainted with his companion, Secretary Stanton. We cheered him right lustily, but he would not gratify our desire for a speech; and after a few words of cheer to those near him, they drove off. This was the first opportunity many of us had ever enjoyed of seeing Lincoln, and the open hearted smile with which he greeted us warmed many a heart toward him.

CHAPTER XIX.

THE same afternoon upon which we landed in Washington, a portion of the Sixth Corps made a determined charge upon the rebels laying siege to one of the many forts which encircle the city. They routed them utterly, so that they immediately raised the siege and that night retreated, followed by the Sixth Corps. This gallant affair was the work of the brigade to which the Forty-ninth N. Y. Vols. (a Buffalo regiment) belonged, and was commanded by Col. D. D. Bidwell. It won for the Colonel the long delayed recognition of his services and made him a brigadier general.

The only portion of our corps (the Nineteenth), yet arrived, was the First Brigade, and even this had reached the city in so many different vessels that the regiments were scattered.

About midnight Col. Love received orders to move the One Hundred and Sixteenth at once some seven miles out of the city, where the balance of the brigade had at last been collected. The object of the night march was to be in readiness to move to the support of the Sixth Corps early the following morning.

No one was sent to guide us, and at midnight, in a city of which we knew but precious little even by daylight, we shouldered our muskets and started.

Up this street and down that, out this one and back by another, round this corner and then that, past mansions and hovels, up hill and down, we went until, completely wearied out and entirely befogged, we concluded we were lost.

A halt was sounded, inquiries made of such inhabitants as could be found, and at last, in some unexplained way to us, we reached the designated point about four o'clock in the morning, and were soon sound asleep.

Three short hours we were permitted to enjoy "nature's sweet restorer," and at seven o'clock the bugle sounded the forward. Without any breakfast we roused ourselves from our slumber, and began what was termed the "Snicker's Gap," expedition.

Passing through a small collection of houses, sporting the name of Tenallytown, we turned to the left, and followed the ridge road leading to Leesburg, Va. Shortly after leaving the town, we passed an ambulance containing Maj. Gen'l Q. A. Gillmore, who had been placed in command of the forces, but had been thrown from his horse and severely hurt. Maj. Gen'l H. G. Wright, of the Sixth Corps, being the next in rank, assumed command.

In Louisiana we had marched upon perfectly level roads, with no hills to ascend or descend, and with no stones to interfere with our movements. Now, however, it seemed as though we had no sooner reached the bottom of one hill than another rose before us but a short distance ahead. Some claim that such roads are easier to travel upon than level ones, from the fact that ascending brings into play one set of muscles, which are relaxed and relieved by others when once the descent is begun. With all due deference to such mistaken souls, the men of the One Hundred and Sixteenth must differ. This was not their experience, and they found themselves much sooner exhausted than ever before. And then our feet were soon covered with blisters from the stones, large and small, over which we stumbled almost continually. Toward night we went into bivouac near Poolsville, all heartily wishing that we were again in Louisiana.

Coming as we did from a much warmer climate, we suffered very much from the cold night air, and found our supply of blankets entirely inadequate to keep us warm.

The Sixth Corps encamped near us, and many friendly visits were made to, and received from, the friends in the Forty-ninth N. Y. Vols., attached thereto.

This corps preceded us in the morning, and from some cause we did not move until ten o'clock. A short distance brought us to the banks of the Potomac, which it became necessary to ford, and we were halted to enable the Sixth Corps to accomplish this.

Hour after hour we waited, busying ourselves in making inquiries of all who chanced to pass as to where we were, and the no less important fact of where the rebels were. By this means we learned that we were at White's Ford, on the Potomac, and that the rebels were at or near Leesburg.

About five o'clock we fell into line, marched down a steep hill, crossed a canal and were upon the banks of the Potomac, which must be crossed without the aid of any pontoon bridge. Hastily we divested ourselves of shoes and stockings, and rolling our "unmentionables" well up, stepped into the stream and commenced the novel and somewhat perilous journey. The sight to any disinterested person must have been ludicrous in the extreme. For six hundred feet a scattered column of soldiers with muskets, shoes, stockings and cartridge boxes, elevated above their heads, were seen floundering along in a very unmilitary kind of a way. Long legs had a decided advantage over short ones, and the water being clear and the bottom covered with stones, it was but natural that a choice should be made between sharp-pointed ones and large smooth ones. No sooner, however, had a foot been placed on these, than away the foot would slip from the accumulated slime, and under would go the owner of it.

Many amusing incidents occurred to mark this our first attempt at fording a large stream. Dripping with water we touched the sacred soil of Virginia, and ascended the bank of the river without the fear of the "F. F. V.'s" before us.

Notwithstanding the sun had nearly disappeared when all had crossed, we moved on, and went into bivouac about ten o'clock that night a short distance from Leesburg.

The next day, July 17th, was Sunday, and was enjoyed in a very acceptable rest, being informed that we should probably remain there some time.

At five o'clock the following morning, however, came the order to "fall in," and passing around the city of Leesburg, we turned in the direction of the Blue Ridge, looming up in all their grandeur before us, and seemingly at no great distance.

One of the necessaries, even of soldier life, we found in greater abundance and of much more inviting appearance here than in Louisiana, and that was water. Clear cold springs issuing from the solid rock were abundant, and instead of satisfying our thirst from dirty stagnant pools, or the turbid fluid from the Mississippi and Red rivers, we drank long draughts clear and delicious.

During the day we passed through Hamiltonville, Purcellville and Snickersville, which latter place is situated just at the base of the mountains at the entrance to Snicker's Gap. Passing this small village we slowly began the toilsome crossing of the Blue Ridge through the gap. Many times we wondered where the gap was, for we seemed to be ascending the sides of the mountains themselves. At last, about eight o'clock in the evening, we reached the summit and began the descent, hardly less difficult than the ascent. By nine o'clock we had accomplished the task, and were bivouaced on the level plain between the ridge and the Shenandoah River.

Here we learned that a portion of the Eighth Corps, under Maj. Gen'l Crook, had been defeated that day by the rebels, who held the opposite bank of the river, and during most of the night a lively cannonading was kept up. The following day was spent in bivouac with nothing to enliven the hours except the shots exchanged by the pickets. Toward night an alarm was given, and considerable confusion manifested from contradictory orders, it being supposed that the enemy were about to attack us. It proved a false alarm, and we lay down and enjoyed a good night's rest.

A reconnoissance early on the morning of the 20th revealed the fact that the rebels had retreated during the night, and the whole command was ordered forward. Descending the banks of the Shenandoah we repeated our experience of a few days before, and reached the opposite bank in a very moist condition.

We proceeded some two or three miles in the direction of Berryville, and forming in line of battle, remained all day long listening to the sound of heavy cannonading. No move was made in the direction from which this sound proceeded. We knew nothing of what it was, but it would seem that the general commanding the forces there assembled, should have found out (what we afterwards learned) that Gen'l Averill with his cavalry was hotly engaged with the rebels. Had this been ascertained and we marched at once to his support, Jubal Early would not have so easily escaped.

A heavy rain set in while we remained here, which drenched us to the skin, and rendered the roads almost impassable. Just as the sun was sinking below th western horizon, we counter-marched, re-crossed the Shenandoah, marched up the rocky mountain side, passed again through the dismal gap, and traveled all night along the same road upon which we had advanced. By ten o'clock the next morning we had made a distance of twenty-three miles, and went into bivouac at Goose Creek, near Leesburg. This had been accomplished in the darkness of night at a break-neck pace, and we could not for the life of us see the necessity for such haste.

Leesburg we found to be a place of some considerable pretensions. Here and there were mansions which told of luxury and wealth, but the terrible hand of war had left its mark. We found in Virginia as well as in Louisiana, that these men who fondly anticipated an easy triumph and an increased wealth, had found, instead, an enemy not so easily conquered, and a terrible decrease in this world's goods. To this we could but say amen.

After going into bivouac, we learned the cause of our forced march. It was rumored that Gen'l Lee had abandoned his position before Gen'l Grant, and was advancing with his whole command upon Washington. Even we poor soldiers could see no foundation for these rumors, and did not find our estimation of Gen'l Wright very much heightened by the belief he evidently placed in them.

Never since our enlistment, not even in the famous

Red River campaign, had we fared as poorly as now. It was with difficulty that we obtained any rations, and when we halted that morning were almost destitute. From those not willing to listen to reason, but ready to grumble, we heard any thing but compliments to the government, which here, within a few miles of its capital, could permit its defenders to go hungry. To those who were inclined to be reasonable, the cause became at once apparent, when they remembered the hurry in which we were sent in pursuit of Early, and the consequent inability of our quartermasters getting supplies along.

The country on the whole presented a much better appearance than might have been expected. Army after army had passed over it, and although desolation was on every hand, still there were traces of husbandry. Enough seemed to be grown to supply the wants of the inhabitants. As was the case in Louisiana, so was it here, but very few able-bodied men were ever seen. All these were either in the rebel army, or very shady when Uncle Sam's boys were around. Only the women, children and negroes, such as were left of them, made their appearance, to do the *dis*agreeable or agreeable, as best suited their color.

At nine o'clock on the morning of the 22d we were again in motion, and passing through the village of Drainsville about noon, halted late at night eighteen miles from our starting point.

A good night's rest enabled us to move at eight o'clock on the morning of the 23d, almost as fresh as new. Marching a good fifteen miles, we crossed the famous chain bridge, and about three o'clock in the afternoon encamped some four miles from Washington, and within its defences.

CHAPTER XX.

It was now very generally expected that, having driven the invading force of Early up the valley, the Nineteenth Corps would be at once dispatched to Petersburg, where we had undoubtedly been destined to go when we left New Orleans. Coming events, however, ordered it otherwise, and the One Hundred and Sixteenth never saw either Richmond or Petersburg.

The 24th and 25th days of July were spent in camp, during which time the Second Brigade of our division joined us, having but just arrived from New Orleans. The troops were well supplied with clothing, of which they stood in great need, and better if possible than this, our commissary arrangements were perfected, so that in future we might reasonably expect our stated allowance of rations.

On the evening of the 25th it was rumored that the rebels were again invading Maryland, and before we turned in for the night orders came for us to advance early in the morning.

Accordingly, at eleven o'clock, July 26th, the One Hundred and Sixteenth started on what the boys afterward termed "the Harper's Ferry roust-about." Moving a short distance toward the city, and near to Tenallytown, from which point we started before, we took the Rockville turnpike, and until midnight toiled on over rocks and stones. During the early evening we passed through the thriving little town of Rockville, bivouacing nineteen miles from Washington, and making perhaps as fatiguing a march as ever the One Hundred and Sixteenth made. But three or four hours' sleep were allowed us, when, at four o'clock the next morning, we moved on. That day we passed the villages of Middlebrook, Clarksburg and Hyattsville, going into bivouac two miles beyond the latter place.

We were forcibly impressed that day with the vast difference between the people and country of a State true to the good old Union and of those false to it. In Louisiana and Virginia the people were few and poorly clad and fed, the country was running to waste, and the cities and villages dilapidated beyond belief. In "My Maryland" all was thrift. The people were well clad, and their countenances bore the unmistakable marks of well-filled stomachs. The country was under splendid cultivation, rich fields of ripening grain meeting us at every turn. The villages through which we passed were real live towns.

At five o'clock A. M. of the 27th our column was again in motion, but halted about eight o'clock on the banks of the Monocacy River, quite a large stream. Here Maj. Gen'l Lew Wallace, with such troops as could be hastily gathered in the vicinity of Washington, had met Early on his advance some two weeks before, and vainly attempted to stay his progress. Evidences of the battle were lying all around us. Broken muskets, bayonets, cartridge boxes, etc., etc., were strewn all about, giving mute tokens of the conflict. A substantial bridge across the river had at that time been destroyed, and another of tressle work, used by the Baltimore & Ohio Railroad, had been considerably damaged.

At four o'clock P. M. we left this point, and fording the river some two miles above the ruined bridge, proceeded on toward the city of Frederick. Just at the close of the day we entered this most beautiful city. With colors flying and drums beating we passed through it, and went into bivouac on the Chambersburg pike, some four miles beyond.

Frederick is a large city and a model one, not only in its beauty but in its loyalty. Never in our soldier experience had we seen so much love for our flag shown as here. Hundreds were flying from the house tops, and the entire population seemed to vie with each other in showing their good-will. Haversacks and pockets were filled with all manner of good things, and from almost every door came the children with pitchers and pails filled with clear cold water. From nearly all the windows the smiling faces of its good ladies looked down upon us.

At six o'clock on the 29th we again shouldered our muskets and proceeded on our way. Jefferson, Knoxville and Sandy Hook were passed that day, and we made a note of the rustier look they had than towns not so near the loyal line. From the latter place the road followed the Baltimore & Ohio Railroad, along a narrow ledge of rocks just at the base of Maryland Heights and on the bank of the Potomac. A short distance from it we turned a bend in the river, and Harper's Ferry, on the opposite bank, was before us. Crossing the river upon a pontoon bridge, we passed through the town and went into bivouac on Bolivar Heights. That day we marched twenty-two miles under a hot July sun, on a dry and dusty road, and were about used up.

Of course we improved the opportunity and took a view of the scene of poor old John Brown's hair-brained operations. One look was sufficient. The streets were narrow and dirty beyond description, and being built upon the side of Bolivar Heights, some of the houses seemed built upon the roofs of others, making it no difficult matter for those above to tell what their neighbors below were going to have for dinner.

We examined the ruins of the government arsenal destroyed by the rebels, but found nothing in or about them or the place to attract our attention, and so turned to the surroundings.

At this point the waters of the Shenandoah unite with those of the Potomac, and by their united power seem to have forced a passage through the Blue Ridge. Three bold peaks are thus formed, called Maryland, Loudon and Bolivar Heights. The scenery is magnificent in the extreme, causing the beholder to wonder at the power and majesty of the great Maker of the universe.

Amid this grand and imposing scenery we passed the night and the next day, until two o'clock in the afternoon, when a rumor having reached the General commanding that the rebels were moving toward Pennsylvania, and had already destroyed Chambersburg, our bivouac was broken up. Hardly rested from our severe marching, we turned our backs upon Harper's Ferry, recrossed the river, and at midnight spread our blankets near the Kittoctan Creek.

At six o'clock on the morning of the 31st we were aroused and once more started on. The day was intensely hot, the road dry and dusty, and hundreds of men were sunstruck. About noon we passed again through Frederick, receiving the same kind attention from its citizens as before. Proceeding a short distance beyond the city limits, we turned from the road and bivouaced in a delightful piece of woods. Here we found that the rumor was false, or at least greatly exaggerated, and one day, August 1st, was allowed us of comparative quiet. This, with the two nights' rest, enabled us to start again on the 2d greatly refreshed.

A short march of seven miles brought us to the Monocacy, where we found the Second Division of our corps, under Gen'l Grover, and once more the Nineteenth Corps was united.

Our old division commander, Gen'l Emory, was assigned to the command of it, with Gen'l Dwight in command of the First Division and Gen'l Grover of the Second. These officers retained their positions to the close of the war.

A word here of our corps commander may not be out of place. An old army officer, well advanced in years, his very presence was calculated to inspire respect. His constant care that his men were supplied with every thing that could be obtained, had gained their love. Of light complexion and sandy hair, he was known throughout the corps as "old brick top," and although rough and stern in his manner, the generous nature within often manifested itself to even the lowest in rank. Above all, on the battle-field we had learned his ability to handle us with intelligence, and this completed our admiration of the man.

Maj. Gen'l David Hunter had been assigned to the command of this army soon after our return to Washton from Snicker's Gap, and now Lieut. Gen'l Grant arrived at the Monocacy. Almost simultaneously it was announced that Hunter was relieved, and that Maj. Gen'l Philip H. Sheridan was assigned to the command of the Middle Military Division. This was a new creation of the war office, and embraced the Departments of Western Virginia, Susquehanna, Middle and Washington, and of which we formed a part.

Of Gen'l Sheridan we knew but very little. His name had been associated with some brilliant cavalry exploits, but much regret was manifested that some man better known, like Gen'l Joe Hooker, for instance, had not been selected. Gen'l Grant, however, knew better than we the duties to be performed, and future events proved that he knew the man, too, whom he had chosen.

The Shenandoah Valley, extending from Harper's Ferry to Staunton, had been the scene of many engagements. They had almost invariably resulted in victory to the rebels, until it had become familiarly known as the "valley of humiliation" to us. When Gen'l Grant made his grand advance through the Wilderness to Richmond, he fully realized the importance of sending a force up this valley to prevent the rebels from invading Maryland and Pennsylvania. Through this gateway these invasions had always been made. Gen'l Siegel was therefore placed in command of a force for this purpose, but failed entirely, being badly defeated. Gen'l Hunter afterward relieved him, but was still more disastrously beaten. He advanced nearly to Staunton, and was then so utterly routed as to make it necessary for his army to leave the Shenandoah Valley, cross the mountains, and retreat by the Kanawha Valley. Thus the way was opened for Gen'l Early, who at once moved down the valley, crossed the Potomac, and, as has been already related, came very near capturing Washington. This was his darling plan, which he was only prevented from effecting by the opportune arrival of the Sixth and Nineteenth Corps.

Now a determined effort was to be made, under the new commander, to retrieve our misfortunes, and hold possession of this key to the whole North.

For this work Gen'l Sheridan was to have the Sixth, Eighth and Nineteenth Corps of infantry, and two divisions of cavalry, with which it was hoped he would succeed.

August 3d was spent in quiet on the banks of the Monocacy, but toward night, on the 4th, we filled our haversacks with four days' rations, and crossed the trussle bridge. About two o'clock A. M., August 5th, our brigade was ordered on board the cars, and amid the darkness we were whirled along toward Harper's Ferry.

The cars were much worse than those upon which the One Hundred and Sixteenth traveled from Elmira to Baltimore, two years before, but not a grumbler was found to cry shame on the government that would compel its soldiers to ride in any thing short of passenger coaches.

At five o'clock the next morning we alighted from the cars at the base of Maryland Heights, and commenced ascending the zigzag road leading to its summit. Before reaching that point, however, and when something more than half way up, we came out on a large level plain, where we went into bivouac. A more magnificent sight it had never been our good fortune to behold, than now opened before us. Towering hundreds of feet above our heads was the bristling summit of the peak, away to the right, for miles upon miles, we looked into Maryland, while across the Potomac the beautiful Shenandoah Valley stretched as far as the eye could reach. Bordered with the blue mountains on either side, carpeted with alternate field and forest, and interspersed here and there with small towns and villages, it looked a perfect paradise on earth. The ascent had been toilsome, but the wonderful sight more than repaid us.

That night we slept in our elevated bivouac, but at seven o'clock the next morning the One Hundred and Sixteenth moved with the rest of the army down from Maryland Heights, crossed the river, and by noon were encamped near the spot occupied by them a week before. Three days of rest — unheard of blessing — were allowed us here. Every moment was improved, and as we smoked our pipes we recounted our movements since our arrival from New Orleans. The conclusion reached was, that bad as had been the management of affairs there, we could see no marked improvement here. We wondered what need there was in moving hither and yon, at the beck of dame rumor, passing three times between Harper's Ferry and the Monocacy in a single week.

On the 7th of August, while we lay on Bolivar Heights, Gen'l Sheridan arrived and assumed command. His order issued to the troops, announcing this fact, was a model one. Unlike the most of such orders, it was short and to the point, with no waste of ink and paper in telling what he could or would do. Twenty-four hours had hardly elapsed before we all felt that the little man who rode so large a horse was equal to almost any emergency, and naming him "Little Phil," we waited his movements.

CHAPTER XXI.

AT five o'clock, on the morning of August 10th, the One Hundred and Sixteenth broke camp and entered upon the Shenandoah Valley campaign, the most glorious of any it had ever participated in.

Our three days' rest had refreshed us amazingly, and with light hearts within our breasts, and a good hard turnpike beneath our feet, we started. Halltown, consisting of one house and the ruins of two others, was soon passed; and by nine o'clock we entered Charlestown, the place where old John Brown was hung. As we passed through its streets every man joined in the song—

"John Brown's body lies mouldering in the ground,
But his soul goes marching on."

The truth of which refrain the citizens of that place had long since learned.

In Louisiana it had been the custom to march the whole army upon the road, by which plan it would occupy miles and present any thing but a bold front if sharply attacked. The folly of this we had seen manifested on our Red River campaign, and now we saw, on the very first day's march, Gen'l Sheridan's method. The artillery and wagon train were allowed the undisputed use of the road, while all the troops were marched in the fields along both sides of the road four and five columns deep.

By this disposition of his army he not only effectually guarded his artillery and train, but should he meet the enemy he had but to deploy or spread out his troops, and he was ready for them. It requires no knowledge of military science to see the advantage of this mode of advancing over the "Banks' system."

A toilsome march of eighteen miles enabled us to bivouac near Berryville. At five o'clock the following morning our column was again in motion, and before noon our cavalry advance seemed to have met the enemy. The reports of cannon could be distinctly heard; but they were easily driven, and we slowly advanced. Winchester was left on our right, the column passing some four or five miles to the left of it. Toward night we bivouaced near a small place called White Post.

Bright and early on the morning of the 12th we were aroused from our slumbers, and to the sound of artillery in the front, marched twelve miles, encamping just beyond Middletown.

If the Shenandoah Valley had looked inviting from Maryland Heights, we found as we traversed it that it was even more beautiful than it had appeared. The desolating hand of war was seen on every side, to be sure, in ruined houses, burned buildings, and destroyed fences; yet for all this, it was beautiful, more like our northern farming land than any we had seen, and consequently seemed more like home. Some splendid mansions, sadly in need of the care of loyal owners, were passed every day. Every thing betokened this to have been the abode of plenty and one of the most fruitful portions of the earth.

The next day our cavalry found the rebels posted on the line of Cedar Creek, a strong position, which they did not appear anxious or willing to relinquish. A portion of the Sixth Corps was despatched to the assistance of the cavalry, and at length succeeded in driving them across the stream and in the direction of Fisher's Hill. After this had been accomplished, we moved up to the line abandoned by the rebels, where we remained August 13th, 14th and 15th. Whether it was Gen'l Sheridan's intention to continue the advance we had no means of knowing; nor do we know that the news received while we remained there determined him to return. This news was to the effect, that a fresh division from Richmond was hastening down to Early's assistance, and that it was expecting to gain our rear by coming down the Luray Valley. This is really a part of the main valley, separated from it by the Massanutten Mountain, which rises at Strasburg, a few miles beyond Cedar Creek, and extends many miles.

Whether it was through fear of this reinforcement, or from a desire that the enemy should so construe it, that Gen'l Sheridan ordered his army to fall back, is of no moment; suffice it that about ten o'clock on the night of August 15th, we buckled on our equipments, and, amid a rain storm, proceeded toward Winchester, where we arrived by five o'clock the next morning.

The whole day was spent here, affording ample time to see such sights as were to be seen. Winchester is the largest, and by far the most important place in the valley. It contains two banks (which were not, however, in a very flourishing condition), ten or twelve churches, a town hall, a hotel, and some elegant residences. During the war it was captured and re-captured by the contending forces no less than seventy times. As may be imagined, this fact made it a difficult matter for its inhabitants to tell, for any length of time, just how loyal it was prudent to be.

Their real sympathy with the rebellion would, however, manifest itself, and leave no doubt as to their want of loyalty to the Union.

There was no business done, except such as we enabled them to do, and here, as at New Orleans, we noticed the eagerness with which the most arrant rebel would clutch our greenbacks.

At four o'clock the following morning we were once more under way upon the Berryville pike, which place we reached about two o'clock P. M.

During our stay at Cedar Creek, Mosby, the guerrilla, with his band of desperadoes, attacked a supply train near Berryville, and completely destroyed it, capturing quite a number of our men. This man Mosby was deserving of a better cause than that in which he was engaged. He was indefatigable, and caused our army very much trouble. His movements were made with great celerity, and although attempts were often made by our cavalry to capture him, his ways were past finding out, and he remained the terror of the Shenandoah Valley to the end of the war.

Early on the morning of August 18th, the column was again put in motion, and a march of some thirteen miles brought us to within three miles of Charlestown. Here we went into bivouac, and remained until noon of the 21st. During all this time we heard almost constant firing in the direction of Berryville, making it very sure that the rebels had followed us.

At noon, on the 21st, the army was moved back through Charlestown, and the Nineteenth Corps formed in line of battle on a road running at right angles with the turnpike. The One Hundred and Sixteenth was placed in position in a corn field of immense growth, which was leveled with the ground in much less time than would seem possible. With such implements as were at hand, the rail fences were torn down, placed in position, and soon covered with sufficient earth to form a good protection from bullets. All this time the firing in our front and a little to our left was growing more rapid, indicating that the Sixth Corps were having lively times.

All fully expected an engagement, but the sun went down without our having fired a shot.

Quietly we prepared our evening meal of coffee and hard tack, and then rolling ourselves in our blankets, slept as soundly as did our friends at home.

At midnight this line was abandoned, and we continued the retreat to Halltown, reaching there before daylight. Twice before we had occupied nearly this same camping ground, and from our almost periodical return to the vicinity of Harper's Ferry, our army received the cognomen of "Harper's Weekly."

The heights which Gen'l Sheridan now occupied were exceedingly well located for defensive operations. The line extended from the Potomac on the right, to the Shenandoah on the left. It was not so long but that the troops he had easily covered it, and thus made it impossible for the rebels to flank the position.

The right was held by the Sixth Corps, the centre by the Nineteenth, and the left by the Eighth, while the cavalry were left for reconnoitring. A deal of labor was again expended in building breastworks, which were now planned and built under the supervision of an engineer officer. They were very strong and secure, and behind them we waited in hopes that the rebels would attack us, and give us a chance to give them such a reception as their comrades had given us at Port Hudson.

Vain hope! Not a shot was ever fired from behind them, nor were we ever in our experience permitted to fight behind works erected by us, although, again and again after this, we shoveled earth sufficient to bury the whole rebel army.

It soon came to be known that our "Little Phil" was being governed by orders from Gen'l Grant. At present he could not do better than to hold Early right where he was, and thus prevent the return to Richmond of any of his troops. From Early's movements, he was seemingly there with the same object in view with reference to us.

Day after day passed, and except constant firing by the pickets, and a daily reconnoisance, nothing of interest transpired. On the morning of August 27th, our brigade was ordered out on one of the reconnoisances; but had proceeded only a short distance when the orders were countermanded, the enemy having fallen back. Soon after reaching our quarters, orders came that the whole command would move the following morning.

Accordingly, at seven o'clock on the 28th, we left our works, and that night bivouaced near Charlestown. This position, on the road leading to Winchester, was also fortified with a strong line of earthworks. All expected to move in the morning, but as the hours passed away and no orders were received, we settled down to enjoy the rest and listened to the distant connonading. This, we learned, was from a portion of our cavalry who attacked the enemy near Bunker Hill, and would have been badly defeated but for the timely assistance of a division of the Sixth Corps sent to them.

Five days of delightful repose, free from care, were spent here; during which time the glad news of the capture of Atlanta by Gen'l Sherman was received.

On the evening of September 2d orders were received to move at day-light the next morning. At the appointed time we moved from out our fortifications, and filing to the left, took up our line of march in the direction of Berryville. Crossing meadows and cultivated fields alike, we made sad havoc with vegetation, such as there was, and about noon halted on the same ground occupied by us on our retreat. Toward night we were moved to the right a couple of miles, and just as we got into the position selected for a camp, and were about to stack arms, the heavy rattle of musketry startled us, just beyond a belt of woods and a little to our left. Expecting every moment to be ordered into the engagement, we grasped our muskets with nervous energy, and in the growing darkness waited. The sounds soon died away, however, and as this danger to a good night's sleep vanished, another in the form of a heavy rain storm set in. Supperless we rolled ourselves in our blankets, and each selecting as dry a spot as could be found, went soundly to sleep despite the rain.

The alarm was occasioned by the sudden coming of a party of the Eighth Corps upon a force of rebels, who, after a short but stubborn resistance, retreated.

Notwithstanding the storm continued nearly all night, we awoke quite refreshed and found the sun just rising with warmth and comfort in his beams. A substantial breakfast finished, and we once again entered upon the construction of a line of intrenchments. Immediately in front of the One Hundred and Sixteenth was a small house, which offered good timbers with which to construct the works. Besides, it would, in case of an engagement, seriously interfere with our movements. Without so much as "by your leave" to the owner, it was, therefore, quickly demolished and used for this loyal purpose Before the works were completed our position was advanced some twelve hundred yards, and other troops took posession of them while we commenced, not without some grumbling at this injustice, another line in our new position.

As there were evident signs of an attack upon us, we went to work with a will, and before nightfall had completed as formidable a line of earthworks as could be found. Again we trusted our rebel enemies would favor us with a visit; they failed, however, to gratify us, although on the morning of the 5th they drove in our pickets, making quite a demonstration. Owing, probably, to the strength of our position, they satisfied themselves with this, and, as we afterward learned, fell back to Winchester.

For two weeks we quietly occupied our works, busying ourselves with drilling and target practice. An occasional reconnoisance varied the scene somewhat, furnishing the only excitement we enjoyed, for soldiers in time come to really enjoy excitement. During one of these, an entire South Carolina regiment was captured.

Sunday, September 11th, was set apart by President Lincoln as a day of Thanksgiving to God for our victories at Mobile and Atlanta. By direction of Col. Love the One Hundred and Sixteenth was assembled and listened to the reading of the Proclamation and a prayer from the Episcopal service. All duties were suspended for the day, except such as were absolutely necessary, and we spent it in as happy a manner as was possible under the circumstances.

On the 17th we learned that Gen'l Grant had arrived, and conjecture was rife as to what this meant. It was the general conclusion that the time had come for us to strike a blow. The next day an order was received directing all surplus baggage sent to the rear, and then we knew that such was the fact. Hurriedly all articles not essentially necessary were speedily packed and sent to Harper's Ferry, and by night every thing was in readiness to move at a moment's notice.

At midnight reveille was sounded, and in a short time hundreds of camp fires were throwing their light upon the dusky forms of thousands of hungry soldiers preparing their frugal meal. But little time was occupied in this very necessary duty, and long before daylight, on the 19th day of September, the army had left its bivouac, and was slowly wending its way toward Winchester.

CHAPTER XXII.

At five o'clock forty-four minutes, the sun rose on that eventful 19th day of September, 1864. One of the most glorious in the calendar of the One Hundred and Sixteenth, and yet the last many of us were ever to spend on earth.

As the sun rose, our cavalry in the advance came upon the enemy strongly posted on the banks of the Opequan Creek. This made it impossible for the column to advance, but the rapid reports of cannon, to which we listened at first, ere long died away, the cavalry having driven them from their position. The wagon train interfered somewhat with our movements, and our progress to this point was slow. Here the train was turned aside, and, passing the Eighth Corps, we forded the wide but shallow stream, and entered a deep gorge, along which flowed a small stream.

This gorge is about a mile in length. Through it runs the main valley turnpike and upon this road our army must proceed should it advance up the valley. This fact was as well understood by Early as by Sheridan, and the defeat of the force he had left to prevent our entering it, left him but this course to pursue: which was, to seize with his whole force the opening, and prevent our coming out on the open fields in the vicinity of Winchester; or, failing in this, to permit us to pass through it; and then by one dashing charge regain it, and thus cut off our retreat. By this he hoped to capture Sheridan's whole command.

He failed in preventing our entrance, and was equally

unsuccessful in keeping us within the gorge. Consequently the battle of the Opequan or "Sheridan's Winchester" was fought for the possession of this gorge: by Early to cut off our retreat, and by Sheridan to maintain a line of retreat, should one be found necessary.

The Sixth Corps were in the advance, and passing out of the gorge filed to the left, forming their line of battle with their right resting opposite to, and some hundreds of yards in advance of it.

As the Nineteenth Corps entered the gorge, the sound of artillery was becoming more rapid every moment, and in the intervals we could hear the cracking of musketry. Had any thing more been needed to make us sure that we were in for a fight, we had it in numerous hospital tents already erected, in which we could see a few wounded. All along the road were the splendid cavalrymen of Wilson's Division, who, having driven the enemy from the Opequan and developed his position, coolly held their bridles while they consoled us with the information that the "rebs" were ready for us. Besides all this, among the rocks and bushes which lined the road, were seen the still more certain evidences of an approaching battle in the persons of skulkers, of whom the One Hundred and Sixteenth had its share. No barometer ever more truly indicated the approach of a storm than do these cowards the approach of a battle. By hook or by crook, despite the vigilance of their officers, they will manage to get out of the column, and not be seen until toward the close, or after the engagement is over.

Firmly the men of the Nineteenth Corps, who had won victories and suffered defeat thousands of miles away in the lowlands of Louisana, marched into this their first engagement on the sacred soil of Virginia. As they came out upon the open fields and caught a glimpse of the beautiful valley before them, they determined that no disgrace should attach to the cross of the "Legion of Honor" (their corps badge) that day. The whole corps was moved some distance to the right, and Grover's Divison formed in line of battle, their left connecting with the right of the Sixth Corps. Our Division (Dwight's) was placed in position to support them, with each brigade in close column by regiment.

The same movements necessary to put us properly in position, were probably executed by our whole army; and as Gen'l Sheridan is one of those particular commanders who must see that every order is executed to the letter, considerable delay was experienced. During this time, occupied no doubt by the rebels in the same manner, the artillery entirely ceased, and only an occasional musket shot was heard. From this, many reasoned that after all we were not going to have a fight, the "wish being father to the thought," no doubt.

To every general officer Gen'l Sheridan had said, "Remain as you are until you hear my bugle sound the forward, then *go for them.*" The moments seemed hours, but at last away to our left the well known bugle sound was heard, and being repeated by each commander the whole line arose and slowly advanced. Clearing the field where we had rested, we entered a heavy piece of woods through which we proceeded with difficulty.

Not a war-like sound could be heard. All was as still as death, to which every man felt he was possibly advancing. By those only who have "been there," and experienced the stillness which always attends such a movement, made in the bewildering recesses of a forest, expecting every moment to find themselves upon a concealed enemy, hearing only the cracking of dry branches beneath their feet, can our feelings that morning be appreciated.

Ere the One Hundred and Sixteenth cleared this forest, Grover's Division, in advance of us, were seen by the rebels, and with a roar like ten thousand thunder claps they opened upon them. Our fears all at once vanished like dew before the sun, the peculiar swelling in the throat, which no doctor was ever able to explain or cure, was effectually removed by the very first shot fired.

The point held by Grover's Division and the right division of the Sixth Corps, was the vital point in our line, covering as it did the gorge. Here Early made an immediate and furious attack, which came well nigh being successful. Firing one volley the rebels dashed across the open field, and before our men had time to look, they were upon them. Bravely they resisted the overpowering numbers, but were forced to give way. All this happened in half the time occupied in reading it, and now our Division (Dwight's) was deployed into line of battle to meet the on-coming conquerers, and with them dispute the possession of the coveted gorge.

It has been stated that the brigades were in column of regiments, the deployment of which those versed in military science will understand. The leading regiment of our brigade was the gallant One Hundred and Fourteenth N. Y. Vols., and while the One Hundred and Fifty-third N. Y. Vols. and One Hundred and Sixteenth faced to the right and moved their length beyond it, it was subjected to the most awful fire that ever a regiment received. Most nobly did they maintain their position, losing in killed and wounded one hundred and eighty-eight men, two-thirds of their number. By this time Grover's Division was rallied, and forming on our left, we presented once more a continuous line of battle to the enemy. We were now annoyed, and a number of our men killed, by the fire of a battery placed in position on our flank by the rebels. Two regiments of our brigade, the Thirtieth Mass. and Twenty-ninth Maine Vols., were disposed to care for this flank, but did not succeed in driving the battery away.

For one long hour or more we remained holding firmly our ground, giving and receiving a heavy fire.

It is astonishing how much ammunition is wasted in every engagement. Not one ball in a thousand ever does any one any harm, and it has been estimated that it takes a man's own weight in lead to kill him.

At last an order came for the line to advance to a rail fence some five hundred yards distant. It was a perilous undertaking, but forward we went in as short a time as possible, the shells whistling over us, and the bullets singing about our heads in great numbers meanwhile. For some time we remained on this line, and then an order was communicated to the One Hundred and Sixteenth by the regiment on our right, to return to our first position. Hardly had we regained it, however, before the order was found to have been unauthorized, and back again to the rail fence we hurried.

These movements were not as easily made as they are described, nor were they bloodless ones, two men of Company "H" being killed by the bursting of one shell.

Soon after our second return to this fence, Company "G," Capt. Rohan, was deployed as skirmishers, and advanced under a terrible fire some distance. It was found to be a useless exposure of the men, and they were recalled. All this time the enemy could be seen in the edge of a piece of woods which partially concealed them, and they made a great display of their battle-flags as if courting our fire.

In the early part of the engagement we all showed the quick nervous movements of excitement, but after a few volleys had cooled us, we settled down to our work, and found fighting in Virginia very much the same as in Louisiana. We perceived that a puff of white smoke from the woods occupied by the rebels, was certain to be followed by a shrieking shell, in honor of which we invariably bowed ourselves low.

Thus far the battle had resulted alike to both armies. Each occupied substantially their original positions. Had all Gen'l Sheridan's troops been engaged, the result of that engagement, and consequently of Grant's movements before Petersburg, must have been far different from what they afterward were.

Gen'l Sheridan, however, fully appreciated the value of a reinforcement of fresh troops, and had, therefore, held the Eighth Corp in reserve, and now, when the Sixth and Nineteenth Corps were exhausted, and the enemy were, doubtless, feeling sure of a drawn battle, the sound of advancing troops coming to our relief was heard. It was the Eighth Corps clean and fresh. They came up in splendid order, and as they halted we fell back a short distance and rested. Without delay Gen'l Crook reformed his line, extending away beyond the one we had held, in order that it should swing round on the enemy's flank. While this was being done, Gen'l Sheridan directed an aide to give Gen'l Custer his compliments and tell him to break for the enemy's rear, and not to spare "one d——d ounce of horse flesh."

When all was in readiness, the Eighth Corps moved forward slowly at first, but as they caught sight of the rebels, faster and faster, their right swinging round and doubling up the enemy. With a yell they entered the woods where we had seen the rebel line all day, and then we were ordered to follow them. As we passed over the ground, disputed for so stubbornly during so many hours, the sight was sickening in the extreme.

The charge of the Eighth Corps, with that of Custer's cavalry, had been entirely unexpected. Flesh and blood could not resist them, and in confusion the enemy fled, leaving us the victors.

Our brigade passed through Winchester, and as darkness came on encamped in its outskirts, and snatching a hasty supper we were soon dreaming of the events of the day.

While resting from our fatiguing labors, and while the Eighth Corps were forming preparatory to their charge, a detail of men from the One Hundred and Sixteenth was made, who collected our dead, and with tender care buried them, marking the spot as best they could. These numbered nine brave boys, and besides these there were forty wounded.

Truly, that 9th day of September was a glorious one for the One Hundred and Sixteenth, and the army to which it belonged. It was the beginning of hard work, as exhausting, perhaps, as any we had ever performed, but it was in pursuit of an enemy soundly whipped and badly demoralized; not a retreat from one elated with victory.

Gen'l Grant's visit to Gen'l Sheridan *did* mean something, and those two pithy words of command which he gave, "go in," were fruitful of more glorious results than any other one so brief. Our victory had been complete; several rebel generals were killed, and their loss was estimated at five thousand men, with five pieces of artillery and fifteen battle flags.

CHAPTER XXIII.

HAD some of our earlier generals of "masterly inactivity" been in command of the army which had won so brilliant a victory as that recorded in the last chapter, we should have remained at Winchester two or three weeks. Thus the rebels would have been enabled to recover from their defeat, and be ready to meet us again on an equal footing. Not so with Gen'l Sheridan. He fully realized the advantage he had gained, and did not propose thus to lose it.

Accordingly, at five o'clock A. M., September 20th, the One Hundred and Sixteenth was again in motion, following the same road it had traveled about a month before. Kernstown, Newtown and Middletown were successively passed, and about two o'clock in the afternoon we reached our old camp near Cedar Creek. Fording the creek — the bridge having been burned by the rebels — we continued our march until four o'clock, and went into bivouac a short distance from Strasburg.

As we pitched our shelters we heard the sound of guns, and soon learned that our cavalry had followed close upon the heels of the retreating army the night before, to Fisher's Hill. Here they made a bold stand, and the cavalry found it impossible to dislodge them.

The point selected for this stand was well nigh impregnable. No force could ever have routed them by direct assault. The hill is an abrupt cliff, at least a hundred feet high, upon the crest of which they had built a strong line of earthworks, and were again ready to dispute our further advance. Just at this point, too, as if to afford a sure place from which to defend the valley against us, the Massanutten mountain rises and divides the valley, making it very narrow here. This enabled them to cover the whole line extending from mountain to mountain.

As we took a survey of this position on the morning of September 21st, our faith in our ability to route them became very weak, and in the breasts of some entirely vanished. As the day wore on we discussed the probabilities of the success of an attack; and as we heard the firing of the pickets and saw the evident signs of coming battle, we nerved ourselves with the remembrance that Sheridan was our leader, and found our confidence brightening. Toward noon our brigade was ordered into line, and proceeded across the Manassas railroad, where we remained until about five o'clock, when the One Hundred and Sixteenth left the brigade and went on picket. The line was along the banks of the Shenandoah river, and before the posts were all established we saw the sun descend below Fisher's Hill. Just before dark we listened to some very fine music from a rebel band, the wind being in the right direction to waft the sound to us.

The prospects of a fight having, for the present, disappeared, and our disposition for the night being, as we supposed, made, we congratulated ourselves, and proceeded to make our arrangements accordingly. Alas for all human calculations. About ten o'clock P. M., the One Hundred and Fourteenth N. Y. Vols. came down with orders to relieve us, and directing us to rejoin the brigade. Considerable time was spent in relieving the different posts, but toward midnight the One Hundred and Sixteenth was groping its way in the dark, in a vain endeavor to find the First Brigade. Had it remained in the position in which we left it, we might possibly have found it, but during our absence it had been moved some distance, and although an aide from Gen'l Beal, our brigade commander, was with us, we stumbled along, surrounded on every side by sleeping soldiers, and yet lost.

Tired out at last, and vexed beyond expression, we were halted by Col. Love, who informed the aide that he was going to remain where he was until daylight, or until Gen'l Beal would send an officer who could conduct us to the brigade. Selecting the best spot of ground available, each man was soon asleep. Not long, however, were we permitted to enjoy our rest, for long before daybreak on the morning of the 22d, another staff officer found us, and at last enabled us to rejoin our command in a heavy piece of woods.

Here we were again set at work upon a line of breastworks. Axes, shovels and picks were furnished us; and while some swung the axe and felled the trees, others brought them to the line selected and placed them in position; and still others dug deep into the soil and covered them with earth. The result of all this labor was that before noon we had erected as formidable a line of entrenchments as was ever constructed. We felt more secure after they were finished than before, but not a shot were we ever enabled to fire from behind them.

A detail of skirmishers from the One Hundred and Sixteenth, under the command of Lieut. Shepard, was sent out to the edge of the woods in which we were at work, who kept up a lively fire with the rebel skirmishers, some five hundred yards distant. These fellows were snugly ensconced in what were termed "bull pens," a slight structure of rails hurriedly thrown together and covered with earth, scattered along at intervals of ten or twelve yards, and sufficiently large to cover five or six men each.

Gen'l Sheridan had, during the day previous, thoroughly examined the ground, and during the night had placed the Sixth and Nineteenth Corps in the position he desired them to occupy. We were busily employed at these earthworks for the undoubted purpose of misleading the enemy with the impression that we were preparing to resist his attack upon us, while away upon the right, climbing the rugged sides of the mountain, Gen'l Crook, with the Eighth Corps, was slowly gaining the enemy's rear, preparing to repeat his brilliant charge of the 19th on their flank.

The time which it would take for him to reach the desired point had been figured to a moment, so that when that hour arrived, and he charged down upon them, the Sixth and Nineteenth Corps were advanced, and the simultaneous movement of the three corps it was hoped would give us victory.

About twelve o'clock M., Gen'l Dwight, our division commander, directed Col. Love to take the One Hundred and Sixteenth and drive the enemy from the "bull pens" in front of his division. The task was no easy one, and he was instructed to deploy his regiment as skirmishers, and advance in that manner. Forming in line behind the works, we leaped over them and moved forward to the edge of the woods, when Col. Love, knowing that a sudden dash for them would be more certain of success and less disastrous to us, at once gave the command to charge upon them. With a deafening cheer the One Hundred and Sixteenth cleared the wood, and at its first appearance received a heavy discharge of musketry from the rebel pens. Across the open field we went like mad men, never returning a shot, and ere we reached the line the "rebs" incontinently fled. In less than fifteen minutes from the time of receiving the order, the One Hundred and Sixteenth were in possession of the line, and found that three companies of the Thirtieth Mass. Vols., sent upon a like errand, were sharers in the credit of the capture.

For two or three hours we remained here exposed to a severe fire from the enemy, which, however, did no harm, shielded as we were by the rails. At four o'clock P. M. we heard the cheering of the Sixth Corps as it advanced, and at the same moment all our artillery opened, which seemed to make the very mountains quake. Simultaneously the solid columns of our own Nineteenth Corps were seen emerging from the woods. The fire from the rebel works was now terrific in the extreme, but on came our boys seemingly unmindful of it. Waiting until they reached us, we joined our brigade and went forward with them.

Gen'l Sheridan's only reliance was upon the success of the flanking column, the nature of the ground in front making an attack there impracticable. The movement, therefore, of the Sixth and Nineteenth Corps was simply for effect. The Eighth Corps were as victorious as at Winchester, and ere we reached the base of Fisher's Hill the enemy were routed even worse than before. As this intelligence reached us we were toiling up the hill, and, exhausted as we were, we gave expression to our joy in hearty cheers.

The loss of the One Hundred and Sixteenth, in the battle of Fisher's Hill, was very slight, being but one killed and nine wounded.

The rout of Early was the most complete of any, thus far, during the war. It utterly demoralized his army, the men fleeing by hundreds into the mountains for safety. He lost over two thousand prisoners, twenty-one pieces of artillery, and small arms and battle flags without number.

To say that we were tired would not in any measure express our condition. We were exhausted with the hard and constant duties of the preceding four days. Since the morning of the 19th, the One Hundred and Sixteenth had had but eight hours' sleep, had been engaged in two battles and marched and countermarched many miles, and now fondly anticipated a good night's rest.

As we mounted Fisher's Hill, we met hundreds of prisoners going to the rear. From them we learned how the appearance of the Eighth Corps on their flank and rear had astounded them. Never dreaming that such a thing as getting a force up the rugged sides of the mountain was possible, they had given their undivided attention to us in their front. When, therefore, Gen'l Crook's corps made its appearance, they fled in great confusion. No regrets were expressed that the fortunes of war had made them our prisoners. On the contrary, they manifested real joy at falling into our hands, knowing that they were sure of good rations and better treatment than while in the service of the C. S. A.

Daylight was fast fading away, and at every step we expected an order to halt and make ourselves comfortable for the night, but still on we moved with hardly energy sufficient to drag one foot before the other. Darkness had now enveloped every thing, and the only sound to be heard, except an occasional wish that our generals were in our places, was the clatter of the bayonets and canteens as we jogged along. The darkness was intense. It was literally impossible to see your hand before your eyes, and there were those who thought it bad policy thus to advance into any trap the enemy might set for us.

We had proceeded perhaps five miles in this impenetrable darkness when a brilliant flash of light, immediately in front of us on the road we were following, almost blinded us; the well known report of a gun, and the screech of a shell as it flew over our heads, told us that it was *not* a flash of lightning. Of course it created considerable confusion. As soon as was possible in the darkness, our division, which was in advance, was placed in line of battle across the road, and skirmishers sent out to the front. No further demonstration was made by the rebels, and, notwithstanding the scare they had given us, we were grateful for the rest it afforded.

The sound of artillery was a summons for "Little Phil," and down the hard pike we heard him coming with the speed of the wind. Riding up to Gen'l Dwight, our division commander, he inquired the trouble, and was speedily informed. He at once ordered us forward, but Gen'l Dwight with accustomed caution — which we of his division called by a different name — presumed to remonstrate, calling it rashness to proceed. Sheridan's reply was the key note of his wonderful success, and furnishes a valid reason why he "sent the enemy whirling up the valley." Said he, "Gen'l Dwight, I have completely routed Early, taken a very large number of prisoners, and captured every piece of artillery he had but one, and now do you suppose that I am going to let that one gun stop my army? No Sir, this army must move forward at once, and if you, Sir, do not wish to go to the front, you can go to the rear."

It was rash to proceed, but he knew that his only hope of complete victory was in keeping Early "whirling up the valley," thus preventing him from collecting his scattered forces. Dwight's plan was the plan of all our early generals, the carrying out of which had many times lost us the fruits of hard-earned battles. We were worn out—or at least thought so—but neither horse-flesh nor man-flesh was allowed to stand in the way of gathering the fruit of victory with Sheridan.

The event proved that we were *not* worn out, and when, twenty-four hours later, we came up with Early and all day long followed him so closely as to make the remnant of his army fade like snow before the summer sun, we saw both the object and effect of that hard night march.

A word more of the difference between campaigning under Banks and under Sheridan. On the Red River campaign every regiment was allowed at least one wagon, and some of the time two, to carry the officers' baggage, etc. It was very convenient, but the result was a train of nearly one thousand wagons, each drawn by six mules. No wonder that campaign was a failure! The train alone required an army to guard it.

Now the army was fully as large, but the train amounted to nothing. Every regimental wagon was sent to the rear when we moved on the 19th, and for six weeks not a regimental officer in that army had a rag of clothing except what he had on his back. No wonder this campaign was a success.

But to return to our movements. It is needless to

say that the army *did* move on, notwithstanding the alarm; and although as tired as before, we kept a bright look-out ahead. Nothing more occured, and all night long we kept on our course. Every hour we were allowed a rest of ten minutes, and toward morning an hour was granted us, every moment of which was improved in sound sleep. At seven o'clock we entered Woodstock, a small village twelve miles from Fisher's Hill. Passing through it we went into bivouac and remained until noon.

Our supply of hard tack was now nearly exhausted, and four days' rations were speedily issued to us. During the forenoon it rained very hard, but very much refreshed by our rest, we obeyed the command "forward" with alacrity.

A march of six miles enabled us to cross one or two streams, pass through Edinburg, and encamp in a pine forest just beyond. As we pitched our shelters we could hear a scattering fire of musketry, and learned that our advance had come up with the rear guard of the retreating enemy. That night we enjoyed a good eight hours' sleep, and never were men more in need of it. At six o'clock on the morning of the 24th we were once more on the road. At Hawkinsville, the enemy — who had undoubtedly rested as we had — made something of a stand, but our cavalry soon routed them and the pursuit was continued. After passing over about eight miles we entered Mount Jackson, quite a large town, where we found many storehouses filled with munitions of war. These were all destroyed, but the hospitals, filled with wounded rebels from the battle fields of Winchester and Fisher's Hill, were left undisturbed, and every assistance given to relieve the sufferings of these unfortunates.

On the outer edge of the village the rebels now made a determined stand. Every thing seemed to indicate another battle, but our arrangements for the engagement were lost, as, after fording a rapid stream called Mill Creek, their retreating columns were seen making excellent time up the valley. Hurrying through the north fork of the Shenandoah River, we pursued them. It was the good fortune of the One Hundred and Sixteenth to be deployed as advance skirmishers during the balance of the day, and a more exciting day we never spent. Away in the distance we could distinctly see the retreating rebels hurrying on as for dear life. Much nearer us was their rear guard with skirmishers to protect them. All along this portion of the valley were hills which afforded splendid positions for our artillery. From one of these hills a piece of artillery would belch forth an admonition to the enemy to "hurry up," and while this was being done, another would dash along as fast as horses could drag it, to the next hill, and their repeat the warning.

As the shells left these guns, we watched them descend, exploding sometimes high above them, and then again right in their midst. Occasionally we passed some poor fellow who had thus received his discharge. We could but pity these men, knowing from experience how terrible it was to be thus harrassed, and yet there was a satisfaction in being able to play the part of pursuers as well as pursued.

During the afternoon we passed through the village of New Market, and toward sundown the enemy once more disputed our further progress.

In view of the movements of the cavalry, which, under Gen'l Averill, had been sent around through the Luray

Valley in hopes to get in the rear of the retreating army, and thus enable us to capture it entire, they were not pressed very hard, and after dark we bivouaced in the fields and there remained all night.

Whether Early received information of the movement of this cavalry force or not, he let no grass grow under his feet that night, and thus escaped, as we saw nothing more of him.

At seven o'clock on the morning of the 25th our bivouac was again broken up, and a march of fifteen miles put us in camp at Harrisonburg about four o'clock P. M.

CHAPTER XXIV.

We remained at Harrisonburg three days, and as the devastations of war had hardly penetrated to this point, we found plenty of rail fences for fuel, and did not suffer much from a lack of good eating.

The cavalry pursued the enemy to Staunton, destroying immense quantities of grain, and all mills which could supply a rebel army with flour. On the 29th Gen'l Sheridan advanced his army to Mount Crawford, on the south fork of the Shenandoah River, and within seventeen miles of Staunton. About noon of the 30th we retraced our steps to Harrisonburg.

The four days' rations which we had received at Woodstock were now nearly exhausted, and it being an exceedingly difficult matter to bring supplies so long a distance, and there being no particular advantage to be gained in holding a position so far up the valley, Gen'l Sheridan determined to move back to Cedar Creek and there establish his army permanently. This would have been done at once, but there were indications that the enemy were going to offer him battle. He therefore delayed the movement to give them the opportunity should they desire it, and also to allow our cavalry to burn every thing which could possibly subsist another rebel army.

This having been well begun, and the enemy keeping themselves at a respectful distance, at five o'clock A. M., October 6th, we moved back from Harrisonburg to a point three miles beyond New Market, a distance of twenty-two miles. The next day the One Hundred and

Sixteenth formed the extreme rear guard of the army, being deployed as skirmishers, and in consequence of waiting until every thing was in motion, did not get off until ten o'clock A. M.

Our duty that day was fatiguing in the extreme. We were constantly annoyed by the advance cavalry of the enemy, besides which, each man was obliged to move straight ahead, regardless of streams, fences and other obstructions, our line extending across the road away into the fields on either side. None of the One Hundred and Sixteenth will ever forget that toilsome march, and when, after twenty miles had been scored, we threw ourselves down on the ground about nine o'clock P. M., it was to sleep soundly.

At four o'clock A. M., on the 8th, we were roused from our slumbers, and after a light breakfast once more started. The enemy had now grown very bold, and after a march of eight miles we were halted at Fisher's Hill, where we remained until the 10th. During this time Gen'l Sheridan with the cavalry had a severe engagement with the enemy's cavalry at Tomsbrook, who, under Gen'l Rosser, the new "saviour of the valley," were going to perform wonders. He easily routed them, capturing three hundred prisoners, forty-five wagons and eleven pieces of artillery.

At one o'clock P. M., October 10th, we moved from Fisher's Hill, and before night were occupying the line of Cedar Creek.

Our march back from Harrisonburg was remarkable for the wholesale destruction of every thing which could render the occupation of the valley by another rebel army possible. It has been characterized as barbarous warfare, but that it was justified by the known sympathy of the inhabitants with the rebels, none of Sheridan's army for a moment doubted.

A large portion of the supplies for the rebel army at Richmond were drawn from this exceedingly rich section of country. It supplied Early entirely, thus making his occupation of it an easy matter. Had this supply been sooner cut off, it would have been impossible for him to have constantly threatened Maryland and Pennsylvania with invasion. War is terrible, and this was but one of the evils which the chivalry should have expected.

Cedar Creek rises near the North Mountain, and empties into the Shenandoah at the base of the Massanutten Mountain, running diagonally across the valley. At some seasons of the year it assumes large proportions. At this time, however, it was a small and shallow stream, but as its bed lay between high banks it afforded an excellent line to hold.

Necessarily the three corps of Sheridan's army were disposed in what is termed *echelon.* On the left, or where the stream empties into the Shenandoah, was the Eighth Corps, their line extending from the base of the mountain along the bank of the creek to the valley turnpike. In the centre was the Nineteenth Corps, by necessity in the rear and to the right of the Eighth, as the line followed the creek. Still further to the right and rear, came the Sixth Corps. Upon the extreme right was the cavalry to protect that flank, the left being, it was presumed, securely shielded by the Massanutten Mountain.

Elaborate earthworks were planned, and with much labor constructed, so that the position was considered almost impregnable; and glad of a respite from fatiguing marches and terrible battles, the army quietly settled down to the routine of camp life.

Seeing every thing in proper shape, Gen'l Sheridan improved this season of quiet in making a flying trip to Washington, leaving Gen'l Wright, of the Sixth Corps, in command.

Early had, so soon as we left Fisher's Hill, immediately taken possession of his works there with the army he had collected and Longstreet's Division from Richmond. He gave no evidence, however, of a desire to break another lance with "Little Phil," and had he not learned of Sheridan's trip to Washington, the battle of Cedar Creek would hardly have been fought.

An occasional reconnoisance by the two armies only resulted in the discharge of some few pieces of artillery, except upon one occasion when our cavalry had quite a severe engagement with them.

Tuesday, October 18th, was a beautiful day, passed as those days all were in delicious relief from active duties, and as we of the One Hundred and Sixteenth "turned in" that night, it was remarked that just a month previous we started on the march which eventuated in the glorious battle of Winchester. How kind the Providence which hid from us the morrow. In perfect peace and quiet the hours of that night passed away until four o'clock on the morning of the 19th, when suddenly the stillness was broken by the roar of musketry on the left of the line.

Jumping from our blankets, we rushed out of our shelters to see what was the trouble. Our benumbed faculties were not slow in understanding that the Eighth Corps were attacked in force, and, we made no doubt, surprised.

The "long roll" soon called the One Hundred and Sixteenth into line of battle behind our breastworks, but not a shot was fired from in front of our position, nor did there seem to be any commotion in front of the Eighth Corps. All the musketry, which seemed to be increasing in volume, came from their rear. This, with the evident confusion and hurry with which staff officers were riding hither and yon, enabled us to make pretty sure that the Eighth Corps had not only been surprised, but their position flanked.

Our fears were soon confirmed by a rush of demoralized men over our works and through our line, who told us the sad story of the utter defeat and rout of the Eighth Corps. Not a regiment was able to form its line, but attacked simultaneously in both front and rear while yet asleep in their shelters, they could but jump and run for dear life. Many were not permitted an opportunity to do this, being bayoneted as they lay upon the ground. Twenty-four pieces of artillery were captured by the enemy, besides large quantities of small arms and equipments, with the entire camp of the Eighth Corps.

The position of the Nineteenth Corps was now very critical. The enemy had gained possession of the road and, now that the Eighth Corps was *hors de combat*, was turning his attention to us. Bullets began to reach us, but not from the front, and we saw plainly that if we were going to use *this* line of breastworks, which had cost us so much hard work, we must get upon the wrong side of them. An occasional shell screeched past us, and although it seemed impossible for us to remain where we were, not an order to move in any direction was received. By this time daylight had fully dawned upon us, but revealed no enemy. Bullets came thicker and faster, and ere long the dusky forms of the rebel lines could be seen extending well over the pike.

The position of the One Hundred and Sixteenth was upon the crest of quite a large hill, immediately to the right of which ran Cedar Creek. At length an order was received from Col. Davis of the One Hundred and Fifty-third N. Y. Vols., our brigade commander, to leave our works, and moving by the right flank, cross the creek and join the brigade. As soon as this movement was attempted we became the targets for hundreds of rebel muskets. But without delay we found ourselves on the opposite bank, and were soon in a new position, attempting to hold the rebels in check. On they came with renewed determination, and turning the guns captured from the Eighth Corps upon us, forced us to abandon the place. O how unmercifully they did send those howling messengers after us as we rose from our cover and fell back across an open field. About half way across this field was an orchard, and here another stand was made.

When Gen'l Wright became aware of the rout of the Eighth Corps, and of the necessity which compelled the Nineteenth to fall back, he caused the Sixth Corps, which from its position so far to the rear was intact, to change front to the rear and thus hold the rebels until the Nineteenth could get in position on its right. This we were enabled to do in this orchard. The range of the rebels was most excellent. While attempting here to hold them, Capt. Rohan of Co. "G" and a large number of men were wounded, besides four killed in less than ten minutes. Capt. Kinney, serving upon the brigade staff, had his horse killed under him while carrying orders.

A very short time proved our inability to hold this point, and again we retreated to a piece of woods, and tearing down the rail fences formed a sort of breast-work, which we were able to hold some time.

The crisis had now passed, and by direction of Gen'l Wright we at once commenced a well ordered but humiliating retreat. The Sixth Corps remained in line of battle while the Nineteenth in column of brigades moved a half mile to the rear.

With what gloomy thoughts we thus fled before an enemy which under Gen'l Sheridan we had twice driven before us. It was indeed a sad march, our only hope being to reach Harper's Ferry, which we knew we could hold until reinforced. But while to us it was so mournful an occasion, it was a jubilant day to our enemies. They had wiped out of existence for the time being the Eighth Corps, had captured their entire camp, from which hardly a thing had been removed, besides some two thousand prisoners, twenty-four pieces of artillery and the hospital supplies of the Nineteenth Corps. But above and beyond all this, they had redeemed the valley, erased the disgrace attending their defeat at Winchester and Fisher's Hill. Truly they had as much reason for joy as we had for sorrow.

Had Early been content with his victory thus far, and gathering up his trophies, at once returned to his works at Fisher's Hill, it would have been a terrible blow to the good cause we were engaged in, and undoubtedly have prolonged the struggle. But beside himself with his unexpected success (and apple brandy) he pushed on after our retreating army, not even taking care that his forces were all kept well in hand. Hundreds of his ragged and starving soldiers, unable to resist the desire to plunder the still standing camps of the Eighth Corps, left the column and commenced an immediate overhawling of them.

For four miles we continued our retreat, all the time wishing that "Little Phil" had been with us, when towards the pike, from which we were about half a mile distant, we heard genuine Yankee cheering, which betokened good news at any rate. At the same moment an aide rode up to Col. Davis, our brigade commander, and informed him that Gen'l Sheridan had arrived upon the field, and directed him to face about and return to the line we had just left.

The order was obeyed at once, and forming on the right of the Sixth Corps we (the Nineteenth) demolished all the rail fences with which to throw up a rude fortification. When this had been done, and skirmishers had been sent well out to the front, orders came for us to get our dinners, as we should have some time to rest. This was hailed with delight. We had been routed long before our breakfast hour that morning, and had consequently been without any thing to eat since the night before, and this too, while constantly moving or fighting; and now the near prospect of a good cup of coffee was of itself exhilerating. While engaged in its preparation, rousing cheers were continually being given on our left, which gradually approached us. Ere many minutes our gallant "Little Phil," upon his coal black horse all reeking with foam, rode along the line of the One Hundred and Sixteenth. "Boys," said he, "this should never have happened if I had been here; but we are going back to our old camp to sleep to night, for we're going to get the tightest twist on them you ever saw; I tell you we'll lick them out of their boots before night, if you'll only fight." To attempt a description of the frenzied excitement which the sight of him and these familiar words of confidence from his lips stirred up within our breasts would be folly. It cannot be done. Only those who saw and heard can have any conception of it. Cheer after cheer rent the air, old caps were flung high, and we vowed that we would fight as we had never fought before if only he would lead us.

About two o'clock P. M. the skirmishers of the Nineteenth Corps were driven in and a determined attack made upon us by the rebels, which, however, we handsomely repulsed, and all was again quiet. We remained there nearly three hours, the time being occupied by Sheridan in giving confidence to the troops by his presence, in a careful survey of the ground, and in disposing the cavalry and artillery for the coming attack.

At three o'clock, when every man had taken a good square meal, which is one of the first requisites to good square fighting, the order was received for the whole line to advance. Realizing that the time had now come for us to wipe out the stain of the morning's defeat, and perhaps add to our victories, we grasped our muskets and moved forward. The line was in a heavy forest, and as quietly as possible we penetrated its darkness for perhaps twenty rods, when we came to an open field some fifty rods across, along the outer edge of which, and behind a stone wall, was the rebel line. Our appearance was the signal for them to pour a withering volley into us, opening on us with their artillery very heavily, besides following it up with so steady a fire as to somewhat dampen our ardor, and cover the field with the smoke of battle. The quick eye of Col. Davis saw at once that his brigade could not remain there, but must go forward, or it would go backward. Preferring the former, he rode before us and waving his sword above his head ordered us to charge the enemy. The One Hundred and Sixteenth had been there before, and seeing Col. Love before us upon his sorrel horse, "rebel," we leaped the fence which divided the woods from the field and followed him. On we went, every moment telling among us as one and another fell, but bearing us to the stone wall which the enemy seemed determined to hold. As we neared them, however, their determination began to falter, and just as we reached the wall they left it in great confusion and over it we went. Just here, Col. Love's horse, a splendid animal which had been captured in Louisiana, fell dead, being shot in the side. We followed the retreating rebels for some distance, when from our right and rear we began to receive a fire which we knew must proceed from a concealed enemy. We afterward learned that it was a force dispatched by Early to flank the Nineteenth Corps while it lay quietly resting in the woods.

Halting his brigade, Col. Davis reformed the line and again we charged, finding, however, but few of the rebels, the main body having in some way rejoined their comrades. We now came out into another field separated entirely from the balance of our army, which was still heavily engaged with the enemy, as was evinced by the constant and rapid discharge of both musketry and artillery.

We had hardly emerged from the woods into this field, when Gen'l Sheridan made his appearance, and seeing the position we had gained at once dispatched an aide to Gen'l Emory with this order, "Tell Gen'l Emory that the First Brigade has burst through the enemy's line; send them reinforcements at once." Such an order needed no repetition, and in a very short time we were joined by the Second Brigade of our division, commanded by Brig. Gen'l McMillen. As our division commander, Gen'l Dwight, was nowhere to be found, being either indisposed or over cautious, Gen'l McMillen was placed in command of the division.

Under the immediate supervision of Gen'l Sheridan our line was then reformed. When all had been arranged to suit his practiced eye, he said to Gen'l McMillen, "You are now in just the position I want you in, don't be in a hurry, but wait until you see Custer's cavalry charge up that hill to the right yonder, then swing round your right and push them! push them!!"

We had not long to wait, for before many moments we saw the cavalry mount the designated hill as if on the wings of the wind. Their bright and glistening sabres flashed for a moment in the sunlight, and then disappeared. Immediately the command "forward" rang out, and slowly and quietly we advanced. The whole division line wheeled to the left so that we entered another piece of woods at right angles with the rebel line which we were sure of striking in the flank. Previous to this, Company "C," Capt. Morgan, had been sent out as skirmishers, and as our line advanced moved ahead of us. When they had nearly cleared this wood, word was sent in that a strong rebel force were awaiting us. This was unexpected, and nothing but a dashing charge would drive them.

Accordingly the order was at once given, and with a cheer of exhultation we "went for them." The suddenness of our onset made resistance impossible, and they fled before us, thus exposing the flank of the main line, upon which we now poured down with a still fiercer shout.

As far as the eye could reach we now saw the rebel army rise from its position and start for Cedar Creek much faster than we had left it in the morning.

The chase now began in real earnest. Up hill and down hill, over streams and across fields, through mud and water we followed the retreating mob of utterly demoralized rebels, happy and exultant in being able so soon to repay them for the morning's work. At almost every step we overtook some poor fellow who could not get on as fast as his pursuers. It was during this exciting chase that Col. Love saw ahead of him a color guard of four or five men, striving to make off with the battle flag of what proved to be the second South Carolina regiment. Riding after them — for he had secured an apology for a horse — he demanded the surrender of the flag. They showed fight at first, but drawing his revolver and threatening to use it if his demand was not instantly complied with, they considered discretion the better part of valor, and gave it into his hands. In acknowledgment of this the Colonel was afterward sent to Washington with all the flags captured in the battle of Cedar Creek, and there received a bronze medal for the exploit.

We were now as disorganized a mass of men as the rebels, every man seeking to outstrip his neighbor in reaching our works at Cedar Creek. We had gained the turnpike, upon which a few of the rebels had just one piece of artillery, which they were striving to save, and yet were using against us. To capture this piece was now the ambition of twenty or thirty officers and men of the One Hundred and Sixteenth, among whom was

Sergeant Geo. Townsend, the color bearer, with our good old flag. During the whole day he had proudly borne it, and while engaged in this chase its standard was cut entirely in two by a musket ball. On we went, panting at every step, until we saw our coveted capture descend the bank of Cedar Creek, and we knew it was beyond our reach. Still on we pressed, and when within a hundred yards of the works, we saw from this gun which had been run up on to a hill across the creek, a cloud of smoke issue, followed by a shell which burst just above the party. At the same instant our flag fell, the brave Sergeant being, as was supposed, killed. We took up the flag and tenderly bore its bearer behind the works, and then found that he was still alive. He lingered about two days and died. Geo. Townsend was a noble specimen of the Christian soldier, for while fighting for his country he ever remembered God, and his whole life was worthy of his profession of religion.

The men of the One Hundred and Sixteenth were the first of our army to re-occupy our works at Cedar Creek, and plant our flag upon them, but were constantly receiving accessions to their number from those who followed close after them. We had no sooner planted our flag upon the works than we saw the cavalry dash across the creek, mount the hill from which the gun had been fired, and before the smoke had cleared away we saw them capture the gun as well as the rebels whom we had followed so eagerly. Still on they pressed, capturing prisoners without number, and countless articles which go to make up the outfit of an army, until they sent in word that they were unable to care for their captures, and asked that a force of infantry be sent to their assistance.

Accordingly Gen'l Sheridan directed Gen'l Emory to send a portion of his corps, and he ordered our brigade to proceed to the vicinity of Strasburg. Weary and foot sore, but full of the spirit which so glorious a victory gives, we buckled on our belts, and by the pale light of the moon passed out of the fortifications, crossed Cedar Creek and picked our way along the pike. It required considerable exertion to make any progress; squads of cavalry taking in hundreds of prisoners were met every few rods, while all along the road were pieces of artillery, caissons, battery wagons, forges, and ambulances filled with the wounded, many of them overturned. Our path was literally strewn with muskets, cartridge boxes, belts, haversacks and every conceivable part of a soldier's equipment, which had been thrown away to facilitate their flight. Such another sight was probably never seen.

Our progress was necessarily slow, but by nine o'clock we filed off from the road and went into bivouac. For some reason no fires were permitted us, and, as it was intensely cold, but very little sleep was enjoyed by us, and we welcomed with joy the dawn of October 20th.

During the day, Companies "E," Lieut. Swartz, and "I," Lieut. Tibbetts, were sent out on a reconnoisance to Fisher's Hill, to ascertain if the enemy were in the vicinity. Without much difficulty they penetrated into the works at that point, but found no force of rebels. Three prisoners who had found the "last ditch," were captured, and with these and the shell of a demoralized drum they returned.

The day was spent here, and toward evening orders came for us to return to Cedar Creek. We did not, however, reach our old position that night, but halted in a piece of woods before we reached it, and there remained.

Early the next morning we again re-crossed Cedar Creek, and were soon encamped on the same ground from which the rebels had driven us on the morning of the 19th.

The loss of the One Hundred and Sixteenth in the battle of Cedar Creek, was seven killed, forty-four wounded and ten prisoners; and our first care, after our return, was to collect our dead, see them decently interred and their graves properly marked.

This was the last engagement in which the One Hundred and Sixteenth took part, a finale as grand and satisfactory as was Plain Store, our first fight.

No more wonderful battle was ever fought. Napoleon lost Marengo and saved it only by the arrival of De Saix with re-inforcements. Shiloh was lost by Grant, and only won by re-inforcements under Buell; but Cedar Creek was a still more disastrous defeat, and the tide was turned, and victory won, by the arrival of but one man, Gen'l Phil Sheridan.

His brilliant achievement won for him an imperishable name, and the service was recognized by his promotion to be a full Major General in the regular army.

The final charge of the First Division Nineteenth Army Corps was what gave Sheridan his victory at Cedar Creek. No order was received by Col. Davis, our brigade commander, to charge across the first open field which we came to, but seeing a regiment of the Second Brigade breaking, he assumed the responsibility of doing so, and eventually found himself just where he was wanted by Gen'l Sheridan, upon the flank of the rebel army.

No display of gallantry or daring by the Sixth Corps and Second Division of the Nineteenth Corps, could ever have routed that line. It was solely the final charge of our division which gained the battle of Cedar Creek.

For the display of bravery shown by Col. Davis, he was subsequently breveted a brigadier general.

CHAPTER XXV.

Three weeks were spent in the camp we had fought so hard to regain, but it was found a difficult matter to supply the army, as the roads were becoming almost impassable from the mud. As the enemy were so badly used up, it was determined to fall back some distance and establish the army in winter quarters.

On the morning of November 9th, therefore, our bivouac was demolished, and passing through Middletown and Newtown, we pitched our camp a short distance from the latter place on a line of hills, the Nineteenth Corps in the front with the other corps in the rear.

The One Hundred and Sixteenth occupied the extreme right, and as this was to be our winter abode, we lost no time in erecting, from the timber of the adjoining forests, very comfortable huts with fire places and chimneys, which the cold weather made very welcome.

In honor of Gen'l Russell of the Sixth Corps, who fell at Winchester, it was called Camp Russell. Here again we constructed elaborate fortifications, much more so than any we had built, and working parties were kept constantly employed upon them for weeks.

A small and insignificant cavalry force of the enemy, not content with the thrashing they had received, kept annoying our picket line. On the 12th they made so determined a show, that the One Hundred and Sixteenth was ordered out to the support of the pickets, and were soon after, by order of Gen'l Sheridan, deployed as skirmishers and advanced through the village of Newtown. The town was occupied by the enemy, but upon our approach they concluded to retire, and left it as we entered.

All day long we remained on the outer edge of the town exchanging shots with them, and toward evening were ordered still further to the front. We, therefore, proceeded some distance beyond the town, Co's "H," Capt. Clark, and "C," Capt. Morgan, being deployed as skirmishers. The skirmishers advanced to the crest of a hill which the rebels had held during the day, but the day being now far advanced we were recalled, and shortly after dark were relieved by a brigade of cavalry, and returned to camp Russell. This brigade of cavalry succeeded in getting in the rear of the enemy, and made one hundred and seventy-six of them prisoners, and added two more to the number of Sheridan's captured guns.

The One Hundred and Sixteenth lost in this skirmish one man wounded.

This was the last annoyance we received from the enemy, who left that night and fell back to the vicinity of Staunton and Waynesborough. Some four months later, Gen'l Sheridan with his cavalry, on his way to join Grant, met and captured some seventeen hundred of them, scattering the remnant.

The weather was now becoming very cold, and we, who had enjoyed the beauty of a real southern winter, found ourselves hard pushed to keep comfortably warm. Especially was this the case when duty called us to the picket line. Our camp was in the midst of a plowed field, and as it rained almost every day, we could neither keep ourselves nor our houses in a decently clean condition.

When we entered upon the Red River campaign, all

surplus baggage was stored in New Orleans, and subsequently sent to Washington. On the 7th of December this almost forgotten property reached us, and was distributed to its owners. Not more than half of what was stored was found, it having been levied upon whereever it had been, and what there was of it we found of but little value.

While lying at Camp Russell the Sixth Corps was sent to Petersburg, and the Eighth to garrison portions of Western Virginia. This left the Nineteenth Corps alone, except the cavalry, and even this corps was subsequently reduced to one division, the Second Division, Gen'l Grover's, being sent to Savannah to occupy it, and thus enable Gen'l Sherman to continue his great march.

Constant as had been our service ever since our experience at Port Hudson, and acceptable as was this season of rest and quiet from the fatigue of the march and battle, still, as we read of the wonderful march of Sherman and of the constant victory which attended him, or of the great triumph of Gen'l Thomas over Hood at Nashville, we could but wish that we were with the one or the other. As this was impossible, we contented ourselves with the thought that no more brilliant achievements than our own could be attained by them.

Thanksgiving, November 24th, was to be a day of feasting, as the good people of the North had sent to their soldiers a bountiful supply of turkeys. Notwithstanding the gift was well intended and doubtless munificent, many were unable to get more than a taste, the supply being far short of the demand. In the afternoon the brigade was paraded, and appropriate services held by the Chaplain of the Thirtieth Mass. Vols.

Christmas, that day of all days, was observed on Saturday, December 24th, by the officers of the One Hundred and Sixteenth. A dinner, as complete in its arrangements as was possible under the circumstances, was given by the officers, at which a number of invited guests sat down. After thoroughly discussing its merits the time was spent in songs and speeches, and all felt that they had passed an enjoyable time.

On Friday morning, December 30th, we again left our comfortable shanties at camp Russell, and passing through Winchester, encamped toward evening at Stevenson's Depot, the terminus of a military railroad from Harper's Ferry.

As we reached this place and saw the almost forgotten locomotive, and heard its shrill whistle, our joy found vent in lusty cheers. Here we were to remain for the balance of the winter, at least, as our supplies could reach us by rail entirely, thus saving the tedious wagon transportation over very muddy roads. That night it snowed considerably, and as the lateness of our arrival made the erection of our shelters impossible, we found ourselves covered with winter's white mantle when we turned out the next morning. It disappeared, however, before the heat of the sun, which shone out clear and beautiful; and before night the One Hundred and Sixteenth was once again in a fair way to secure good warm huts. Our camp was in a heavy piece of black walnut timber, which furnished the material in abundance. This timber, so valuable, was used not only in the construction of our shanties, but served through the whole winter as our supply of firewood. Cords upon cords of it, which at the North would have enriched us all, were utterly destroyed.

A very few days enabled us to make "Camp Sheridan" a very comfortable place of abode, but we had hardly completed our labors, and begun to enjoy it, when the Third Brigade of our division was sent to Winchester, and the Second distributed along the railroad to Harper's Ferry; and it was rumored that our brigade would be drawn in closer to the depot, in order to effectually guard it from Mosby, who was hovering around.

Many of the men and officers for the first time since entering the service, were, while we remained here, granted furloughs and leaves of absence to visit their homes. Col. Love was one of these. On his return to the regiment, January 12th, 1865, he brought with him a splendid new flag, the gift of Mr. Henry A. Richmond, and some other prominent dock men of Buffalo. With all due ceremony he presented it to the regiment in the name of the donors, and said he had promised that it should be as well defended as the others had been.

In this connection the following action of the "Buffalo Board of Trade" is inserted:

BOARD OF TRADE ROOMS,
January 5th, 1865.

At a meeting of the "Buffalo Board of Trade," January 3d, 1865, on the occasion of their presenting a National Flag to the 116th Regiment, N. Y. S. Volunteers, through their Colonel, Geo. M. Love, a committee, consisting of Messrs. S. V. R. Watson, Richard Williams and Capt. D. P. Dobbins, was appointed to draft resolutions, to be reported on the 5th, expressive of the appreciation of Col. Love's services and those of his Regiment by the Board of Trade, the Citizens of Buffalo and county of Erie generally.

The following resolutions were accordingly presented and unanimously adopted by the Board "on 'change," on the 5th instant:

Resolved, That we regard the present as a proper occasion for returning to the 116th Regiment, N. Y. S. Volunteers, on behalf of the city of Buffalo and county of Erie, no less than on our own, profound acknowledgments and hearty thanks for the long and glorious services it has rendered to the country.

Resolved, That the citizens of Buffalo and Erie county have just cause for pride in having given to the country a regiment which from its first organization under the late lamented Col. E. P. Chapin, to the present time, has borne so conspicuous and honorable a part in the great struggle for the salvation of our country.

Resolved, That in the present commander of the regiment, Col. George M. Love, we recognize no "holiday soldier," but one who has richly earned his promotion from the ranks of the 21st Regiment to his present position, by long, faithful and distinguished services in that regiment, in the 44th, and in the 116th, at the "Siege of Yorktown," the battles of "Hanover Court House," "Malvern Hill," "Plain Store," the "Siege of Port Hudson," and the battles of "Cox's Plantation," "Sabine Cross Roads," "Pleasant Hill," "Cane River," "Mansura," "Winchester," "Fisher's Hill," and "Cedar Creek;" and that we would regard his further promotion as only the just reward of a meritorious and gallant soldier and patriot.

Resolved, That the Secretary is hereby instructed to see that these resolutions are suitably engrossed, signed by the officers of this Board, and presented to Colonel Love.

Resolved, That the Secretary be instructed to procure the printing of 600 copies of these resolutions, and that Col. Love be requested to distribute them in the regiment.

[SEAL.] GEORGE S. HAZARD, *President.*
ALBERT SHERWOOD, *Vice President.*

WILLIAM THURSTONE, *Secretary.*

Buffalo, Jan. 6th, 1865.

NOTE.—The flags (three in number) which the One Hundred and Sixteenth carried during its term of service were disposed of as follows, viz: The first one, presented by the citizens of Buffalo, and the second, presented by Capt. D. P. Dobbins, are deposited with the Buffalo Historical Society. The last one is deposited at Albany, in the Bureau of Military Statistics.

CHAPTER XXVI.

As was anticipated, on the 5th of March we were obliged to leave our snug quarters and move about a mile nearer the depot. There being no especial hurry, two or three companies were allowed to move each day, in order that our huts might be moved to the new camping ground. Notwithstanding all this required considerable labor, we were, in about a week, once more settled, as housekeepers say.

About this time Col. Love, for meritorious services at the battle of Cedar Creek, was made a brevet brigadier general. On the 15th of March he was assigned to the command of a brigade of new troops, and ordered to report to Brev. Maj. Gen'l Brooke, at Halltown, by Maj. Gen'l Hancock, who had been placed in command of the Middle Military Division, when Sheridan started up the valley for Petersburg. The following day he left us, and Maj. Carpenter assumed command of the One Hundred and Sixteenth, Lieut. Col. Sizer being still on the staff of Gen'l Emory.

The weather was now most beautiful. The roads and fields were soon free from mud, and, as a consequence, drilling was again the order of the day.

Our long-continued campaigning, we could readily see, had put us far behind our former proficiency; but constant attention, irksome as it sometimes was, enabled us to gradually regain the precision upon which we had prided ourselves.

Some time in December, Gen'l Emory received from the Ordinance Department at Washington a quantity of "gun cappers," which he was directed to issue to the best regiment in his corps, for trial; and forward the report of the colonel of the regiment to the department. He selected the One Hundred and Sixteenth, an honor of which we had good reason to be proud.

Col. Love, after making his report, in which he disapproved of them, received the following:

"HEAD QUARTERS MIDDLE MILITARY DIVISION,
"OFFICE CHIEF ORDINANCE OFFICER,
"WINCHESTER, Va., Feb. 5, 1865.

"COL. GEO. M. LOVE, Commanding One Hundred and Sixteenth N. Y. V. Infantry:

"SIR,

"Your report on Seely's 'gun cappers,' for infantry, has been received at this office, and forwarded to the War Department, with the following endorsement:

'Respectfully forwarded to Brig. Gen'l A. B. Dyer, Chief of Ordinance, Washington, D. C.

'The regiment of Col. Love enjoys the reputation of being the best in the Nineteenth Army Corps, and the Colonel states that the men do not want these gun cappers, as they consider them worthless. I forward the report of this efficient officer with no further comment than that his opinions are endorsed by me fully.

'P. H. SHERIDAN,
'Maj. Gen'l Comd'g.'"

March 20th orders were received discontinuing the Nineteenth Army Corps, and assigning our brave old Gen'l Emory to the command of the Department of the Cumberland. We had loved him despite his roughness, and parted from him with unfeigned regret. Our sorrow, however, at losing him, and at the breaking up of an organization to which the men of the One Hundred and Sixteenth may well be proud to have belonged, was in a measure relieved by the fact that it would return to us Lieut. Col. Sizer, who had now served upon the staff of Gen'l Emory over a year. He at once joined us, and remained in command of the regiment until we started for Buffalo, after being mustered out of the service.

The old First Division remained intact to the close of the war, and was known simply as "Dwight's Division."

Every thing now indicated the final success of our armies over rebellion, and among us much speculation was indulged in as to when we should make our grand entree into the good old city of Buffalo. Almost all thought that the Fourth of July, at the furthest, would see us there.

April 3d the glorious news of the fall of Richmond, and its occupation by our forces under Gen'l Weitzel, reached us; and this with the gallant achievement of "Little Phil" at Five Forks, was announced by the thunder of artillery at Stevenson's Depot.

Every preparation for an advance up the valley had been made days before, and now, in order to prevent the retreat of Lee with his army down this valley, we were ordered to move early the next morning, April 4th. By five o'clock our winter quarters were abandoned, and to the stirring strains of our band, the One Hundred and Sixteenth took its place in the column, and moved along the well-known road through Winchester. Near our old "Camp Russell" we bivouaced for the night, and over our camp fires talked of the sudden collapse of the confederacy bubble. We could not but feel that, although not present with the army which drove Lee from his capital, we had struck hard blows, which aided materially to bring about this glorious result.

Two days were spent here, at the expiration of which time, no signs of the retreating army being visible, we again turned our faces toward Winchester, and when within sight of the city turned from the road and went into camp.

Here we remained three days, all the time hearing the glad news of victory upon victory achieved by our armies. At last the finale came, and to attempt a description of the joy manifested when we heard of the surrender of Gen'l Lee to Gen'l Grant would be useless. Virtually the war was at an end, and we could now look forward to our return home with good prospects. Gun after gun was fired in honor of the hero who had "fought it out on that line;" but how differently they sounded to us now from what they had only a few short weeks before. Then they told of danger and death; now of peace and coming happiness among loved ones at home.

At seven o'clock, on the morning of April 10th, Dwight's Division again left its camp and took up its line of march on the main valley turnpike. The day was a dreary one, the rain pouring down in torrents, making the roads almost impassable. It ended at last, as all days eventually do, and about dusk we entered a piece of woods in the vicinity of Summit Point, a station on the Harper's Ferry and Winchester Railroad. With but very little preparation for the night we dropped our weary bodies down, and, despite the damp condition of the ground, enjoyed a very good night's rest. The following morning saw the One Hundred and Sixteenth busy again, clearing up the grounds selected for our camp, and making our shelters as comfortable as might be. But a close observer would have detected something never seen before, and that was a sort of indifference, arising no doubt from a conviction that our soldier life was nearly over, and that it was a waste of time to do more than make it comfortable.

On the morning of April 15th the astounding intelligence reached us, that President Lincoln had been assassinated the night before, at Ford's Theatre, in Washington. No one believed it at first, it was too monstrous to believe. It could not be that a man had been found so base as to take the life of so good a man as Lincoln; but as the news was repeated, with additional particulars, we found it impossible longer to doubt, and then our feelings were beyond expression. Deep and loud were the curses uttered against the assassin, and had Booth been captured by the men of the One Hundred and Sixteenth, while their feelings were so wrought up, short work would have been made of him. Yet with all these baser feelings there was an under current of heartfelt sorrow and sadness, as deep as would have been felt had each of us lost a personal friend. No man was ever more universally mourned than Abraham Lincoln; and as time rolls away, Washington and Lincoln will become the two dearest names to an American.

The following day was Sunday, and as throughout the country the people assembled to listen to sermons upon the all engrossing subject, so we of the First Brigade quietly gathered beneath the spreading branches of the forest to do likewise. Chaplain Gorton, of the One Hundred and Sixteenth, pronounced an eulogy on the life and character of the departed President, full of earnest eloquence.

On the 19th, the day set apart for the funeral at Washington, the brigade was again assembled, and listened to an address from the chaplain of the Twenty-ninth Maine Vols.

Throughout the length and breadth of the land there was mourning. Seldom, if ever, has the death of any man been the cause of such profound sorrow. Some of this may have been due to the manner of his death, but this alone could never have so roused the sympathies of an entire people. Lincoln was one of the people. He sympathized with them, and showed the kindness of his nature on many occasions. He was simple and honest, and in almost every heart there was a feeling nearly akin to love for him.

CHAPTER XXVII.

It was now rumored that we were soon to be ordered to Washington, and at nine o'clock on the morning of April 21st, Dwight's Division gathered all its effects together, and loading them upon cars made ready for them, before night reached Harper's Ferry. Across the Potomac River we rolled, and following the Baltimore and Ohio Railroad, took the direction of Baltimore. Toward morning the One Hundred and Sixteenth reached the Relay House, at which point we branched off for Washington, crossing the Patapsco River upon the magnificent bridge which spans it.

Expectation was all alive to see the funeral train of the lamented Lincoln, which was to leave Washington that morning. At every station we found large crowds assembled, awaiting in sorrowful silence its coming. We passed Annapolis Junction without meeting it, but when about twelve miles from Washington our train slackened its speed, and the slow tolling of our engine bell announced the approach of the funeral cortege. Slowly it passed us, and then we sped on our way to the capital, where we arrived about noon, and proceeding to the Soldiers' Rest, were provided with a good meal.

Although the One Hundred and Sixteenth had been nearly three years in the service, had been landed at its wharf and traversed its streets in the darkness of night, this was really our first advent to the city of magnificent distances. As the huge dome of the Capitol rose before us in its grandeur, we wondered at its immensity.

During our stay in the city every opportunity was given us to visit the many places of interest, which were all embraced with eagerness. The White House, Treasury, Patent Office, War Department, and other public buildings were visited, and impressed us with the greatness of our country. We crossed the Long Bridge, of which we had heard so much, as well as the Aqueduct, and strolled out to the forts which encircle the city, until we felt as well acquainted with it as though all our soldier life had been spent there.

We remained but a short time in the city. About two o'clock P. M., the colors of the different regiments having been draped in mourning, we proceeded out Pennsylvania Avenue and through Georgetown to the identical ground occupied by a part of our division upon our arrival in Washington from New Orleans, after our tedious tramp in the dark.

Camping grounds were assigned to each regiment, and the One Hundred and Sixteenth went to work once again to grade the streets, and embellish it somewhat. This work had not, however, progressed very far, when an order was received from the War Department, detaching the One Hundred and Sixteenth from Dwight's Division, and directing us to report to Maj. Gen'l Augur, commanding the defences of Washington, for provost duty in the city. The order was hailed with delight by both officers and men. As it was presumed that Booth, the assassin of our President, was still within the city, the duty of picketing the whole east side of the city was assigned to Dwight's Division. Our old First Brigade was obliged to cover a line some three or four miles long, and the duty was arduous in the extreme. Besides this, we had no great respect for the division commander, and were going from his control into the hands of Gen'l Augur, whom we all respected and loved. It was he who had ordered and watched the first charge the One Hundred and Sixteenth ever made at Plain Store.

The only regret was that we were to be separated from two regiments, the One Hundred and Fourteenth and One Hundred and Fifty-third N. Y. Vols., between whom and ourselves a very strong attachment had for a long time existed.

With little delay we retraced our steps, and passing the Capitol were assigned a camping ground on Capitol Hill. The men were supplied with "A" tents, and the officers with wall tents, and very great care was taken that the camp should be laid out in strict conformity to army regulations. This had often been done before, and without much trouble it soon assumed a look of which we had no need to be ashamed.

The dress coats and shoulder scales which had been our pride in Camp Emory, at Franklin, Louisiana, were obtained from the store house, and we were ready to mount guard, have our dress parades and perform guard duty with any regular regiment in the service.

The duty assigned to the One Hundred and Sixteenth was the entire care of the old Capitol and Carroll prisons, incarcerated within which were a number of those charged with being accomplices of Booth. This required a detail of something like one hundred men each day, so that we found our coming into the city did not enable us to idle away our time. It was, however, much more pleasant than picket duty outside the defences of the city, and we were content.

The lieutenants of the regiment relieved each other

as officers of the guard in charge of this detail. The captains were placed on the roster of field officers of the day, whose duty it was to visit not only these prisons, but many other points where guards were stationed in various parts of the city. At night they visited, in addition to these, the White House and the residences of Secretary Seward and some other prominent personages, to see that no more assassins were allowed to prowl around.

Every effort was now made by Lieut. Col. Sizer, in command of the One Hundred and Sixteenth, and all the officers, to bring the regiment up to its old standard in drill, and if possible to surpass it. In this they had the hearty co-operation of the men, and it was, therefore, a matter of course that very soon our dress parades were witnessed by hundreds of spectators drawn to our camp by the report that our evening parade was worth seeing.

Many general officers rode out at different times, and on one occasion Gov. Fenton, of our State, with a party of friends viewed the exercise. At its conclusion he made us a speech, the import of which was his pride that so well drilled a regiment hailed from the State of New York, and that we might expect, as the result in part of our efforts, to return to our homes very speedily.

All these hours of drilling were with an object in view, which was, that when we arrived in Buffalo, we might show its citizens that the One Hundred and Sixteenth was entitled to the reputation it had won for proficiency in drill.

The bayonet exercise, the most advanced part of a soldier's schooling, was the drill now ordered. Although at Camp Emory, Franklin, La., we had become very proficient in it, still constant practice enabled the regiment on dress parade to execute the most intricate combinations as one man.

Troops were constantly arriving in the vicinity until it seemed that more soldiers were now assembled than had ever been borne on the muster and pay rolls of Uncle Sam; and yet they came.

As it was understood that Gen'l Grant and the President were to review the whole vast army, thousands upon thousands of citizens from the North came flocking into the city to witness one of the grandest sights ever seen. It was announced that the grand review would occupy the 23d and 24th day's of May, that the army of the Potomac would pass in review the first day, and Sherman's army the last.

On some accounts the members of the One Hundred and Sixteenth would have preferred to participate in this review, and yet on other accounts were glad to be relieved from it. We could enjoy the sight very much better as spectators than as participants, and all things considered were inclined to consider ourselves fortunate.

The night before the grand gala day all the vacant portions of the city were temporarily occupied by the troops of the army of the Potomac, many of whom were encamped a number of miles outside the defences.

At nine o'clock precisely, on the morning of May 23d, a cannon announced the moving of the column. The arrangements were most complete, and Gen'l Meade, who had been waiting the signal gun, started at once. The sight from the Capitol grounds was grand beyond description. The day was a beautiful one. Looking away down Pennsylvania Avenue to the Treasury building, a distance of over a mile, nothing could be seen in the street but one vast compact mass of soldiers swaying from the right to the left as each man kept step to the music. Every gun and sabre shone like polished steel, as they were, and this glittering pageant was continued hour after hour until nearly night. The sidewalks were crowded with eager lookers-on, while from every window and roof thousands upon thousands looked down upon these war bronzed heroes, and gave them honor.

In front of the White House a stand was erected, upon which were Gen'l Grant, the President, and many other dignitaries. Among these latter were most, if not all the foreign ministers, upon whom the sight of such a vast army of *volunteers* must have been indeed wonderful. It must have also impressed them with a more exalted view of the power of the Yankee nation than they had ever had before, and was no doubt, in this respect, beneficial.

All this was repeated the next day, as Gen'l Sherman with his sturdy Western veterans filled the broad avenue from curb to curb.

Such another sight, none of those who witnessed it will ever see again; and in years to come, to have seen it will be worth telling to grand children.

CHAPTER XXVIII.

On the 5th day of June, the following order was received and hailed with joy:

"Head-quarters Dwight's Division,
"June 5th, 1865.

"General Orders, No. 13.

"I. Pursuant to General Order No. 94, War Department, Adjutant General's Office, current series, and General Order No. 58, Head-quarters Middle Military Division, current series, the 114th, 116th and 153d N. Y. Vols. are hereby ordered to be mustered out of the service of the United States.

* * * * * * * * * * * *

"III. In parting with these gallant regiments, after so long a period of service, the General commanding feels regret, mingled with pride, when he recalls how patiently they have endured, how bravely they have fought, and how nobly they have won. Fort Bisland, Plain Store, Port Hudson, Sabine Cross Roads, Pleasant Hill and Cedar Creek, bear witness to this. To all these regiments the General commanding renders his heartfelt thanks.

"By command of Brig. Gen'l Dwight,
"J. G. LEEFE,
"A. A. A. G."

The balance of our division had a longer time to serve than the regiments mentioned in this order, and they were accordingly ordered to Savannah, Ga., for garrison duty. They sailed about this time much against their will, and after their arrival there were distributed throughout the State of Georgia.

All was now hurry and bustle. Muster-out rolls were obtained, and although every two months, during our service, had seen each commanding officer of a company complete his muster and pay rolls, still these were so much more intricate and comprehensive, that many hours were spent before they were pronounced complete and ready for the mustering officer. At ten o'clock on the 8th, Capt. Pellett, mustering officer on the division staff, arrived at the camp of the One Hundred and Sixteenth. Taking one company at a time, he soon performed the ceremony which was to sever our connection with the United States as soldiers. Discharges for each officer and man had previously been made out, and these, with the muster-out rolls, he quietly put under his arm and marched off. They were returned, however, the next day, duly attested.

The instructions now received were to hold ourselves in readiness to move at a moment's notice. We had very often received orders exactly like this, but they did not stir within us the same emotions that this one did, for a reason the reader will readily understand. We were to proceed by the way of Baltimore and Elmira to Buffalo, where the regiment would be paid off, and each man receive his discharge. Until that time the commanding officer of the regiment was directed to hold these discharges, and, with the other officers, was to be held strictly responsible for the conduct of the men, and for all arms and equipments. Transportation was all that now detained us. Hundreds of cars were running over the road to Baltimore every day, carrying those who, like us, were "homeward bound."

June 9th and 10th were very long days to the One Hundred and Sixteenth. Every thing was packed ready for a move, and to be obliged to wait in almost hourly expectation of the order to march to the depot was terribly annoying.

On the 9th Gen'l Love, having been relieved of his command in the Shenandoah Valley, joined us and assumed command of the regiment.

At last transportation was secured, and at ten o'clock, June 11th, the One Hundred and Sixteenth broke camp for the last time, and with lighter hearts than ever marched to the depot. A train of cattle and platform cars was in waiting for us, but not a hoot (as at Elmira nearly three years before) was heard. Two tedious hours were occupied in getting all on board, and at one o'clock P. M. we moved out of Washington on our way to good old Buffalo. Nothing occurred worthy of mention, and about seven o'clock that evening we reached Baltimore.

Stacking our arms in the street, the regiment was marched into the Soldiers' Rest, near at hand, and provided with a substantial lunch. After this had been well attended to, we took our arms, and passing through the city, found at the Camden Station depot of the Northern Central Railroad another train of cars in readiness to receive us.

All our effects were speedily loaded, the men as comfortably accommodated as was possible, and in the darkness of midnight the One Hundred and Sixteenth moved out of Baltimore. Our train was of course an extra, which forced us to wait for all regular trains; and as the regiment and its effects occupied a large number of cars we made very slow progress. All that night, and the following day and night, we wound our slow course along, until the boys, some of them, proposed that we get off and march to Buffalo, being confident that, as we had made forced marches under far less advantageous circumstances, we could reach our destination almost as soon as by rail.

However, we at last reached Elmira on the morning of June 13th, and found there awaiting us a committee of three citizens of Buffalo, Messrs. James Adams, Isaac Holloway and Dr. E. Storck, who had been sent down to see that there was no unnecessary delay. They gave us the welcome intelligence that great preparations had been made at Buffalo to make our reception as gratifying and imposing as was possible, and assured us that it was to be indeed a gala day, as we should see in due time.

They had secured a sufficient number of passenger coaches for our accommodation, so that our ride the remainder of the way should be more pleasant.

In less than two hours from the time we arrived at Elmira, every thing was transferred to the new train, and at seven o'clock A. M. we moved from the depot on our way home.

It had been determined by the officers of the regiment —in which the men fully concurred—that we should enter Buffalo as neat and clean as we would have presented ourselves for a review or inspection. We knew that it was customary for troops returning from active service, to rather pride themselves on their ragged and dirty appearance, presuming that it was to be expected, and only gave evidence of hard service. But the One Hundred and Sixteenth had gained a reputation for neatness in its absence, of which we knew our friends were aware, and were determined that they should see that it was well deserved. Accordingly, before leaving Washington, a sufficient quantity of blue ribbon was purchased to give every man a necktie. At Elmira a number of boxes of blacking were bought, which the men were directed to use upon their shoes; and after the train was in motion, they were also directed to put on their dress coats and shoulder scales. As a consequence of this care, long before we came in sight of Buffalo, each man presented an appearance worthy of the number of his regiment.

The hours now passed all too slowly to satisfy our anxious minds. The nearer we approached the good old city, the slower, it seemed to us, did we progress. The news that the One Hundred and Sixteenth was *en route* for home had been flashed along the wires from Elmira, and at every station we found large numbers assembled to welcome us. As we neared the end of our journey the numbers increased, until at Batavia, where we stopped for a few moments, the crowd was very large.

At Attica we were met by a deputation of some thirty or forty of our old comrades. With the two old flags which we had carried in many a battle, they had come to greet us, and bear some share of the honor to be conferred upon any who had belonged to the One Hundred and Sixteenth.

Receiving them on board, the engine whistled a warning, and on we rolled. At Darien, Alden, Town Line, Lancaster and Cheektowaga, every evidence of joy was manifested by crowds of excited people.

At last the spires of Buffalo met the gaze of hundreds of noble fellows, who for nearly three years had never set eyes on them. Then the prominent buildings came in sight, and soon the slackened speed of our engine showed that we had entered the city limits. Slowly we crawled along, crossing Exchange, Louisiana and Chicago streets, passing old familiar buildings, and some that had grown into being during our absence.

At 3 o'clock in the afternoon of June 13th the train stopped at the depot, and the One Hundred and Sixteenth were home from the wars.

CHAPTER XXIX.

The approach of the train was the signal for a general outburst, and the cheers and shouts were for a time almost deafening. An attempt was made to prevent the crowd from getting within the enclosure, but the policemen were unable, or unwilling, to deprive anxious friends of the earliest possible meeting with their soldier boys. The consequence was such a scene of glorious joy as is not often witnessed.

We had hardly come to a stand still before the fire bells rang out an alarm, and the planing-mill of E. & B. Holmes, close by, was discovered to be on fire. The whole fire department were out as part of the procession to escort us to Fort Porter, but duty called them, and all, save Eagle Hose Co. No. 2, responded. Gen'l Love was an old and honored member of this company, and Capt. Tuttle, who was killed at the battle of Cox's Plantation, had also belonged to it, and it was from a desire to do honor to them that they were permitted to remain. The fire attracted many who were crowding in and around the depot from mere curiosity, and thus gave us a better opportunity to begin our triumphal march.

With very great difficulty the companies were formed, and the regimental line at last completed, and facing to the right we entered Exchange street by the flank. The crowd, partially controlled by a strong police force, surged back and forth as if anxious to eat us up, but with much labor we found ourselves in the position assigned us in the procession. This was composed as follows:

Brig. Gen'l WM. F. ROGERS, Marshal.
Staff Officers.
Union Cornet Band.
74th Regt. N. Y. N. G., Lieut. Col. G. M. BAKER.
Union Continentals, Capt. N. K. HALL.
21st N. Y. Vols., Capt. JOHN M. LAYTON.
Officers in the U. S. Service.
Officers discharged from U. S. Service.
Car containing thirty Young Ladies representing the States.
Buffalo Liedertafel.
Buffalo Saengerbund.
Buffalo Turners.
Drum Corps.
Eagle Hose Company No. 2.
Citizens' Committee of Reception.
Miller's Band.
Ex-members 116th N. Y. Vols.
Regimental Band 116th N. Y. Vols.
116th N. Y. Vols., Brev't Brig. Gen'l GEO. M. LOVE.
Citizens in Carriages and on foot.

The jam throughout the entire line of march was beyond any thing Buffalo had seen more than once or twice before, and our expectation that we would be able to show some model marching at company front, was in a fair way to be disappointed.

At the junction of Exchange and Main streets, we passed beneath a beautiful arch covered with evergreens, interspersed with the names of Grant, Sheridan, Sherman and Farragut, and of the battles in which the One Hundred and Sixteenth and other Buffalo regiments had been engaged. Conspicuous on the Exchange street front were the words "Welcome Home."

Immediately after passing this arch we turned into Main street, and the sight was one to send a thrill of pride and pleasure through our hearts. As far as we could see, the street was filled with a mass of human beings, while the roofs and windows on either side were crowded with ladies who waved their handkerchiefs and tossed an occasional bouquet at some lucky fellow in our ranks. Most of the buildings were decked in gay colors, festooned from the roof to the walk, while it would have been utterly impossible to count the flags flying from house tops and windows. Truly it was worth all our months and years of toil and suffering to find our friends at home so mindful of us on our return.

As we turned into Main street, Gen'l Love gave the command, "By company into line—*march*," and taking a light touch of elbows to the left, every man carried himself as became his schooling.

Amid the booming of cannon and the ringing of bells we reached Niagara street, and wheeling to the left continued our march. At Niagara square another beautiful arch spanned the street, bearing among many other things the words "Your glorious deeds claim triumphant laurels." Turning up Delaware avenue the same sight opened before us as upon Main street, except that the display was from residences instead of stores.

At Public School No. 10 we were greeted by the stirring strains of "Victory at last, Boys," sung by the entire school, marshaled upon the sidewalk. At the corner of Delaware and Huron streets was a third arch, embellished by the fair hands of Gen'l Love's sisters, and devoted to the memory of our departed hero, Gen'l Chapin.

Our march was continued up Delaware to Chippewa, through Chippewa to Georgia, down Georgia to Niagara again, out Niagara to York, through York to Sixth, and out Sixth to Fort Porter. As we entered these grounds, where almost three years before we had enlisted and eaten our first meal in Uncle Sam's service, we could not but thank God that we had done so, and bless Him for sparing us to return. Sad thoughts of those who had left it with us, but were now sleeping beneath a summer sun the sleep that knows no waking, would mingle with our joy and cause a tear to start in memory of them.

A bountiful lunch was provided by the ladies, and stacking our arms we entered the old mess-house and ate our fill of every thing good. This pleasant duty completed, we were called to our stacks, and taking our muskets, Lieut. Col. John M. Sizer gave the assembled multitude an exhibition of our dress parade, including the bayonet exercise. This done, we were addressed by Hon. Geo. W. Clinton, as follows:

"Thanks to Almighty God, the Author of light, and Giver of victory, you have come home. The great rebellion has been crushed, and our country, purified by suffering, is free, united, vigorous, able to stand up against a world in arms! And while at this time we adore the good God and wonder at his providence, and admire and praise the more conspicuous instruments through which we have been so secure and happy, how can we forget you, our noble soldiers? While we would award a just tribute to the statesmanship which has swayed our counsels, and to the wonderful generalship and strategy which have found their clearest manifestations in Grant, Sherman and Sheridan, how can we forget you, 'bone of our bone, and flesh of our flesh,' most gallant soldiers, most worthy fellow-citizens.

"You have heard our shouts, you have seen our triumphal arches, our decorations, and all the signs of our rejoicing at your return. But you cannot see, nor is it possible for any tongue to tell you the great joy, the pride, the exultation, with which we welcome you back to Buffalo, and take you to our hearts. War-worn soldiers you are welcome indeed. Buffalo has a warm place in her great heart for all her worthy children, and especially for those who, like you, have exemplified in wretchedness and blood, her loyalty and heroism. It was a pity, I had almost said a burning shame, that through the failing of the telegraph the worthy One Hundredth received no welcome. But fellow-citizens of

Eaton's Battery, Weidrich's Battery, and of the illustrious One Hundred and Sixteenth, you have not escaped us. We have caught you, and with a spontaneous unanimity which evinces our sincerity, and cannot but reach your hearts, we now unite to do you honor, and greet you with a most hearty, loving welcome. We are proud of your achievements, and the story of them will thrill and animate the souls of our descendants throughout all time. Your trophies must be preserved, your banners, tattered and soiled by the smoke of battle and the bullets of the enemy, must be hung up for monuments." * * * * * * * * *

After Judge Clinton had concluded his address of welcome, Gen'l Love and some others responded to calls. When speech-making was at an end, Gen'l Love informed the men that his orders were to keep the entire regiment in camp until they were paid off and discharged. But the paymaster not having arrived, he should take the responsibility of allowing all to go to their homes, trusting that every man would be on hand the next Monday, June 19th, as he had promised the Major commanding the post they should be.

This was indeed good news, as we had feared that an attempt would be made to keep us in camp, and all felt gratified that we were to be permitted to spend the intervening time at home.

A very short time sufficed to store the arms and equipments of the men, and before dark the One Hundred and Sixteenth were seeking their homes in all parts of the city and county.

Promptly on the day appointed every man appeared at the fort, but found that no paymaster had arrived to liquidate their claims against Uncle Sam. A request had been made by many of the citizens that we should give a battalion drill upon the Terrace. In accordance with this desire, the regiment that afternoon marched down Sixth street to the Terrace, but found so great a crowd assembled as to make it impossible to comply with the request; and after several vain attempts to drive back the vast multitude, we retraced our steps to the fort.

A detail was now made from each company, who were required to remain at the fort, and the balance of the regiment were again permitted to seek their own pleasure at home, with directions to return on Saturday, June 24th. At that time every man again answered to his name. However, the paymaster was still unable to pay us, but promised to do so on Monday, the 26th.

This promise was kept, and by ten o'clock P. M., June 26th, 1865, every enlisted man in the One Hundred and Sixteenth was fully paid and discharged from the service of the United States, and the gallant regiment was no more. It had fought a good fight, it had finished its course, and henceforth there is laid up for all who bore an honorable part in its history a crown of glory.

APPENDIX.

MEMORIAL SKETCHES.

BRIGADIER GENERAL EDWARD P. CHAPIN.

BY COL. JOHN B. WEBER.

EDWARD PAYSON CHAPIN, the subject of this sketch, was born August 16th, 1831, in the village of Waterloo, Seneca Co., N. Y.

He was purely American in his nationality, a descendant of deacon Samuel Chapin, who settled in Springfield, Mass., in the year A. D. 1642.

Of six children belonging to the Rev. Ephraim and Elizabeth Chapin, he was the youngest, the pet and pride of the family. His father was a regularly ordained minister of the gospel, and a Presbyterian by persuasion, who spared no pains to bring up the son in the nurture and admonition of the Lord.

The first rudiments of his education were attained in a common village school, where his ability both to acquire and retains howed above the medium standard. Perseverance was among the first developed traits of his character—pursuing to the very end whatever he undertook, and never admitting "give up" as part or parcel of his creed.

For fishing and hunting he early acquired a passionate love—the desire following him to manhood, growing, you may say, with his growth, and yet never forgetting duty or interest in controlling his love for this natural and exciting sport. He was a great lover of the water, and the river being within a few rods of his paternal home, a good opportunity was afforded him to gratify his every desire in that direction. Many of his old friends and schoolmates can recall to memory the youngster as he appeared in his fishing and hunting costume. He was almost always accompanied by the great farm dog Hector (his special pet), whom he had taught every thing within the limits of dog-knowledge, and who could make his mile with packet speed, towing his young master along the banks of the river, stopping occasionally to give him time for a shot or a bite.

In warm weather, and while pursuing his studies at the village academy, rather than walk around by the road, he would swim the river, with his clothes in one hand and the other holding fast to Hector's tail—who enjoyed the sport equally with his master.

Many are the little incidents of his boyhood that might be told as applicable here, insomuch as to show to those who knew him in after life, how much of the man was developed in the boy; but time and space in a work of this character forbid; besides, why needs it that of the boy, when the record of the man is of so brilliant and imperishable a character, and of a reputation whose limits are not confined to his native State alone.

As stated before, the rudiments of his education were attained in a common village school, but the academy of his native place furnished him with a thorough classical and English education; and when about seventeen years of age, having adopted the law as his profession, he entered the office of John McAllister, Esq., of Waterloo, with whom he continued for a year and a half. He finished his legal education at Buffalo and Ballston Spa, where he graduated with his class August 11th, 1852, and was admitted to the bar soon after attaining his majority.

He opened an office in the city of Buffalo, where he continued in the practice of his profession until the breaking out of the rebellion. In his practice he met with decided success. Energetic and talented, he built up for himself an enviable reputation, and was fast rising to the front rank of his profession when the news of the attack on Fort Sumter touched a chord in his patriotic heart, which changed the whole current of his thoughts, and directed anew every object of his being.

Thoroughly imbued with a generous patriotism and an ardent desire for the preservation of the Union, he immediately began to prepare himself for the struggle in which he was destined to take so prominent, and, to him, so fatal a part. His connection with the militia at Buffalo gave him some idea of the details of the new work; but he nevertheless entered upon a course of military studies, which he pursued with unceasing industry, and which he intended never entirely to neglect, so long as he should remain in the service.

Upon the death of Col. Elmer E. Ellsworth, of the New York Fire Zouaves—the first victim of distinction in the war—it was proposed by some of the leading citizens of this State to organize a regiment in which every city, town and village, throughout the State, should be represented, and to be known as the "People's Ellsworth Regiment," or the Forty-fourth New York State Volunteers.

Money was to be raised by subscription (one hundred thousand dollars, or one hundred dollars per man) with which to organize, arm and equip the regiment, free from any expense to the State; and at Washington, within sight of the spot where Ellsworth fell an early victim to his country's struggle, the command was to be tendered to President Lincoln, as an evidence of the loyalty of the Empire State, and an indication of the earnestness with which its people should respond to the calls made on them for the material so necessary to the preservation of our Government. This plan was not fully carried out, owing to the fact that there were few men of Chapin's metal to take up and push the matter to a successful issue. Through his energetic efforts a company was raised to represent Erie county in this regiment, composed of as fine material as ever wore the blue, of which he was elected captain, with a unanimity to which he always referred with pride: a unanimity never marred by a single regret on the part of his men.

The regiment was officered principally by men of ability and experience—Ellsworth's Fire Zouaves furnishing quite a number,—and with these Capt. Chapin was pitted for a test of superiority in the great work. With his limited experience, it required, and he gave to the work, all the strength of his nature; and "give up" was still as foreign to his creed as when this trait developed itself so prominently in his character while yet a boy.

It was not long, however, before he took the lead among his brother officers, and when, shortly after the departure of the regiment for the seat of war, there occurred a vacancy in the majority, to which Captain Chapin was promoted, it was an event which lacked the usual murmurings and complaints, and all conceded it to him as a matter of desert as well as right.

He felt and expressed a sincere regret upon throwing up his company command to assume the higher and more important position, and while this regret was a mutual feeling, yet his company knew that the good of the service required Major Chapin for more responsible duties. He never forgot them, however, and the careful consideration with which he always attended to their interests, showed conclusively that his first love still kept warm in his heart.

Major Chapin on entering upon his new duties carried with him his usual energy and consequent success, as shown by the improved state of drill and discipline of the regiment. The first opportunity for active service which occurred to the Forty-fourth was at the seige of Yorktown, where the Major made himself conspicuous for his courage and daring. At the battle of Hanover Court House, which took place on the 27th of May, 1862—just one year to a day previous to his death—he was severely wounded, and sent North as soon as his condition would permit of his removal. The nature of his wound was such that it was impossible to determine for a few days whether it would prove mortal or not, and many a heart beat freer when the surgeon pronounced him (with good care) out of danger. This he received from the time he reached White-house landing, where he was at once taken charge of by the agents of the Sanitary Commission, the beneficial results of which system he always spoke of in terms of the highest praise.

He improved quite rapidly considering the severity

of the wound, and after remaining home about a month, enjoying the tender care of his anxious parents, he proceeded to Buffalo to take charge of a recruiting office for the Forty-fourth Regiment, now standing sadly in need of material to repair, in numbers at least, the loss incurred by reason of the bullet, or the silent and more dreaded swamp fever. He did not continue long in the performance of these office duties before he was tendered the colonelcy of the One Hundred and Sixteenth Regt. N. Y. Vols., then forming, with head-quarters at Buffalo.

Owing to the difficulties of getting his documents of transfer through the circumlocution office at the War Department, he was considerably delayed, and this delay finding him improved in condition and with rather a slim prospect of success in his application for transfer, he reported for active duty to the Secretary of War. He had been recommended to the lieutenant colonelcy of his own regiment in the meantime, but his friends persevered in pressing his case at Washington, and finally the long-looked-for order arrived, assigning him to the command of the new regiment.

I will pass over the detail of its organization by saying that it was a task of no small import, as those only can realize who have been taught by experience. Suffice it to say, that upon its completion he proceeded with his regiment to Baltimore, thence to the Department of the Gulf, where he was directed to report to Gen'l Banks, of whose expedition his command formed a part. His superiors had already singled him out as one worthy of a higher position than that he held, and shortly after arriving at Carrolton, near New Orleans, La., his regiment was detached from the brigade and assigned to another, where the date of his muster as colonel entitled him to command.

Col. Chapin accepted the trust not without some misgivings, for he fully appreciated the nature of the duties and responsibilities devolving upon the position of a brigade commander. It was a position not of his own seeking, and he accepted it simply because he was ordered so to do, being too good a soldier to obey an order reluctantly, even though its performance involved personal unpleasantness. His regiment had already taken post in the front rank for drill and discipline, and had been specially commended for their soldierly qualities in general orders from department head-quarters. He felt he could rely upon them, for as men the material was good; as soldiers, he had moulded them according to his own particular ideas. He could obtain more personal glory by remaining with the regiment than by assuming command of a brigade, three regiments of which were nine months' men, whose time had nearly expired. The difficulty of enforcing and keeping up a state of discipline among men who are revelling in the anticipation of a speedy meeting with their loved ones at home, is observable even among veteran troops; and those only who saw can appreciate what it is to fight battles with such a set of men, who had hardly known what discipline meant, which, with the exception of his own regiment and the Forty-ninth Mass. Vols., was the case with Chapin's Brigade.

Active service was in immediate prospect, for Banks' army was largely composed of nine months' men, who were anxiously numbering their days of service, and whatever was expected of that expedition must be attempted at once, or time would deplete his army by nearly one half.

Col. Chapin entered upon his duties as brigade commander with that quiet determination which characterized all of his important undertakings: a determination which expressed, to those who knew him, a resolution that his brigade must be equal to any task assigned to it. He coveted the advance for his command on the march to Port Hudson, aware, however, that, as a matter of seniority simply, it did not belong to him. Although this at first was given to a brigade commanded by his senior, and a regular army officer, yet after the affair at Plain Store, May 21, 1863, this question as to who should lead was measured by a different standard than that of dates of muster, and from that time his brigade, and after his death, his regiment, was never far from the front.

His regiment and brigade made their debut on the battle-field of Plain Store, and with a success that argued well for their morale and discipline. The first battle is an important event in the history of a soldier, and victory is as certain to bring with it a beneficial confidence that will influence his whole future career, as defeat will carry with it instability and indecision, in critical moments, ever after. From his first entry into the service, every thing done for the soldier is purely of a preparatory nature; every thing tending toward his efficiency on the battle-field; and nothing but an actual battle can establish that confidence between officers and men so necessary to success. To a commanding officer this is a moment of fearful anxiety, for now comes the test of his fitness for the position he occupies, to be judged by a public whose standard for ability is measured only by success, and who are as unsparing in their damaging criticisms as they are wise in planning campaigns after they are over.

Col. Chapin's demeanor on that occasion, to all outward appearance, was as cool and determined as if he was leading a band of battle-scarred veterans; yet the look of relief which illuminated his features when victory was assured, was a pleasure to behold.

From that day he was more than ever attached to his "boys," if such a thing were possible, and a tender affection was begotten toward them akin to the feeling which an anxious parent experiences on the success of a favorite child.

The One Hundred and Sixteenth was now no longer an experiment, but an assured fact. They had established their reputation, had been weighed in the scale of battle, and purchased a victory, made doubly precious by the blood of their brave comrades who had fallen in the struggle. Chapin was satisfied, and while we may wonder at and mourn his untimely fate, it is a melancholy pleasure to his surviving comrades to know that he tasted the fruits of his labors before he left us to bewail his loss.

On the 27th day of May, 1863, in the terrible charge over the slashing at Port Hudson, and while leading his brigade, he was struck by a bullet in the face, which crashing through the brain, produced instant death. His body was found far to the front, a smile resting upon his calm and placid features, as if his soul was glad to be released from earthly bondage in so glorious a cause. Loving hands performed the last sad offices, and although he met his death far away from the scenes of his happy childhood, and in a strange land, yet they were not strangers who lifted him from his death-bed in the slashing, and deposited him a corpse under the tree in front of his head-quarters, which he left in the morning, in the pride and strength of a bright and glorious future. One by one his boys came up for a last farewell look upon the face of him whom they had all learned to love as a father, and the silent tear as it moistened the cheeks of his battle-begrimmed followers, in the dusk of so eventful a day, was a tribute to his memory than which none could be more touching or beautiful.

His remains were taken to Baton Rouge, thence to New Orleans, where they were embalmed, and sent home in charge of his servant Tim; and in his own loved Waterloo he sleeps the peaceful sleep of the brave soldier, the Christian gentleman, and God's most perfect work—the honest man.

He was buried on the 14th of June following, with all the honors due his rank. The "Tigers," of Buffalo, under command of Capt. Wardwell, attended in a body, and did duty as the funeral escort during the ceremonies. The deceased had been a member of this company previous to the war, and it was with them he obtained the rudiments of his military education. A large number of the citizens of Buffalo testified their appreciation of the brave soldier by their attendance, and from among them the following named gentlemen were selected as pall-bearers:—Gen'l Wm. F. Rogers, Lieut. Col. C. W. Sternberg, Lieut. Col. Horace G. Thomas, Lieut. Col. W. G. Seely, Lieut. Col. H. C. Blanchard, Capt. Robt. P. Gardner.

The procession marched to the residence of the father of the deceased, and receiving the corpse continued to the Presbyterian Church, where services were held by the Rev. Dr. Gridley, who delivered a beautiful and touching address, referring in appropriate and eloquent terms to the life, services and character of the gallant dead.

The church was filled with friends and acquaintances, the whole affair being conducted in a most perfect manner.

Upon the conclusion of the ceremonies the procession was reformed, hundreds of citizens joining, headed by the Union Cornet Band of Buffalo, whose solemn strains floated out upon the still air in sweet but sorrowful cadence.

At the cemetery appropriate ceremonies were performed, and the lowering of the coffin and the farewell shots over his grave, betokened the burial of all that was mortal of our beloved chief.

On the 28th day of September following his father received from President Lincoln a commission appointing his son a brigadier general, for gallant and meritorious services in the assault on the fortifications at Port Hudson. The commission was dated May 27, 1863, the day of his death, and was issued in acknowledgment of his services, as a tribute to his memory, and in testimony of the rank he should occupy on the roll of his country's defenders. The act was one of most delicate respect to the grief of his bereaved parents, of whom he was their youngest born, and for whom, spite of his glorious memory, they must go down into the grave mourning.

Few men of as much real worth have lived and died without more of an acknowledgment of that worth than he, and this because of his modesty in all his intercourse with those in authority. He was fully appreciated, both in his character as a man and soldier, by his immediate commander, Gen'l Augur, and none expressed deeper sorrow at his death than did he. Two years later, at Chicago, in the summer of 1865, Gen'l Augur, in speaking of Gen'l Chapin, said: "The army could illy afford to lose such an officer, or the country such a man." A tribute of this character from such a soldier is a tribute indeed.

Chapin, as a soldier, possessed a peculiar talent of keeping up that line of distinction between the different grades, so necessary to the preservation of discipline, without seeming tò encroach upon natural privileges, or resorting to severity of measure. There was something in his look, his manner and actions, which betrayed a superiority that required not the shoulder strap to indicate, nor the exercise of any of the powers attending his position, to interpret. Frequently descending to familiarity in his conversation with his inferiors in rank, there were none so bold as to take advantage of this condescension. Always kind and attentive to his men, no personal sacrifice was too great for him to make, by which their health or comfort might be improved. I venture to say that no officer in the army had a more complete hold upon the affections of his men than did Gen'l Chapin.

He was of steady and excellent habits. Temperate almost to abstemiousness, setting an example to his men in this respect which was a novelty in the army, on account of its rarity among commanding officers. He was a Christian by profession, and decidedly one by practice. He was a subject of the awakening in Buffalo, and joined the First Presbyterian Church while under the pastorate of the Rev. Dr. Thompson.

From the time he first went to Buffalo he kept a diary, in which he made daily entries. In its introduction he writes: "As a means of resisting temptation I promise myself that I will do no act but what I will write in this book, and leave for posterity to read." This sentiment so beautifully and sublimely expressed, and so faithfully carried out, as attested by the yearly volumes, carried up to the date of his entrance into service, and found in his safe at Buffalo after his death, is a monument to his character which in the hearts of his friends will live forever. What a pleasure to his parents it must be to look over those pages, and read the thoughts, the promises and struggles, the bright hopes of the future, which the buoyancy of his spirits and the well-controlled ambition of his nature must have indulged in. To his parents he was a source of infinite pleasure and comfort. His whole life was a study how to add to their happiness, and to repay them, as far as lay in his power, for the cares and anxieties attendant upon their endeavors in training him to be a man who would gain the esteem of his friends and reflect credit upon themselves. His love for his mother was almost reverential in its character, and the writer, who passed a week in her society after the General's death, can never forget the exhibition of a mother's pride, struggling with a mother's affection, in reviewing his life and the many touching incidents connected with it, during his absence in the army. Though time may have seared over the wounds of her affliction, the beauties of his nature, and the extent of her loss cannot be effaced from her memory this side of eternity. May the path of the few remaining years which she will be compelled to pass upon earth be smooth and pleasant, sustained by the recollection of the glory of his death, and the anticipation of meeting in the other world the darling son, the idol of her heart.

The following extracts from letters to his friends, and from himself to his family, are, perhaps, applicable here, as an exhibition of his soldierly spirit and the motives which actuated him in giving himself to the cause; and these will close the sketch of a subject that requires greater ability than mine to do it justice:

From CHAPIN to his Parents; written the evening before the battle of Hanover Court House, May 27, 1862.

"We leave with two days' rations, in light marching order, and expect a fight. I am not anxious to be shot, but I hail with joy the approaching conflict, for I believe if it turns out a grand battle it will be the finishing stroke of the rebellion. God only knows what is in store for your beloved son, my dear parents; but of this I feel assured, it will be either an honorable life or a glorious death: and if the latter, I trust in God that you may have strength to bear it as cheerfully as I freely lay it down for our glorious country. Good night, and farewell. I fully realize my position, and my trust is in my Heavenly Father, who caused me to be born of Christian parents, and reared me in the knowledge and love of our dear Saviour."

From same to his Sisters; written August, 1862, apologizing for not visiting them before leaving Buffalo.

"I have been extremely anxious to see you before my return to the seat of war. The thing is altogether impossible, however, until we may once more sit together, when a peaceful country shall be the reward of our great and trying self-denial. You know I am the father of a large family, one thousand hard-fisted men, and I am going back again to do my whole duty, come what may to me. I hate war, and every thing pertaining to it, except as a means to peace; but now I am forced as a loyal citizen to love it. My heart is in my vocation, and I count not my life at a pin's fee, if by any means I can help to secure again a great and a glorious union.

"I hope to survive this war, but not this union. Girls, I have a great responsibility, and I feel that I need the prayers of all, and the aid of our Heavenly Father to enable me to discharge my awful undertaking, with credit to the cause and honor to myself."

From CHARLES P. CROSBY, Esq., an old schoolmate, to the "Waterloo Observer," June 21, 1863.

* * * "Of a warm, unselfish nature, a noble, generous and loving heart; and although naturally quiet and undemon-

strative, he was possessed of a lion-like courage. He was careful of the feelings of others, and during the existence of an acquaintance, I have never known him intentionally to cause any one pain.

"He had proved himself, prior to the battle in which he lost his life, to be a fine specimen of the American soldier, careful of his men, and attentive to their real wants, obedient to the orders of his superiors, courteous to his equals and inferiors, always, and in all places, doing his duty, he has left behind him a record of which his friends have just reason to be proud. He has died young, but on his name as a lawyer, citizen or soldier, there is no spot. * * * * * * * * * * *

"He died with his last glance toward the flag he loved so well, and for whose supremacy he was yielding up his life. Another name has been added to the roll of those whose memory through all time shall be immortal, who died to support the cause of freedom, law and Christianity. Among the victims of this unholy and unrighteous rebellion, there are none whose remembrance will be more tenderly cherished.

"He sleeps in consecrated ground, in the home of his youth. For him no more the shout of battle nor the clang of arms. The sods of the valley cover his broad breast, and the noble heart is pulseless and still. May the God of our armies in his infinite mercy sustain the hearts of his aged parents in this their awful affliction. May they be comforted in this their dark and solemn hour, by the hope that in the hereafter, when war shall be no more, and earth shall have passed away, that they will meet their dear son in the realms of the holies beyond the stars. He sleeps well. True friend, loyal soldier, Christian gentleman, greeting and farewell."

From JOHN B. WEBER, Act'g Asst. Adjt. General, to the General's father, informing him of his son's death.

* * * * "He fell about four P. M., yesterday, in the assault upon the enemy's works at Port Hudson, while gallantly leading his men on in the glorious work for which he so nobly and cheerfully offered himself a sacrifice. I found his remains far to the front and within speaking distance of the enemy's entrenchments. He was shot in the face, the bullet crashing through his brain, and producing an almost instant death. His remains I take to New Orleans this evening, and will forward them, with his effects, from there to your home by his faithful servant Timothy.

"I hardly know, my dear sir, how to console you for this great loss—the once fervent supporter of your aged days. We all loved him as a brother, confided in him as we would repose confidence in a father, and followed him as our brave leader on many a hard fought field. He died in a glorious cause: a cause made more holy by the many brave hearts that have ceased their pulsation —victims to the insatiate demand for noble blood. He was our friend, our adviser and leader. One blow has bereft us of all these, and has deprived us of a tower of strength by taking away the brave and cheerful example which he exhibited in all his actions.

* * * * * * * * * * * * *

"While we mourn his loss as an esteemed friend, to ourselves, and a brave and devoted laborer in the good cause, we cannot help but feeling consoled that he died the death he would have chosen above all others—his face to the foe and on the advance line. A purer Christian there was none; and with his bright spirit looking down from the throne of his Maker, upon his own gallant band, and the influence which his memory will ever carry with it, will, I am sure, go far to sustain the honorable reputation which "his boys," as he loved to call them, have obtained through his unwearied and untiring exertions.

"Accept, sir, our heartfelt sympathies in this sad hour of affliction, and may God give you strength to bear up under the trial which he in his infinite wisdom and goodness has seen fit to impose upon us all." * * * * * * * * *

CAPTIAN JAMES AYER.

BY REV. H. M. DANFORTH.

Among the brightest ornaments of the One Hundred and Sixteenth Regiment of New York State Volunteers, was Capt. James Ayer, of Evans, Erie Co., who died in camp at Baton Rouge, May 22d, 1863. He was born in the town of Evans on the 14th day of August, 1813. His parents removed from Haverhill, Mass., in the fall of 1811, and were among the earliest settlers of this section. His whole life was spent in this his native town, and no man was so universally loved and respected. His love for his country was second only to that for his God, and when traitorous hands were lifted against the flag, he felt it his duty to offer himself to defend it. Accordingly he received authorization papers from the committee having in charge the raising of the One Hundred and Sixteenth N. Y. S. Vols., and immediately set about the raising of a company.

His military ability was very highly appreciated years before the war commenced. From the office of captain he was promoted to that of major, then to lieutenant colonel, and finally, in 1838, to that of colonel, in the Forty-eighth Regiment, Forty-seventh Brigade, Twenty-fourth Division of N. Y. State Militia. In all these positions he was beloved and admired.

As a man in every day life, it is no exaggeration to say that a better model of Christian excellence cannot be found in any community. His life without any shade of coloring would make a volume so richly ornamented with noble deeds as to awaken the admiration of all, and especially of those who appreciate goodness and know the worth of those examples which lead to virtue, to moral purity and to God. We can but regard Capt. Ayer as emphatically a benefactor of his race, one who delighted in acts of usefulness, and laid himself out to do good. But very little of his precious life will ever be written except in the Book of Records, for it is made up to a great extent of little acts of kindness and usefulness which memory cannot collect, and some of which were known to very few beyond those immediately concerned, for to do good was always a greater pleasure to him than to publish it; he never sounded a trumpet before him, but did good for pleasure rather than show.

He was a liberal soul, always ready to lend a helping hand to every good cause. His large benevolence was often much relief to the poor and needy, and a great help to those institutions which have for their object the moral elevation and salvation of our race. The wide fame of his generosity drew around him a large number of those who sought aid for the destitute, for the institutions of the gospel, or for the sufferers in the service of their country; and few, if any, will say they were ever sent empty away. Having for a long series of years acted the part of a Christian, a patriot and a philanthropist, in giving bountifully of his property, for the good of his fellow men, he crowned the whole by giving himself for his country a willing sacrifice.

Many have realized his tender sympathy, and will long remember his acts of kindness to them and their families, in sickness, sorrow and death; his business was never too urgent to be set aside by the calls of the afflicted and bereaved.

Though he was naturally retiring, yet easy in his manners, and regarded by all who knew him as a model of true politeness. His kind words, like apples of gold, in pictures of silver, were always ready for the aged and the young: not a little child was passed unnoticed, and no infant was ever more tenderly cared for than his venerable mother Terry. His respect for the aged, his personal modesty and kind attention to all around him, we would commend to the rising generation as worthy of their imitation. If they would cultivate personal refinement and secure the love and good-will of all around them, they should copy the example of James Ayer.

Among the excellencies of this noble specimen of humanity, we would not forget to mention his tender regard for every man's reputation and character. He cared for it as for his own. I say it boldly, for those to read who knew him best, he never was heard to speak ill of any man, and when others did it in his presence, and in a way to call for some response, they received nothing but a gentle reproof for themselves or a handsome apology for the injured. He was anxious to think that everybody meant well, and manifestly had a disposition to be pleased with the conduct of others lying back of all external action, and constituting a part of his character or habit of feeling. This propensity to be satisfied rather than dissatisfied, to look on the favorable rather than the unfavorable side in the conduct of others,—rather to attribute to them good motives than bad ones,—stands opposed to a spirit of faultfinding and complaining which nothing satisfies. A man possessed of such a character, such a heart, such a fountain, out of which are the issues of life, is a great blessing to any community. But he was not only possessed of a good heart, but of a good mind. He was decidedly a man of talent, and one who used his talents for the best of purposes. Though very unassuming, yet wise in counsel and a man of much forecast and prudence.

A short time before the war commenced he became the subject of many deep afflictions, being called to bury his wife, and having previously buried two children. Hence when he heard the call of his country, he had a large farm upon his hands and two motherless children, one eleven and the other eight years of age. But few could have been placed in more trying and difficult circumstances to heed such a call. Considering his time of life, his impaired constitution, the situation of his little, dependent family, and his estate, we may safely say it was a sacrifice which not one in a thousand would have made. The motives which led to this great undertaking, this sacrifice of all that was dear on earth, were as pure as the crystal fountain. It was not to gratify combativeness or any feeling of party strife, but to do his duty, save his country, and bless the world; to do all in his power to save *government by the people* from a dreadful overthrow; to help it in its last struggle for existence among the nations of the earth. In deciding to do this there must have been a painful struggle with the tender affections of his heart. To leave the old homestead, sacred to the memory of all that was interesting and solemn in his whole life, together with his little dependent, motherless children, endeared by successive bereavements and deep afflictions, and with such strong probabilities that he might never return, required greater fortitude than to meet the enemy in open conflict. No wounds are so painful as those which make the heart bleed. Having made arrangements for a stone to mark the spot where his beloved companion is sleeping the long sleep of mortals, he stepped upon the stage to respond to the ladies who presented him with a sword, was able to read the most of his production with composure; but when he came to his sainted wife, and spoke of the mother and the babes, utterance failed, and a pause was necessary to suppress the deep emotions of his heart. When he thought of loved ones he was to leave in the grave, and of others he was to leave in a world of dangers and uncertainties, language was powerless — tears must tell the rest. Having at the family altar commended his little ones to God for the last time, they followed him to the train which was to bear him away, where he gave them a parting kiss as the last expression of a father's love, stepped upon the cars and was out of sight for ever.

The company who enlisted on condition that he should be their captain, found him to be all they had anticipated; the longer they proved him the stronger were their attachments. In the army he manifested the same spirit of kindness, and exhibited the same good sense as in every other position. Having been in the service eight months, disease began to prey upon his system; old pulmonary difficulties were hurried on by the exposure of camp life; but finally he was taken with fever, followed by inflammation of the bowels, which ended all hope of his recovery. On Wednesday morning, May 20th, Mr. John F. Wilcox was released from his march with the army, and went to see him. He seized his hand with an expression of great joy, "O, I am so glad you did not go," and repeated it three times. But still he was not conscious of being very near his end. On Friday noon, the day of his death, when a hope was expressed that he might recover so as to go home to his children, he replied, "I am confident I shall recover from this in a few days." He spoke of the preciousness of Christ as an all-sufficient Saviour, but was too weak to talk much. "I will rest," said he, "a little while, and then I should like to have you come in again and read and pray with me." In a short time he went in again and found Mr. Elijah Smith, of Brant, trying to rouse him to take his medicine; but, alas! it was too late. He took him by the hand and asked him if he knew that he was going, but he showed no signs of consciousness; he was never to hear the chapter read or the prayer offered, but breathed shorter and shorter for about fifteen minutes, and expired about 5 o'clock, May 22d, 1863, aged 50 years.

In his absence from the world he has done so much to enlighten and save—from the country for which he gave his life—from the town and the church he has so abundantly blessed—there is one consolation for all: "He being dead yet speaketh." "The echoes of his words are to be reflected along the ages." It has been truly said, "A man has two immortalities—one he carries with him to a loftier sphere, and the other he leaves behind, and it walks the earth and still represents him; what he said sounds along the years like voices amidst the mountain gorges, and what he did is repeated after him in ever-multiplying and never-ceasing reverberations."

The influence of James Ayer is not dead. Those who have been blessed by his godly example are scattered to the four winds, and will live to bless others in geometrical ratio till the end of time. "The lessons he taught, the grand sentiments he uttered, the noble deeds of generosity by which he was characterized, the moral lineaments and likeness of the man, still survive to bless the world forever."

LIEUT. ELISHA B. COTTIER.

Lieut. Elisha B. Cottier was born in the city of New York, November 23d, 1831.

His education was received in the public schools of that city, where his attention to his studies soon made him proficient.

Upon arriving at a proper age, his parents selected for him the trade of a gold beater, which he very soon mastered, and was able to earn good wages as a journeyman.

In 1849 he removed to Buffalo, N. Y., where he had two brothers residing. One of them, Lieut. Col. Robt. Cottier, was then engaged in the gold leaf manufacturing business, and he at once entered his employ.

The year following he joined Company "D" (at that time an independent organization, but since then a part of the Seventy-fourth Regiment, N. Y. S. M.), commanded by Capt. D. D. Bidwell, who afterward, and during the late war, became a brigadier general. He very soon won the love and respect of his comrades, and for four years served them as a sergeant, three of them as orderly sergeant, *vice* Adrian R. Root. He entered with spirit into the work, and in those palmy days of Company "D's" history, bore a prominent part.

In 1855 he was married to Miss Carrie Hoff, and shortly after returned to New York city, where he remained until the breaking out of the rebellion.

His connection with Company "D" in Buffalo had given him an opportunity to acquire considerable skill in the science of military, which he had improved; and now, when volunteers were called for, he felt the duty of offering his services to his country pressing him sorely. Had he been unmarried, those who knew him best are confident he would have at once enlisted; but his young wife and little ones needed him, and, like many others, he waited.

In 1861 he returned to Buffalo with the promise of a lieutenancy in the Forty-ninth N. Y. Vols., then being raised there, but for some reason the promise was not kept, and the regiment proceeded to the seat of war without him.

When the work of raising the One Hundred and Sixteenth was commenced, he secured from the committee in charge authority to enlist men for it, and at once entered upon the work. In the consolidation of the several detachments, which became necessary to the final organization of the regiment, he, with some others, was thrown out. So highly, however, was he recommended for a position, that Col. Chapin appointed him to the first vacancy occurring in the regiment.

About the first of October, 1862, he received notice of his appointment as Second Lieutenant of Company "K" and on the 8th left Buffalo for the regiment, then encamped near Baltimore, Md. On the evening of his departure, his old comrades of Company "D" presented him with a sword, sash and belt, as a slight token of their esteem.

Lieut. Cottier served faithfully with his regiment at the battle of Plain Store, and in the two fearful assaults upon Port Hudson of May 27th and June 14th was among the foremost.

Escaping the dangers of these terrible places, he fell a victim to the malaria of the climate, and on the 2d day of July was sent back to Baton Rouge sick with a fever. Every attention was paid him by those at Baton Rouge, and hopes were entertained that an opportunity to visit his home in Buffalo would fully restore him to health. An application for a leave of absence was prepared and sent to head-quarters at New Orleans, but from some technical informality it was returned for correction, although Surgeon Hutchins, in his endorsement on the paper, stated that Lieut. Cottier's life depended upon its being at once granted.

Upon its receipt Surgeon Hutchins at once repaired to New Orleans, by personal effort secured the leave, and returned to Baton Rouge. But, alas, too late, poor "Leish," within twelve hours, received a final discharge from all service below, having died on the 21st day of August.

His remains were interred at Baton Rouge with military honors, and the following winter were removed to Buffalo. On the 14th day of February, 1864, at one o'clock in the afternoon, the funeral was attended from Grace M. E. Church. The remains were escorted to Forest Lawn Cemetery by his old companions, Company "D," led by the Union Cornet Band, and with the honors due his rank deposited in its final resting place.

Lieut. Cottier was one of those men who could not but make friends wherever his lot was cast. Coming into the One Hundred and Sixteenth almost an entire stranger, and unknown to a single member of the company to which he was assigned, he very speedily gained the respect and esteem of every member of it. He was prompt in the discharge of every duty, however it may have interfered with his own comfort, and by this won the good will of his superiors.

He was a remarkably genial companion, ever ready to join in all amusements not in themselves degrading. There was in his organization a quaint humor which never failed to enliven the most dreary hours of camp life or to while away the tediousness of the march; and even after he was taken sick at Port Hudson, and unable to perform duty, this humor would break out in such expressions as would cause those whom he addressed to burst into laughter.

He loved his absent wife and little ones with a pure

and holy affection which nothing could shake. The writer has often conversed with him of his home, and can never forget the light which always beamed in his eye when the subject was introduced.

Lieut. Cottier was a general favorite with all, and it is not saying too much to assert, that no one could have been taken from the circle of officers who would have been so much missed, and as we pay this our last tribute to his memory we mourn his loss from that circle.

LIEUT. DAVID JONES.

The facts necessary to the writing of a complete sketch of the life of Lieut. David Jones are unfortunately shrouded in mystery, absolutely nothing of his life, previous to his entering the One Hundred and Sixteenth, being known; and yet it has been deemed best to give the little that is known, inasmuch as no officer in the regiment served the good cause more faithfully than he.

He appeared at Camp Morgan, in Buffalo, one morning, an entire stranger to all, and requested authority to recruit for the regiment. His request was granted, but being entirely unknown in the city, his success was far from satisfactory, either to himself or to the committee. However he soon came to be very valuable in the many duties to be performed in camp; and his time was, in consequence, principally devoted to these duties. He was found to be very energetic and reliable to the last degree.

When the time came round for Col. Chapin to select

from the large number who had been recruiting for the regiment, a sufficient number to fill the positions, his attention was directed to the subject of this sketch, as a person who would fill a lieutenancy with credit to himself and the good of the regiment.

He thought favorably of it, and in the list of nominations to the Governor, we find the name of David Jones, who was duly commissioned and mustered into the service of the United States as second lieutenant of Company "H."

Upon the arrival of the regiment at "Camp Chapin," Baltimore, Lieut. Jones at once took his place among the very best of the officers, proving conclusively the wisdom of Col. Chapin's selection. Throughout all the long months of preparatory drilling, he was untiring in his efforts to make the company to which he was attached as good as the best, and the reputation which Company "H" attained for cleanliness and efficiency was due very much to Lieut. Jones.

He was among the few who always undertook a tour of duty, whatever it may have been, without a murmur of complaint, entering upon it with his whole soul, whether it was the care of an important picket line, or the policeing of the camp.

But true as he was ever found in these lesser duties of the soldier, it was on the battle-field that he proved himself most worthy. His brilliant exploit at Winter's Plantation, where he sought adventure, and captured six prisoners, was an exhibition of that peculiar desire for action which ever characterized him, and proved the only redeeming feature of that failure. He was never still, but always on the move.

At Plain Store the captain of his company was sick,

and the command devolved upon him. He assumed it with good grace, and his conduct was worthy of especial mention for the gallantry displayed.

He led his company in the fearful assault of May 27th, on Port Hudson, and was mortally wounded. The wound was of a very painful nature, and for nearly two days he lingered in sufferings the most intense. Very tenderly he was conveyed to New Orleans, where he died on the 29th, and where his remains now lie.

Lieut. Jones was never heard boasting of his bravery, but when the time came, and duty called him, none were more prompt to respond.

He was of a most cheerful disposition, a general favorite with every one. His peculiar laugh was almost hourly heard, and with his original expression "*By Joram,*" made his presence desirable among all the officers.

This is all that can be given of one we all became very much attached to. Enough was learned after his death to indicate plainly that he was of German parentage, and that he was serving the land of his adoption under an assumed name. What his real name was is still a mystery, but the name of David Jones will ever have a warm place in the memory of the members of the One Hundred and Sixteenth.

LIEUT. CHARLES BORUSKY.

BY CAPT. R. C. KINNEY.

We have been unable to learn much of the early history of Lieut. Chas. Borusky, who was mortally wounded in the regiment's first battle at Plain Store, La.

He was a man not much given to loquaciousness, and never spoke of his former life except to a few of his comrades with whom he had formed more than ordinary relations of intimacy. From them we learn that he had served in the Prussian army, though for how long a period they do not remember.

Certain it is that from the beginning of his term of enlistment he displayed those many little evidences of discipline which mark the trained and experienced soldier. Always prompt and efficient in the discharge of duty, appearing on all occasions of parade, review and guard mounting, with every bit of brass on his uniform and equipments shining; with boots and belts well blacked and polished, and musket in the most perfect condition of cleanliness, he soon became noted in his company and throughout the regiment, as a model soldier.

First promoted to a sergeantcy in his company, his name was shortly after sent to the Governor for a commission as lieutenant, and he was at once assigned to duty in that capacity. His courage under fire was in keeping with the high character for soldierly qualities which he had established.

He was shot in the neck with a musket ball while engaged at his post in the front rank of the battle, and was borne from the field by two of his comrades. After the dressing of his wound at the field hospital, he was conveyed to the hospital at Baton Rouge, where he died on the 25th of May, 1863, four days after the battle of Plain Store.

MUSTER ROLL.

FIELD AND STAFF.

COLONELS.

Edward P. Chapin—Killed May 27, 1863, Port Hudson. In command of a Brigade at time of his death. Promoted to Brig. General, May 27, 1863. (See page 281.)

George M. Love—Wounded May 27, 1863, Port Hudson. In command of a Brigade for a portion of the time. Promoted to Brevt. Brig. General. Mustered out with regiment.

LIEUTENANT COLONELS.

Robert Cottier—Resigned May 27, 1863.

John Higgins—Resigned Sept. 17, 1864.

John M. Sizer—Detached on staff of Gen'l Emory for a time. Mustered out with regiment.

MAJORS.

Geo. M. Love—Promoted to Colonel, May 27, 1863.

John Higgins—Promoted to Lieut. Colonel, Sept. 14, 1863.

John M. Sizer—Promoted to Lieut. Colonel, Oct. 30, 1864.

Geo. W. Carpenter—Mustered out with regiment.

ADJUTANTS.

John B. Weber—Detached on brigade staff for a time. Promoted to Colonel 89th U. S. Colored Troops, Sept. 19, 1863.

John C. Nial—Mustered out with regiment.

QUARTERMASTERS.

James Adams—Resigned Sept. 14, 1862.

Willitt H. Fargo—Resigned Nov. 23, 1862.

Alexander Goslin—Promoted to Asst. Quartermaster U. S. A.

Geo. W. Miller—Mustered out with regiment.

SURGEON.

Chauncy B. Hutchins—Detached on staff of Gen'l Emory for a time. Mustered out with regiment.

ASSISTANT SURGEONS.

Uri C. Lynde—Resigned Oct. 18, 1863.
Carey W. Howe—Resigned Jan. 6, 1863.
John Coventry—Resigned Sept. 14, 1864.
M. Eugene Shaw—Mustered out with regiment.

CHAPLAINS.

Welton M. Modisett—Resigned June 23, 1863.
Hiram J. Gordon—Mustered out with regiment.

NON-COMMISSIONED STAFF.

SERGEANT MAJORS.

Orton S. Clark—Promoted to 2d Lieutenant, Nov. 8, 1862.
John C. Nial—Promoted to 2d Lieutenant, July 23, 1863.
Rich'd M. Hair—Promoted to Adjutant 89th U. S. Colored Troops, Sept. 19, 1863.
Raymond McGowan—Wounded May 27, 1863, Port Hudson. Promoted to 2d Lieutenant.
Oloff W. Stadin—Wounded May 27, 1863, Port Hudson. Mustered out with regiment.

QUARTERMASTER SERGEANTS.

Alexander Goslin—Promoted to Quartermaster, Nov. 23, 1862.
Michael Danner, Jr.—Mustered out with regiment.

COMMISSARY SERGEANTS.

Josiah L. Claghorn—Promoted to Quartermaster 89th U. S. Colored Troops.
Warren K. Russell—Discharged for disability, March 1, 1865.
Wm. H. Matthewson—Mustered out with regiment.

HOSPITAL STEWARD.

Chas. F. A. Nichell—Mustered out with regiment.

PRINCIPAL MUSICIANS.

John Martin—Leader of Band. Mustered out with regiment.
Julius L. Knapp—Mustered out with regiment.

COMPANY A.

CAPTAINS.

Ira Ayer—Resigned March 1, 1863.
Chas. F. Wadsworth—Resigned.
Jacob C. Newton—Resigned Sept. 8, 1864.
Geo. H. Shepard—Mustered out with regiment.

FIRST LIEUTENANTS.

Jacob C. Thompson—Resigned Sept. 21, 1862.

Orton S. Clark—Promoted to Captain Co. H, April 12, 1864.

William Tibbetts—Promoted to Captain Co. I, March 1, 1865.

John G. Dayton—Mustered out with regiment.

SECOND LIEUTENANTS.

Warren T. Ferris—Promoted to 1st Lieutenant Co. K, Nov. 23, 1862.

Orton S. Clark—Promoted to 1st Lieutenant, June 1, 1863.

Jacob C. Newton—Promoted to Captain, April 12, 1864.

FIRST SERGEANTS.

Jacob C. Newton—Promoted to 2d Lieutenant, June 1, 1863.

Samuel Leonard—Wounded May 21, 1863, Plain Store. Promoted to 2d Lieutenant Co. B, April 21, 1864.

John H. Dingman—Wounded May 27, 1863, Port Hudson; and April 8, 1864, Sabine Cross Roads. Promoted to 1st Lieutenant, Jan. 13, 1865.

Horace W. White—Mustered out with regiment.

SERGEANTS.

Rollin C. Hubbard—Wounded May 21, 1863, Plain Store. Taken prisoner July 13, 1863, Cox's Plantation. Promoted to Captain 89th U. S. Colored Troops, Sept. 1, 1863.

Charles H. Grant—Wounded May 27, 1863, Port Hudson. Died June 29, 1864, Buffalo, N. Y.

Wm. H. Bartlett—Mustered out with regiment.

Geo. H. Davis—Mustered out with regiment.

Jacob Gottschalk—Wounded May 21, 1863, Plain Store. Mustered out with regiment.

Frank Bentley—Wounded July 13, 1863, Cox's Plantation. Musout with regiment.

CORPORALS.

John W. Hamlin—Promoted to Lieutenant Corps d'Afrique, April 12, 1863.

Egbert Smith—Wounded May 27, 1863, Port Hudson. Transferred to Vet. Reserve Corps, Jan. 10, 1865.

Ira Ayer—Died of disease Sept. 15, 1863, Hamburg, N. Y.

Authur F. Smith—Wounded May 27, 1863, Port Hudson. Died June 9, 1863, New Orleans, La.

Robert B. Foote—Wounded May 21, 1863, Plain Store. Discharged for disability, July, 1863.

Isaac Colvin—Died of disease Aug. 23, 1863, Baton Rouge, La.

William Lepper—Mustered out with regiment.

Leroy G. Bundy—Transferred to Vet. Res. Corps, April 30, 1864.

Jefferson White—Wounded May 27, 1863, Port Hudson; and Sept. 19, 1864, Winchester. Mustered out with regiment.

Channing Smith—Wounded July 13, 1863, Cox's Plantation. Mustered out with regiment.

Edward Barry—Wounded May 27, 1863, Port Hudson. Mustered out with regiment.

Robert H. Woods—Mustered out with regiment.

Philip Linebits—Wounded Oct. 19, 1864, Cedar Creek. Died Oct. 27, 1864, Baltimore, Md.

George Taylor—Wounded July 13, 1863, Cox's Plantation. Discharged for disability, Jan. 3, 1865.

Wm. H. Young—Mustered out with regiment.

Wm. Ross—Wounded May 27, 1863, Port Hudson. Mustered out with regiment.

MUSICIANS.

Eron V. Carr—Wounded May 21, 1863, Plain Store. Discharged for disability, Feb. 19, 1864.

Harlan E. Bundy—Mustered out with regiment.

WAGONER.

John Akeley—Mustered out with regiment.

PRIVATES.

Alfred Agard—Mustered out with regiment.

Luce Bartoo—Transferred to Vet. Reserve Corps, Aug. 22, 1863.

Henry Beach—Died of disease, Oct. 15, 1863, New Orleans, La.

David Bentley—Mustered out with regiment.

Francis Bourne—Mustered out with regiment.

Andrew Burley—Mustered out with regiment.

Herschell S. Butts—Wounded May 27, 1863, Port Hudson. Discharged for disability, Dec. 15, 1863.

Josiah L. Claghorn—Promoted to Regt'l Commissary Sergeant, Sept. 3, 1862.

Norman Carr—Regt'l Band. Wounded May 21, 1863, Plain Store. Mustered out with regiment.

Daniel W. Clapp—Died of disease June 5, 1863, Baton Rouge, La.

James Cook—Died of disease Dec. 26, 1862, Fortress Monroe.

Wallace Calkins—Wounded May 27, 1863, Port Hudson. Died June, 1863, New Orleans, La.

Andrew Cook—Mustered out with regiment.

Daniel Covensparrow—Died of disease August 17, 1863, Baton Rouge, La.

James H. Duffy—Mustered out with regiment.

John Farrell—Wounded May 27, 1863, Port Hudson. Discharged for disability, Sept. 20, 1863.

Joseph Frochley—Regt'l Band. Mustered out with regiment.

George Fuller—Mustered out with regiment.

Bethuell Fuller—Died of disease Dec. 27, 1862, Fortress Monroe.

John Fenner—Died of disease Jan. 6, 1864, Franklin, La.

Homer F. Gould—Mustered out with regiment.

Anselem Glouser—Mustered out with regiment.

Wallace Hambleton—Discharged for disability, Fortress Monroe. Date unknown.

George Herr—Killed May 27, 1863, Port Hudson.

Voltair Heaton—Transferred to Co. E, Oct. 4, 1862, and died at New Orleans, La.

John Heinendinger—Died of disease June 26, 1864, Morgansia, La.

William H. Hines—Mustered out with regiment.

Elgeva V. Horton—Color Guard. Wounded Sept. 19, 1864, Winchester. Mustered out with regiment.

Thomas Hussey—Wounded May 27, 1863, Port Hudson. Mustered out with regiment.

Francis D. Ingersoll—Killed May 27, 1863, Plain Store.

Frederick Jackson—Mustered out with regiment.

Seneca A. Jones—Transferred to Vet. Reserve Corps, Nov. 1, 1863.

Oscar B. Johnson—Transferred to U. S. Navy, June 25, 1864.

Thomas Kelley—Wounded Oct. 19, 1864, Cedar Creek. Mustered out with regiment.

Frank Keiser—Mustered out with regiment.

Christian Keinzle—Wounded Oct. 19, 1864, Cedar Creek. Mustered out with regiment.

Ambrose S. Lawton—Regt'l Band. Mustered out with regiment.

John Martin—Promoted Principal Musician.

John March—Transferred to 2d La. Cavalry, Feb. 10, 1863.

Philip Mumbach—Died of disease Jan. 4, 1863, Fortress Monroe.

Leroy S. Oatman—Wounded May 21, 1863, Plain Store. Regt'l Ordnance Sergeant, Dec 26, 1863. Mustered out with regiment.

Chas. E. Paine—Wounded May 27, 1863, Port Hudson. Promoted to 2d Lieutenant Co. E, July, 1863.

Ezra T. Ridout—Mustered out with regiment.

Henry M. Raymond—Discharged for disability, Aug. 30, 1863.

Charles Riald—Transferred to Co. C, Jan. 20, 1863.

John Roberts—Wounded May 21, 1863, Plain Store. Transferred to U. S. Navy, May 5, 1864.

Arthur Redmond—Died of disease Jan. 16, 1863, Fortress Monroe.

Charles Strassing—Wounded May 27, 1863, Port Hudson. Mustered out with regiment.
Henry Schamel—Mustered out with regiment.
Conrad Schamel—Killed May 21, 1863, Plain Store.
Henry E. Stambach—Discharged to accept clerkship in quartermaster's Department, Dec. 2, 1863.
John Sensor—Mustered out with regiment.
James Smith—Mustered out with regiment.
Charles A. Stanton—Regt'l Band. Discharged for disability, Feb. 19, 1864.
Bee Stout—Recruit. Transferred to 90th N. Y. Vet. Vols. when 116th was mustered out.
Nathanial J. Swift—Wounded May 21, 1863, Plain Store. Died July, 1863, Baton Rouge, La.
Harvey Smith—Mustered out with regiment.
William H. Sawdy—Wounded May 27, 1863, Port Hudson. Furloughed, and never reported to company.
Benjamin R. Train—Mustered out with regiment.
Lobeski C. Trevitt—Wounded May 21, 1863, Plain Store. Mustered out with regiment.
Albion Webester—Died of disease July 31, 1864, Washington, D. C.
John F. Wilcox—Transferred to Co. B, April 20, 1864.
Homer B. Willett—Transferred to Co. B, April 20, 1864.
Abner M. Williams—Wounded May 21, 1863, Plain Store. Transferred to Co. B, April 20, 1864.
Wm. W. White—Killed May 21, 1863, Plain Store.
Henry White—Killed May 27, 1863, Port Hudson.
Andrus Wolf—Wounded May 21, 1863, Plain Store. Mustered out with regiment.
Ephraim Wooderson—Wounded May 27, 1863, Port Hudson. Died June 10, 1863, New Orleans, La.
Peter Yocum—Discharged for disability, Feb. 14, 1863.

COLORED COOK.

Henry Delancy—Recruit. Transferred to 90th N. Y. Vet. Vols., when 116th was mustered out.

COMPANY B.

CAPTAINS.

Albert J. Barnard—Resigned July 29, 1863.
Wilson H. Gray—Wounded May 27, 1863, Port Hudson. Discharged for disability, Aug. 15, 1864.
John G. Woehnert—Mustered out with regiment.

FIRST LIEUTENANTS.

Leander Willis—Resigned Oct. 3, 1862.

John B. Mason—Resigned June 5, 1863.

Wm. F. Feldham—Mustered out with regiment.

SECOND LIEUTENANTS.

Daniel Corbett—Resigned Oct. 1, 1862.

John R. Dobbins—Acting Adjutant for a time. Resigned Nov. 14, 1863.

Oscar F. Tiffany—Promoted to Captain 89th U. S. Colored Troops, Dec. 31, 1863.

Samuel Leonard—Mustered out with regiment.

FIRST SERGEANTS.

John L. Carmer—Promoted to 1st Lieut. 89th U. S. Colored Troops, Oct. 12, 1863.

Chas. J. Bostwick—Mustered out with regiment.

SERGEANTS.

John W. Tuttle—Promoted to Captain 89th U. S. Colored Troops, Sept. 26, 1863.

Chas. Standart—Killed April 8, 1864, Sabine Cross Roads.

James S. Little—Wounded May 27, 1863, Port Hudson. Discharged for disability, June 6, 1864.

George Townsend—Color Bearer. Wounded Oct. 19, 1864, Cedar Creek. Died Oct. 31, 1864.

William H. Rose—Wounded Sept. 19, 1864, Winchester. Discharged for disability, May 27, 1865.

Jacob Kurtz—Wounded Oct. 19, 1864, Cedar Creek. Mustered out with regiment.

Michael Bund—Mustered out with regiment.

Benj. F. Lentz—Mustered out with regiment.

CORPORALS.

Fletcher Montgomery—Wounded April 9, 1864, Pleasant Hill. Discharged for disability, June 27, 1864.

Jehial Woodward—Discharged for disability, May 19, 1865.

Adam Grill—Mustered out with regiment.

Egbert H. Parcell—Wounded Sept. 19, 1864, Winchester. Mustered out with regiment.

Joseph Drudge—Mustered out with regiment.

Warren Keller—Mustered out with regiment.

James H. Atwood—Mustered out with regiment.

John Keintz—Mustered out with regiment.

Joseph C. Standart—Mustered out with regiment.

MUSICIAN.

William Wigney—Mustered out with regiment.

PRIVATES.

Wm. H. Anderson—Mustered out with regiment.
Silas H. Arnold—Mustered out with regiment.
Benj. E. Anderson—Never left recruiting rendezvous.
Joel Avery—Died of disease Sept. 10, 1864, New Orleans, La.
Frederick Baker—Mustered out with regiment.
James A. Bronson—Mustered out with regiment.
Jacob Bergtold—Mustered out with regiment.
Marcus H. Briggs—Wounded June 12, 1863, Port Hudson. Sent to Hospital. No notice of discharge ever received.
Frank Brix—Recruit. Transfered to 90th N. Y. Vet. Vols. when 116th was mustered out.
Palmer Cummings—Regt'l Band. Mustered out with regiment.
A. M. Cunningham—Absent sick since Nov. 12, 1862. No notice of discharge ever received.
Thomas Clements—Discharged for disability, May 17, 1865.
Stephen Cable—Killed May 27, 1863, Port Hudson.
Willard Converse—Killed Sept. 19, 1864, Winchester.
Albert J. Davis—Mustered out with regiment.
William P. Davis—Mustered out with regiment.
Jacob Diffenbach—Mustered out with regiment.
William Dickenson—Mustered out with regiment.
Chas. Edwards—Discharged for disability, Jan. 6, 1863.
Henry W. Fuller—Died of disease Jan. 28, 1864, Franklin, La.
Geo. H. Fenner—Mustered out with regiment.
Gregory Fry—Mustered out with regiment.
Ambrose Fry—Recruit. Transferred to 90th N. Y. Vet. Vols. when 116th was mustered out.
Lorenzo Fromwiller—Wounded June 14, 1863, Port Hudson. Discharged for disability, Nov. 9, 1864.
Jacob Fromwiller—Wounded April 8, 1864, Sabine Cross Roads. Discharged for disability, Aug. 6, 1864.
Sylvester Glass—Wounded Oct. 19, 1864, Cedar Creek. Mustered out with regiment.
Jacob Gribling—Mustered out with regiment.
Adam Getts—Transferred to Vet. Reserve Corps, Sept. 16, 1863.
Philip Gouch—Died of disease Dec. 4, 1862, Fortress Monroe, Va.
Lafayette R. Glass—Killed Sept. 19, 1864, Winchester.
Henry Hall—Mustered out with regiment.
Albert Harvey—Discharged for disability, March 14, 1863.

Peter Hartman—Mustered out with regiment.
Henry Hausholder—Mustered out with regiment.
Frederick Heller—Discharged for disability, Feb. 1, 1863.
Horace Hill—Transferred to Vet. Reserve Corps, Aug. 10, 1864.
Frederick Hopkins—Mustered out with regiment.
William Hutchinson—Wounded Oct. 19, 1864, Cedar Creek. Mustered out with regiment.
Christian Jenke—Died of disease Aug. 24, 1863, Baton Rouge, La.
George W. Jones—Mustered out with regiment.
Wm. H. Keintz—Wounded Sept. 19, 1864, Winchester. Absent sick. No notice of discharge ever received.
William Kroll—Wounded May 27, 1863, Port Hudson. Mustered out with regiment.
Burton L. Kern—Color Bearer. Killed May 27, 1863, Port Hudson.
George Lewis—Mustered out with regiment.
Christian Leibfritz—Mustered out with regiment.
Frederick Martin—Wounded Sept. 19, 1864, Winchester. Absent sick. No notice of discharge ever received.
Richard Mott—Mustered out with regiment.
John Martzolf—Discharged for disability, May 9, 1863.
Andrew D. Neff—Mustered out with regiment.
Howard Palmer—Mustered out with regiment.
David Palmer—Wounded May 21, 1863, Plain Store. Died of disease Nov. 19, 1863, Baton Rouge, La.
James Page—Wounded June 12, 1863, Port Hudson. Died July 1, 1863, Baton Rouge, La.
Eugene Randall—Mustered out with regiment.
David C. Reed—Mustered out with regiment.
John V. Richardson—Mustered out with regiment.
John Richie—Transferred to Vet. Reserve Corps, Sept. 26, 1863.
John M. Rollin—Died of disease Dec. 20, 1862, Fortress Monroe.
Nicholas Reese—Mustered out with regiment.
James H. Sayles—Wounded Oct. 19, 1864, Cedar Creek. Absent sick. No notice of discharge ever received.
Geo. Snyder—Mustered out with regiment.
Geo. W. Skidmore—Taken prisoner Oct. 19, 1864, Cedar Creek. Mustered out with regiment.
Isaac Skinner—Died of disease March 4, 1865, Stevenson's Depot, Va.
Geo. W. Summers—Mustered out with regiment.
John W. Townsend—Mustered out with regiment.
Daniel A. Townsend—Discharged for disability, Sept. 24, 1864.
Jesse Tyler—Transferred to U. S. Navy, June 25, 1864.

Michael Touchy—Died of disease Sept. 18, 1863, Baton Rouge, La.

Lucius A. Townsend—Wounded Sept. 19, 1864, Winchester. Died Sept. 20, 1864.

John Thompson—Mustered out with regiment.

John Voll—Mustered out with regiment.

Frederick Wander—Mustered out with regiment.

Henry Whitman—Mustered out with regiment.

Andrew Warner—Absent sick since Aug. 29, 1863. No notice of discharge ever received.

Wallace Woodward—Wounded Oct. 19, 1864, Cedar Creek. Absent sick. No notice of discharge ever received.

Seldon Woodworth—Wounded Oct. 19, 1864, Cedar Creek. Absent sick. No notice of discharge ever received.

Frederick Wolfe—Mustered out with regiment.

Abner M. Williams—Absent since Aug. 27, 1863.

Homer B. Willett—Absent since Aug. 27, 1863.

Henry W. Weeks—Discharged for disability, Jan. 4, 1863.

E. L. Willis—Never left recruiting rendezvous at Buffalo.

John F. Wilcox—Discharged for disability, July 18, 1864.

Charles Warner—Killed Oct. 19, 1864, Cedar Creek.

Andrew B. Wise—Killed Oct. 19, 1864, Cedar Creek.

COLORED COOKS.

Wm. H. Harrison—Transferred to 90th N. Y. Vet. Vols. when 116th was mustered out.

Samuel Harper—Transferred to 90th N. Y. Vet. Vols. when 116th was mustered out.

COMPANY C.

CAPTAINS.

David W. Tuttle—Killed July 13, 1863, Cox's Plantation.

Robert F. Atkins—Promoted to Lieut. Colonel 89th U. S. Colored Troops, September, 1863.

William J. Morgan—Wounded May 27, 1863, Port Hudson. Mustered out with regiment.

FIRST LIEUTENANTS.

Robert F. Atkins—Promoted to Captain, September, 1863.

George N. Brown—Discharged for disability, July 27, 1864.

SECOND LIEUTENANT.

Edward J. Cornwell—Discharged for disability, June 8, 1864.

FIRST SERGEANTS.

William Tibbetts—Promoted to 1st Lieut. Co. A., April 12, 1864.
George N. Brown—Promoted to 1st Lieut., Sept. 14, 1863.
John Hoppes—Mustered out with regiment.

SERGEANTS.

Orton S. Clark—Promoted to Sergt. Major, Sept. 3, 1862.
William Tibbetts—Wounded May 27, 1863, Port Hudson. Promoted to 1st Sergeant, Sept. 14, 1863.
Michael Danner, Jr.—Promoted Quartermaster Sergeant, Nov. 25, 1862.
John Hoppes—Promoted to 1st Sergt., Sept. 1st, 1864.
Harry H. Enders—Wounded May 27, 1863, Port Hudson; April 8, 1864, Sabine Cross Roads. Mustered out with regiment.
George W. Hammond—Mustered out with regiment.
Edward Eells—Died of disease, July 23, 1863, Baton Rouge, La.
Thomas Caldwell—Mustered out with regiment.
James La Flamboy—Wounded May 27, 1863, Port Hudson; Oct. 19, 1864, Cedar Creek. Mustered out with regiment.
O. D. Laird—Discharged for disability, Jan. 24, 1863.
Geo. E. Ward—Deserted at Washington, July 26, 1864.

CORPORALS.

William Tibbetts—Promoted to Sergeant, Jan. 1, 1863.
John Hoppes—Promoted to Sergeant, Sept. 14, 1863.
Geo. W. Hammond—Promoted to Sergeant, Sept. 14, 1863.
James La Flamboy—Wounded May 27, 1864, Port Hudson. Promoted to Sergeant, Jan. 1, 1865.
Samuel Young—Wounded May 27, 1863, Port Hudson. Discharged at Hospital.
Gustave R. Jacobs—Mustered out with regiment.
James Marks—Mustered out with regiment.
Gustave Sanders—Mustered out with regiment.
John Blank—Mustered out with regiment.
William Bump—Wounded May 27, 1863, Port Hudson. Mustered out with regiment.
Judson Andrews—Sent to Chesapeake Hospital, Nov. 29. 1862. Transferred to Vet. Reserve Corps Nov. 1, 1863.
Chas. H. Bartlett—Deserted July 5, 1864.
Chas. Faul—Promoted to Lieut. 89th U. S. Colored Troops, Oct. 12, 1863.
Louis E. Filbert—Wounded May 27, 1863, Port Hudson. Discharged to accept commission in Corps d'Afrique, March 1, 1864.
George E. Ward—Promoted to Sergeant, Jan. 24, 1863.

WAGONER.

Wm. Shenkle—Taken prisoner June 30, 1863, Port Hudson. Exchanged Nov. 6, 1863.

MUSICIANS.

John Dolan—Mustered out with regiment.

Chas. R. Dunning—Mustered out with regiment.

Geo. E. Bowen—Mustered out with regiment.

PRIVATES.

Wm. Armstrong—Died in Hospital Dec. 11, 1863.

Henry C. Atkins—Killed June 14, 1863, Port Hudson.

John Brooks—Deserted April 13, 1865.

Joseph Brown—Deserted April 13, 1865.

Frederick Bockhover—Received from 5th U. S. Art. by transfer, April 13, 1864. Transferred to 90th N.Y.Vet.Vols., May 31, 1865.

Christopher Beahn—Mustered out with regiment.

Alexander Buchanan—Sent to Ship Island by sentence of General Court Martial, May 2, 1863, for balance of term of enlistment.

John Burt—Mustered out with regiment.

Henry Beverly—Sent to Chesapeake Hospital, Nov. 28, 1862. Discharged there March 14, 1863.

Wallace Calkins—Transferred to Co. A, Jan. 1, 1863.

Conrad Clar—Mustered out with regiment.

Thomas Day—Died at New Orleans May 16, 1864.

Byron L. Davis—Sent to Chesapeake Hospital, Nov. 28, 1862. Transferred to Vet. Reserve Corps, Aug. 22, 1863.

Harry Dannals—Mustered out with regiment.

John Egloff—Wounded May 27, 1863, Port Hudson. Transferred to Vet. Reserve Corps, April 1, 1864.

Herbert G. Emerson—Detached at Gen'l Banks' head-quarters from Jan. 14, 1863, through term of enlistment.

Chas. J. Eddington—Sent to Chesapeake Hospital, Nov. 27, 1862. Transferred to Vet. Reserve Corp, Sept. 16, 1863.

George W. Ebbs—Discharged to accept commission in Corp d'Afrique, March 7, 1864.

Spencer J. Fuller—Wounded at Winchester, Sept. 19, 1864. Discharged at Hospital.

William Frazier—Deserted Sept. 20, 1862.

Peter Foster—Discharged for disability, March 26, 1864.

Ebenezer Ferman—Sent to Chesapeake Hospital, Nov. 29, 1862. Died there Dec. 1862.

Charles Fischer—Mustered out with regiment.

John Feltz—Detached at brigade head-quarters, March, 1863, until discharged.

William Felchmaker—Died July 26, 1863, Baton Rouge, La.

John Gethicker—Wounded Oct. 19, 1864, Cedar Creek, Va. Discharged in Hospital.

Henry Grimes—Wounded May 27, 1863, Port Hudson, La. Died in Hospital at New Orleans, Aug. 14, 1863.

Freeman Goff—Died at Lancaster, N. Y., Oct. 25, 1863.

Alexander Goslin—Promoted to Quartermaster Sergeant, Sept. 3, 1862.

Dennis Grover—Deserted at Camp Morgan, Sept. 5, 1862.

Fred Hildebrandt—Mustered out with regiment.

William J. Hunt—Discharged on account of imbecility, Jan. 22, 1864.

Frederick Hellriegle—Killed May 27, 1863, Port Hudson.

Fred. W. Joslyn—Deserted from Germantown Hospital, Dec. 30, 1864.

Robert Jimmeson—Killed at Winchester, Va., Sept. 19, 1864.

Matthew Johnson—Sent to New Orleans Hospital, Sept. 1863. Transferred to Vet. Reserve Corps, May 15, 1864.

William Johnson—Confined at Fort McHenry by sentence General Court Martial, since Nov. 6, 1862.

Edwin G. James—Mustered out with regiment.

Andrew Kennedy—Deserted at Grand Ecore, La., April 21, 1864.

William Koll—Sent to Chesapeake Hospital, Nov. 1862. Transferred to Vet. Reserve Corps, Aug. 22, 1863.

Charles La Flamboy—Died Aug. 2, 1863, Baton Rouge, La.

Martin Lardner—Sent to Hospital, May, 1863. Transferred to Vet. Reserve Corps, Nov. 1, 1863.

Peter Matthes—Transferred to First Louisiana Cavalry, Feb. 10, 1863.

Peter Melger—Mustered out with regiment.

William McDonald—Transferred to Second U. S. Artillery.

Bryant Nellis—Transferred to First Louisiana Cavalry, Feb. 10, 1863.

Lewis Nail—Killed May 27, 1863, Port Hudson.

David J. Owen—Sent to Chesapeake Hospital, Nov. 26, 1862. Discharged for disability, Jan. 24, 1863.

Christopher Ort—Died July 27, 1863, Baton Rouge, La.

George W. Plank—Killed July 13, 1863, Cox's Plantation.

William Riehl—Wounded at Fisher's Hill, Sept. 22, 1864. Discharged at Hospital.

Charles Riald—Killed May 27, 1863, Port Hudson.

William Seiber—Deserted at Baltimore, Nov. 2, 1862.

Peter Smith—Died Aug. 7, 1863, Baton Rouge, La.

Thomas Shields—Transferred to First Louisiana Cavalry, Feb. 10, 1863.

Herman Shoy—Transferred to Co. H, Oct. 1, 1862.

Peter Swain—Mortally Wounded Oct. 19, 1864, Cedar Creek.

Conrad Swain—Wounded Oct. 19, 1864, Cedar Creek. Mustered out with regiment.

Michael Sullivan—Discharged for disability, March 7, 1864.

Jacob Swartz—Wounded Oct. 19, 1864, Cedar Creek. Discharged at Hospital.

Samuel Scran—Discharged for disability, June 16, 1864.

Fred. Schmiedding—Sent to Hospital, Aug. 7, 1864. Discharged.

Lanson A. Stanbro—Lost an arm June 14, 1863, Port Hudson. Discharged Nov. 9, 1863.

James Sillaway—Discharged for disability, May 5, 1863.

Robert T. Taggert—Wounded May 27, 1863, Port Hudson; and Oct. 19, 1864, Cedar Creek, Va. Discharged at Hospital.

Joseph Trainer—Sent to Chesapeake Hospital, Nov. 14, 1862. Died there Dec. 23, 1862.

Richard Walsh—Mustered out with regiment.

Patrick Walsh—Wounded July 13, 1863, Cox's Plantation. Discharged at Hospital.

Charles W. Wall—Mustered out with regiment.

John Weiser—Mustered out with regiment.

Frank Wolfe—Absent on sick leave from Sept. 2, 1863 to Nov. 30, 1864. Mustered out with regiment.

Dennis J. White—Wounded July 13, 1863, Cox's Plantation; and Sept. 22, 1864, Fisher's Hill Discharged at Hospital.

John Wilson—Transferred to Co. I, Oct. 1, 1862.

John Von Hecker—Recruit from depot, Nov. 30, 1864. Died Jan. 28, 1865.

Peter Zimmer—Wounded Oct. 19, 1864, Cedar Creek, Va. Discharged at Hospital.

COLORED COOK.

Jessie Ream—Mustered out with regiment.

COMPANY D.

CAPTAINS.

John Higgins—Promoted to Major, July 18, 1863.

Elisha W. Seymour—Ordnance officer on the staff of Maj-Gen'l Augur, during siege of Port Hudson. Mustered out with regiment.

FIRST LIEUTENANTS.

Chas. F. Wadsworth—Promoted to Captain Co. A, March 1, 1863.

Elisha W. Seymour—Promoted to Captain, Aug. 6, 1863.

John H. Rohan—Promoted to Captain Co. G, April 12, 1864.

Geo. W. Miller—Promoted to Quartermaster. Wounded Oct. 19, 1864, Cedar Creek.

SECOND LIEUTENANT.

Elisha W. Seymour—Promoted to 1st Lieutenant, Aug, 1, 1863.

FIRST SERGEANTS.

John H. Rohan—Promoted to 1st Lieutenant.

Willard S. Berry—Promoted to 1st Lieutenant 89th Regiment U. S. Colored Troops, Sept. 23, 1863.

Wm. H. Holden—Promoted to 1st Lieutenant, April 12, 1864. Wounded May 21, 1863, Plain Store.

Geo. T. Bale—Taken prisoner Oct. 19, 1864, Cedar Creek. Mustered out with regiment.

SERGEANTS.

George W. Miller—Promoted to 1st Lieutenant, September 14, 1863.

Albert Smith—Promoted to Captain Corps d'Afrique, April 4, 1863.

Morgan L. Faulkner—Promoted to Captain Corps d'Afrique, Aug. 31, 1863.

James Forbes—Killed May 21, 1863, Plain Store.

John M. Carter—Wounded May 21, 1863, Plain Store. Went North on sick leave. Never reported to company again.

Jethro Bale—Wounded May 21, 1863, Plain Store; and Sept. 19, 1864, Winchester. Discharged for disability, May 19, 1865.

Geo. Laible—Wounded Sept. 19, 1864, Winchester. Absent sick in Hospital, Frederick, Md.

Albert Krause—Mustered out with regiment.

Chas. H. Curry—Promoted to 1st Lieutenant, Jan. 12, 1865.

Jacob Boyer—Wounded May 27, 1863, Port Hudson. Mustered out with regiment.

Edward Ackroyd—Mustered out with regiment.

CORPORALS.

Alanson Osborn—Wounded and taken prisoner, Oct. 19, 1864, Cedar Creek. Mustered out with regiment.

Sylvester A. Hubbard—Mustered out with regiment.

Frederick Neiwardie—Mustered out with regiment.

James McNalley—Wounded May 27, 1863, Port Hudson. Mustered out with regiment.

James P. Taber—Promoted to 1st Lieutenant Corps d'Afrique, Sept. 28, 1863.

Chas. Chittenden—Killed May 27, 1863, Port Hudson.

Jacob Eckert—Mustered out with regiment.

William McAndrew—Mustered out with regiment.

Raymond McGowan—Wounded May 27, 1863, Port Hudson. Promoted to Sergeant Major, Sept. 23, 1863.

John B. Sweetapple—Died of disease Dec. 20, 1862, Fortress Monroe.

George W. Warren—Mustered out with regiment.

MUSICIANS.

Ira Rowley—Mustered out with regiment.

Day L. Chapin—Mustered out with regiment.

WAGONER.

John Atling—Mustered out with regiment.

PRIVATES.

Alexander Avery—Mustered out with regiment.

Edwin E. Austin—Wounded May 27, 1863, Port Hudson. Died June 28, 1863.

Samuel Avard—Dropped out on the march near Natchitoches, La.

Theodore Boyd—Deserted Sept. 3, 1862.

John Bushard—Killed April 9, 1864, Pleasant Hill.

Brian Bradbury—Killed July 7, 1863, Port Hudson.

John Blitz—Mustered out with regiment.

Norton Baker—Mustered out with regiment.

Elias B. Baker—Mustered out with regiment.

Edward C. Bacon—Wounded May 27, 1863, Port Hudson. Mustered out with regiment.

Owen Chilcott—Wounded May 27, 1863, Port Hudson. Mustered out with regiment.

William Clancey—Mustered out with regiment.

Robert H. Clark—Promoted to 1st Lieutenant Corps d'Afrique, Sept. 19, 1863.

Oscar E. Corey—Died of disease Aug. 28, 1863, Baton Rouge, La.

Claude L. Crosby—Transferred to 1st La. Cavalry, returned to company, and mustered out with regiment.

William Dober—Deserted Feb. 2, 1863.

Edward Ente—Mustered out with regiment.

Wm. H. Fellowes—Promoted Quartermaster Sergeant Corps d'Afrique, Aug. 22, 1863.

Ambrose Ford—Deserted Nov. 13, 1862.

Michael Geissdoffer—Mustered out with regiment.

Albert L. Gram—Killed May 21, 1863, Plain Store.

James W. Germain—Killed May 21, 1863, Plain Store.

Christian Grawi—Deserted Sept. 15, 1863.

John G. Howarth—Deserted Sept. 18, 1863.

Lewis Hill—Wounded April 8, 1863, Sabine Cross Roads. Mustered out with regiment.

Frederick Henn—Mustered out with regiment.

Chas. B. Holman—Detached as Clerk in Quartermaster's department. Mustered out with regiment.

Loyal C. Ingersoll—Transferred to Co. K, Nov. 1, 1862.

Harrison A. Irish—Wounded Sept. 19, 1864, Winchester. Mustered out with regiment.

Joab Irish—Absent sick.

Phillip Kles—Killed May 27, 1863, Port Hudson.

Frederick P. Klipser—Died of disease May 24, 1863, Baton Rouge, La.

Frederick Klotz—Mustered out with regiment.

William Kellogg—Mustered out with regiment.

Chas. Lederer—Regimental Band. Taken prisoner April 8, 1864, Sabine Cross Roads. Mustered out with regiment.

Christian G. Lessing—Died of disease Aug. 12, 1863, Baton Rouge, La.

John M. McCumber—Died of disease Aug. 7, 1863, Baton Rouge, La.

John Melling—Died of disease Dec. 19, 1862, Fortress Monroe.

Daniel F. McFaul—Promoted to Captain Corps d'Afrique, April 4, 1863.

Stephen Mansfield—Discharged for disability, Feb. 17, 1863.

Wm. W. McCumber—Wounded May 27, 1863, Port Hudson. Mustered out with regiment.

Stephen A. Mathews—Mustered out with regiment.

Francis Oberfiel—Mustered out with regiment.

Luke Pierson—Died of disease July 27, 1863, Baton Rouge, La.

Alexander Pike—Recruit. Transferred to 90th N. Y. Vet. Vols. when 116th was mustered out.

William Pike—Recruit. Transferred to 90th N. Y. Vet. Vols. when 116th was mustered out.

Peter Paule—Mustered out with regiment.

Wm. H. Purdy—Wounded May 27, 1863, Port Hudson. Mustered out with regiment.
Sanford M. Randall—Mustered out with regiment.
Joseph Raymond—Mustered out with regiment.
Thomas Ryan—Mustered out with regiment.
John C. Rusch—Mustered out with regiment.
Geo. P. Rowley—In hospital, Washington, D. C.
Geo. W. Sheather—Wounded at Port Hudson. Died June 19, 1863.
George Shepard—Killed May 27, 1863, Port Hudson.
Philip Shumaker—Wounded May 21, 1863, Plain Store. Died May 22, 1863.
Joseph Stienmetz—Died of disease Jan. 25, 1863, Fortress Monroe.
Alonzo P. Snyder—Died of disease Nov. 17, 1862, Fortress Monroe.
Chauncey Slayton—Transferred Vet. Reserve Corps, Sept. 26, 1863.
Chas. J. Sweetapple—Discharged for disability, April 2, 1863.
John H. Spencer—Mustered out with regiment.
Albert Sweetapple—Mustered out with regiment.
Jacob Steingle—Wounded Sept. 19, 1864, Winchester. Mustered out with regiment.
John Towle—Furloughed July 1, 1863. Never reported to company.
Wm. Wilke—Mustered out with regiment.
Wendell Walheiser—Mustered out with regiment.
Jno. M. Walters—Mustered out with regiment.
John Weber—Discharged for disability, April 11, 1863.
Conrad Weiss—Discharged for disability, April 25, 1865.
John M. Young—Absent sick.

COLORED COOKS.

Edward Lowell—Recruit. Transferred to 90th N. Y. Vet. Vols. when 116th was mustered out.
John Lee—Deserted July 4, 1864.

COMPANY E.

CAPTAIN.

Richard C. Kinney—Resigned June 4, 1865.

FIRST LIEUTENANTS.

Jas. S. McGowan—Promoted to Captain Co. G, Sept. 14, 1863.
John C. Nial—Promoted to Adjutant, April 12, 1864.
Henry A. C. Swartz—Mustered out with regiment.

SECOND LIEUTENANTS.

Geo. H. Notter—Resigned Jan. 8, 1863.

Charles Borusky—Wounded May 21, 1863, Plain Store. Died May 25, 1863. See page 308.

Henry A. C. Swartz—Promoted 1st Lieutenant, Feb. 24, 1865.

FIRST SERGEANTS.

Charles Borusky—Promoted 2d Lieutenant.

Wm. Kelso—Mustered out with regiment.

SERGEANTS.

John Brown—Deserted Sept. 26, 1862.

Wm. Phelps—Died of wounds, Aug. 23, 1863, Baton Rouge, La.

Wm. H. Hustead—Mustered out with regiment.

James Gallagher—Mustered out with regiment.

Albert E. Bleiler—Wounded Oct. 19, 1864, Cedar Creek. Discharged for disability, date unknown.

William Lehman—Mustered out with regiment.

George Wood—Mustered out with regiment.

CORPORALS.

John Graham—Wounded Oct. 19, 1864, Cedar Creek. In Hospital, Philadelphia, Pa.

Philip Lehman—Wounded May 27, 1863, Hort Hudson. Color Guard. Discharged for disability, Sept. 27, 1864.

James W. McMichael—Mustered out with regiment.

James H. Weingarden—Mustered out with regiment.

Lucius E. Ruch—Mustered out with regiment.

Charles Glasser—Wounded May 27, 1863, Port Hudson. Died May 28, 1863.

Voltaire Heaton—Died of disease, Sept. 19, 1863, New Orleans, La.

Wm. B. McMichael—Mustered out with regiment.

Joseph Kleiber—Mustered out with regiment.

Thomas Maloney—Mustered out with regiment.

Frederick Weber—Wounded Oct. 19, 1864, Cedar Creek. Recruit. Transferred to 90th N. Y. Vet. Vols. when 116th was mustered out.

Nicholas Gitterie—Missing in action, April 9, 1864, Pleasant Hill.

MUSICIANS.

William Hazel—Mustered out with regiment.

William McCormick—Deserted Dec. 12, 1864.

WAGONER.

Burton Slocum—Mustered out with regiment.

PRIVATES.

Max Alwens—Mustered out with regiment.

Frederick Addleburg—Mustered out with regiment.

Frederick Busch—Transferred to Vet. Reserve Corps, Dec. 1, 1863.
Chas. D. Ballard—Transferred to Co. H, Oct. 1, 1862.
William Brenchley—Died of disease June 5, 1863, Baton Rouge, La.
Jesse Belton—Died of disease Sept. 18, 1863, Chicago, Ill.
James Bowden—Taken prisoner Oct. 19, 1864, Cedar Creek. Mustered out with regiment.
Joseph Benz—Wounded Sept. 19, 1864, Winchester. In Hospital at Buffalo, N. Y.
John Britting—Wounded Oct. 19, 1864, Cedar Creek. In Hospital at New York.
Joseph Bretcher—Wounded May 27, 1863, Port Hudson. Mustered out with regiment.
William Baldwin—Mustered out with regiment.
John H. Cahill—Mustered out with regiment.
Silas Crisman—Wounded May 27, 1863, Port Hudson. Mustered out with regiment.
Daniel Constantine—Absent sick.
Francis Downs—Transferred to 90th N. Y. Vet Vols. when 116th was mustered out, by sentence court martial.
Francis E. Duffy—Deserted Oct. 8, 1862.
Alfred Enos—Mustered out with regiment.
Geo. W. Fletcher—Discharged for disability, Nov. 27, 1863.
Geo. Funk—Wounded May 21, 1863, Plain Store. Mustered out with regiment.
Cornelius Fitzpatrick—Taken prisoner July 31, 1864, Morgansia, La.
Wm. H. Gale—Transferred to Co. I, Oct. 1, 1862.
Thomas Griffiths—Killed May 27, 1863, Port Hudson.
Geo. Guenther—Taken prisoner Oct. 19, 1864, Cedar Creek. Mustered out with regiment.
Christian Hilfinger—Mustered out with regiment.
John Hennesey—Wounded May 27, 1863, Port Hudson. Mustered out with regiment.
Charles Haines—Mustered out with regiment.
John Hughes—Mustered out with regiment.
Geo. Haley—Discharged for disability, Aug. 29, 1863.
Theodore Hansel—Transferred to Vet. Reserve Corps, Jan. 5, 1865.
Abraham Johnson—In Hospital, New Orleans, La., since May 1, 1863.
Jacob Koch—Discharged for disability, March 15, 1864.
Thos. W. King—Transferred to Co. I, Oct. 1, 1862.
Geo. A. Kogle—Transferred to Co. I, Oct. 1, 1862.

Peter Kiloran--Mustered out with regiment.

Edward Lawson--Wounded Sept. 19, 1864, Winchester. Mustered out with regiment.

Thomas Mooney--Deserted Sept. 7, 1862.

George Mann—Wounded May 27, 1863, Port Hudson. Discharged for disability, June 30, 1864.

John J. Mickle—Discharged for disability, May 22, 1865.

Henry C. Muller—Died of disease June 23, 1863, Port Hudson, La.

George Major—Wounded May 21, 1863, Plain Store. Died of disease Sept. 27, 1863, Baton Rouge, La.

John McElvano—Wounded Sept. 19, 1864, Winchester. In Hospital, Philadelphia, Pa.

Donald McGilvary—Wounded May 27, 1863, Port Hudson. Mustered out with regiment.

Ernest Obermier—Died of disease, July 27, 1864, Buffalo, N. Y.

James O'Keefe--Wounded May 21, 1863, Plain Store. Killed Sept. 19, 1864, Winchester.

Peter Prim--Deserted Sept. 5, 1862.

William Page--Wounded May 21, 1863, Plain Store. Died of disease Dec. 15, 1863, New Iberia, La.

Lloyd Price--Killed May 27, 1863, Port Hudson.

Theodore Ryering--Mustered out with regiment.

Jacob Rinker--Wounded May 27, 1863, Port Hudson. Transferred to Vet. Reserve Corps, Dec. 1, 1863.

Matthew Robinson—Died of disease Dec. 3, 1863, New Orleans, La.

Miles Skillington—Mustered out with regiment.

Gustavus Stedeman—Wounded Sept. 19, 1864, Winchester. Mustered out with regiment.

Patrick Sullivan—Mustered out with regiment.

James Shannessy—Mustered out with regiment.

Peter Starkey—In confinement at Tortugas for balance of term of enlistment, by sentence of court martial.

Joseph Schweider—Transferred to Co. H, Oct. 1, 1862.

William J. Story—Killed while attempting to run the guard.

Cornelius Sullivan—Killed July 13, 1863, Cox's Plantation.

Adam Swartz—Transferred to 1st La. Cavalry, Feb. 9, 1863.

Bruce Smith—Brigade Post Master for a time. Mustered out with regiment.

Charles B. Trowbridge—Mustered out with regiment.

George Welden—Mustered out with regiment.

Henry Weiss—Mustered out with regiment.

John Weckerly—Transferred to 2d La. Cavalry. Rejoined Co. Jan. 23, 1865. Mustered out with regiment.

Christian Weller—Missing in action Sept. 19, 1864, Winchester.

COLORED COOK.

John Greely—Recruit. Transferred to 90th N. Y. Vet. Vols. when 116th was mustered out.

COMPANY F.*

CAPTAINS.

Geo. G. Stanbro—Resigned June 18, 1863.

Chas. S. Crary—Wounded Oct. 19, 1864, Cedar Creek. Mustered out with regiment.

FIRST LIEUTENANTS.

Wilson H. Gray—Wounded May 27, 1863, Port Hudson. Promoted to Captain Co. B.

Chas. S. Crary—promoted to Captain, Feb. 11, 1865.

William W. Grace—On detached service at Portland, Me.

SECOND LIEUTENANTS.

Clinton Hammond—Resigned Dec. 3, 1862.

Chas. S. Crary—Promoted to 1st Lieutenant.

FIRST SERGEANTS.

Chas. S. Crary—Promoted to 2d Lieutentant.

Wm. H. Vanslyke—Mustered out with regiment.

SERGEANTS.

Andrew J. Thomas—Discharged for disability, Jan. 3, 1863.

Joseph Doty—Wounded May 27, 1863, Port Hudson. Discharged for disability, May 7, 1864.

John G. Dayton—Promoted to 1st Lieutenant, March 1, 1865.

Nathan J. Horton—Wounded Sept. 22, 1864, Fisher's Hill. In hospital, Buffalo, N. Y.

Joshua D. Baker—Mustered out with regiment.

Edwin Pingrey—Wounded May 27, 1863, Port Hudson. Mustered out with regiment.

Philemon King—Mustered out with regiment.

CORPORALS.

William H. Ferris—Died of disease, Oct. 2, 1863, Cairo Ill.

Ira C. Horton—Wounded May 21, 1863, Plain Store. Died July 12, 1863.

Madison Reynolds—Transferred to Vet. Reserve Corps, Sept. 26, 1863.

---

* This Company was detached for a time at Corps Head-quarters.

Ozias Brindley—Wounded May 21, 1863, Plain Store. Mustered out with regiment.

Joseph A. Rockwood—Wounded May 21, 1863, Plain Store. Mustered out with regiment.

Joseph Warren—Mustered out with regiment.

Theodore B. Norris—Wounded May 27, 1863, Port Hudson. Mustered out with regiment.

Albern S. Twichell—Mustered out with regiment.

Daniel A. Bond—Wounded May 27, 1863, Port Hudson. Mustered out with regiment.

Henry Shoemaker—Mustered out with regiment.

Cornelius Graff—Discharged for disability, Nov. 30, 1864.

Sylvester N. Blakely—Discharged for disability, July 31, 1864.

Andrew M. Smith—Killed July 13, 1863, Cox's Plantation.

Samuel A. Mayo—Wounded July 13, 1863, Cox's Plantation. Died Aug. 8, 1863.

Anthony Lieser—Mustered out with regiment.

MUSICIANS.

Wm. A. Ferrin—Discharged, by order of Secretary of War, Oct. 29, 1863.

Stephen E. Spaulding—Mustered out with regiment.

WAGONER.

Stephen Weast—Mustered out with regiment.

PRIVATES.

Rollin J. Albro—Mustered out with regiment.

Geo. Auwaerter—Wounded May 21, 1863, Plain Store. Transferred to Vet. Reserve Corps, Dec. 6, 1864.

Edward L. Blakely—Died of disease May 24, 1864, Boston, N. Y.

Peter Brooks—Wounded July 13, 1863. Died Aug. 13, 1863.

Harrison Bond—Died of disease June 5, 1863, Baton Rouge La.

Marshall Bickford—Died of disease May 5, 1863, Baton Rouge, La.

Geo. B. Brindley—Recruit. Transferred to 90th N. Y. Vet. Vols. when 116th was mustered out.

Henry Burge—Recruit. Transferred to 90th N. Y. Vet. Vols. when 116th was mustered out.

Morris Barnett—Wounded Sept. 19, 1864, Winchester. In hospital, York, Pa.

Martin Bury—Mustered out with regiment.

Edward Bement—Discharged for disability, Dec. 11, 1862.

Samuel A. Billings—Discharged for disability, Dec. 16, 1863.

Jacob Chiefferle—Wounded May 21, 1863, Plain Store. Discharged for disability, April 13, 1864.

John Conley—Recruit. Transferred to 90th N. Y. Vet. Vols. when 116th was mustered out.

David Crosby—Wounded May 27, 1863, Port Hudson. Died of disease, July 10, 1864, Cairo, Ill.

Marshall K. Davis—Wounded May 27, 1863, Port Hudson, and Oct. 19, 1864, Cedar Creek. Mustered out with regiment.

Jacob Demerly—Mustered out with regiment.

Jacob Farner—Mustered out with regiment.

Jas. D. Fuller—Mustered out with regiment.

Cassius C. Grannis—Discharged for disability, July 10, 1864.

Benj. S. Goddard—Mustered out with regiment.

Jacob Gampp—Mustered out with regiment.

Alonzo Hilliker—Mustered out with regiment.

John Hoffman—Mustered out with regiment.

Frederic E. Hoverland—Wounded May 21, 1863, Plain Store. Mustered out with regiment.

Alexander Hammond—Wounded May 21, 1863, Plain Store. Discharged for disability, Dec. 3, 1863.

Emory C. Hopkins—Discharged for disability, May 24, 1864.

Marion F. Johnston—Wounded Sept. 19, 1864, Winchester. Discharged for disability, April 3, 1865.

Lorenzo Johnston—Mustered out with regiment.

Jacob Kern—Mustered out with regiment.

Myron Lynde—Transferred to Vet. Reserve Corps, Sept. 16, 1863.

Mark Louks—Killed June 14, 1863, Port Hudson.

John H. Mayo—Wounded July 13, 1863, Cox's Plantation. Died Aug. 11, 1863.

Michael McCarty—Recruit. Transferred to 90th N. Y. Vet. Vols. when 116th was mustered out.

Julius A. McClure—Discharged for disability, May 10, 1864.

Theron Mathewson—In Hospital at Buffalo, N. Y.

Joseph Moss—Mustered out with regiment.

Emory R. Nichols—Discharged for disability, Jan. 18, 1865.

Cornelius Ostrander—Discharged for disability, March 8, 1864.

Robert H. Pingrey—Mustered out with regiment.

Oscar Rolf—Died of disease, Oct. 16, 1863, Baton Rouge, La.

Henry H. Rogers—Died of disease Nov. 5, 1863, Sardinia, N. Y.

William Reed—Recruit. Transferred to 90th N.Y.Vet.Vols. when 116th was mustered out.

Julian H. Rhodes—Mustered out with regiment.

Elbert J. Runyan—Mustered out with regiment.

Henry W. Shulters—Mustered out with regiment.

John Stonger—Mustered out with regiment.
Chas. W. Sherman—Wounded May 21, 1863, Plain Store, and May 27, 1863, Port Hudson. Discharged for disability, July 29, 1863.
Franklin C. Shulters—Discharged for disability, May 1, 1864.
Francis M. Smith—Died of disease April 1, 1863, New Orleans, La.
Franklin B. Stuart—Died of disease May 10, 1863, Baton Rouge, La.
John H. Thurber—Lost at sea, July 10, 1864.
Hiram A. Tyrer—Died of disease May 9, 1864, New Orleans, La.
John W. Twichell—Died of disease Sept. 22, 1863, Cairo, Ill.
Allan O. Underhill—Mustered out with regiment.
James H. Underhill—Discharged for disability, Nov. 1, 1863.
Carlos Waite—Mustered out with regiment.
James B. Weber—Mustered out with regiment.
Abel E. Warren—Died of disease April 16, 1863, Baton Rouge, La.
Fabian Warner—Died of disease July 26, 1863, Baton Rouge, La.
Daniel Wright—Wounded May 21, 1863, Plain Store. Died May 17, 1863.

COMPANY G.

CAPTAINS.

John M. Sizer—Promoted to Major, July 14, 1863.
James S. McGowan—Resigned March 8, 1864.
John H. Rohan—Wounded Oct. 19, 1864, Cedar Creek. Mustered out with regiment.

FIRST LIEUTENANTS.

Timothy J. Linahan—Killed June 14, 1863, Port Hudson.
John H. Rohan—Promoted to Captain, April 12, 1864.
William Holden—Wounded May 21, 1863, Plain Store. Mustered out with regiment.

SECOND LIEUTENANTS.

George Peterson—Resigned April, 1863.
Chas. E. Paine—Resigned Sept. 24, 1863.
Philip J. Weber—Resigned Dec. 31, 1863.

FIRST SERGEANTS.

John C. Nial—Promoted to Sergeant-Major, November 23, 1862.
Philip J. Weber—Promoted to 2d Lieutenant, Sept. 14, 1863.
John S. Voltz—Mustered out with regiment.

SERGEANTS.

Henry A. C. Swartz—Promoted to 2d Lieutenant Co. E, Sept. 14, 1863.
Adam White—Mustered out with regiment..

William Feldham—Promoted to 1st Lieutenant Co. B, April 19, 1864.

James M. Fuller—Mustered out with regiment.

William Duffy—Wounded Sept. 19, 1864, Winchester. In Hospital at Newark, N. Y.

William H. Gauger—Mustered out with regiment.

Olof W. Stadin—Wounded May 27, 1863, Port Hudson. Promoted to Sergeant-Major, April 1, 1865.

CORPORALS.

William H. Scheu—Wounded at Port Hudson. Discharged for disability, April 1, 1864.

Louis Sloat—Wounded Oct. 19, 1864, Cedar Creek. Mustered out with regiment.

Jacob Heinzleman—Mustered out with regiment.

Joseph Parker—Color Guard. Mustered out with regiment.

Emil Ney—Detached as clerk in Quartermaster's Department. Mustered out with regiment.

John A. Wise—Mustered out with regiment.

John M. Stephans—Mustered out with regiment.

Jacob Gaugh—Mustered out with regiment.

Chas. H. Wright—Recruit. Transferred to 90th N. Y. Vet. Vols. when 116th was mustered out.

MUSICIANS.

Lott McInnery—Discharged for disability, May 9, 1863.

Frank Humbert—Discharged for disability, Jan. 22, 1863.

WAGONER.

Seth J. Harrison—Mustered out with regiment.

PRIVATES.

Charles B. Adams—Wounded Oct. 19, 1864, Cedar Creek. In Hospital at Buffalo, N. Y.

August Aman—Wounded Oct. 19, 1864, Cedar Creek. Mustered out with regiment.

Edward Arbor—Wounded Oct. 19, 1864, Cedar Creek. Mustered out with regiment.

Matthew H. Andrews—Died of disease Dec. 7, 1862. Buried at sea.

August Brengardner—Died of disease July 1, 1863, New Orleans, La.

Sebastian Brenner—Wounded May 27, 1863, Port Hudson. Died May 28, 1863.

Michael Brodback—Died of disease Dec. 1, 1862.

William Bentley—Transferred to Vet. Reserve Corps, April 22, 1863.

Jacob Begert—Transferred to Vet. Reserve Corps, May 25, 1864.

John Brooks—Transferred to 1st La. Cavalry, Feb. 10, 1863.
James Brown—Transferred to 1st La. Cavalry, Feb. 10, 1863.
Ernst Buse—Mustered out with regiment.
Chas. Baursfield—Mustered out with regiment.
John Bilger—Mustered out with regiment.
Joseph Baker—Mustered out with regiment.
Jacob Benzino—Mustered out with regiment.
Chas. F. Benzino—Mustered out with regiment.
John Bump—Mustered out with regiment.
Philip Burger—Mustered out with regiment.
Philip G. Bauer—Wounded Sept. 19, 1864, Winchester. Missing since.
William Berger—In Hospital, Frederick, Md.
Peter Cook—Mustered out with regiment.
Chas. Cobb—Transferred to U. S. Navy, May 7, 1864.
John Downs—Mustered out with regiment.
Martin Ellard—Wounded Sept. 19, 1864, Winchester. Mustered out with regiment.
Asa H. Edmunds—Mustered out with regiment.
John Erhardt—Mustered out with regiment.
John Farrell—Deserted April 22, 1864.
Edward Ferguson—Discharged for disability, Nov. 24, 1862.
John Fleischman—Wounded Sept. 19, 1864, Winchester. Mustered out with regiment.
Philip C. Fisher—Mustered out with regiment.
John Fuchs—Taken prisoner Oct. 19, 1864, Cedar Creek. Mustered out with regiment.
Michael Guenther—Mustered out with regiment.
Adam Gerono—Wounded Oct. 19, 1864, Cedar Creek. Missing since.
Simon Grimes—Promoted to 89th U. S. Colored Troops, Dec. 1863.
Wm. Guenther—Killed Sept. 22, 1864, Fisher's Hill.
Oliver Gilbert—Deserted Nov. 5, 1862.
George Hicks—Discharged for disability, May 9, 1863.
Christian G. Hirsch—Detached as Clerk at Army Headquarters. Mustered out with regiment.
Louis Hirzel—Mustered out with regiment.
Daniel H. Hubert—Mustered out with regiment.
Frederick Jost—Furloughed for sixty days. Never reported to company.
Anthony Kramer—Mustered out with regiment.
Chas. Lewis—Deserted March 27, 1864.
Thomas More—Deserted Nov. 4, 1862.

John Moran—Transferred to 1st La. Cavalry, March 13, 1863.

William McNiff—Transferred to U. S. Navy, May 7, 1864.

Philip Moaback—Mustered out with regiment.

William Martin—Mustered out with regiment.

Edward Martin—Mustered out with regiment.

Chas. Maker—Mustered out with regiment.

John Meyers—Wounded May 21, 1863, Plain Store. Deserted while at Elmira, N. Y., on detached service.

Edward Neidhardt—Mustered out with regiment.

James Poneise—Regt'l Postmaster. Mustered out with regiment.

Christopher Panschot—Wounded Sept. 19, 1864, Winchester. Mustered out with regiment.

Martin Ressler—Mustered out with regiment.

Frank Swartz—Sent to Hospital at New Orleans, La. Never reported to company.

Michael Sherman—Died Nov., 1864, Washington, D. C.

John Shaffer—Killed Sept. 19, 1864, Winchester.

John Slate—Wounded Sept. 19, 1864, Winchester. Recruit. Transferred to 90th N.Y.Vet.Vols., when 116th was mustered out.

John Shea—Mustered out with regiment.

Adam Schmitt—Wounded Sept. 19, 1864, Winchester. Mustered out with regiment.

Wm. Smith—Mustered out with regiment.

Peter Scheller—Wounded Oct. 19, 1864, Cedar Creek. Mustered out with regiment.

Lewis Scheib—Mustered out with regiment.

William Shupback—In Hospital at Washington, D. C.

John Vogel—Mustered out with regiment.

Haratio N. Wilds—Mustered out with regiment.

Samuel Whitmore—Mustered out with regiment.

Horatio Watson—Mustered out with regiment.

Felix Weingarden—Wounded May 27, 1863, Port Hudson. Discharged for disability, May 4, 1865.

Christopher Weinraber—Transferred to Vet. Reserve Corps, April 22, 1863.

Henry Winell—Wounded May 21, 1863, Plain Store. Died May 22, 1863.

Gotleib Wahl—Deserted Sept. 7, 1862.

COMPANY H.

CAPTAINS.

William Wuerz—Resigned July 25, 1863.

Orton S. Clark—Wounded July 13, 1863, Cox's Plantation. Detached on Brigade Staff for a time. Mustered out with regiment.

FIRST LIEUTENANTS.

David Jones—Wounded May 27, 1863, Port Hudson. Died June 2, 1863, New Orleans, La. See page 306.

John G. Woehnert—Promoted to Captain Co. B, Jan. 7, 1865.

Chas D. Ballard—Mustered out with regiment.

SECOND LIEUTENANTS.

Fred Sommer—Resigned March 28, 1863.

Andrew Brunn—Resigned Sept. 16, 1863.

Wm. C. Gillespie—Resigned Sept. 26, 1863.

FIRST SERGEANTS.

Andrew Brunn—Promoted to 2d Lieutenant, March 31, 1863.

August Lilia—Discharged for disability, June 28, 1863.

Chas. D. Ballard—Wounded Sept. 19, 1864, Winchester. Promoted to 1st Lieutenant, Jan. 13, 1865.

Chas. Kanklewitz—Taken prisoner Oct. 19, 1864, Cedar Creek. Mustered out with regiment.

SERGEANTS.

John G. Woehnert—Wounded May 27, 1863, Port Hudson. Promoted to 1st Lieutenant, Sept. 14, 1863.

Henry Wahly—Wounded May 27, 1863, Port Hudson. Discharged for disability Aug. 24, 1863.

Edwin Very—Acting Sergeant Major for a time. Killed July 13, 1863, Cox's Plantation.

Wm. C. Gillespie—Promoted to 2d Lieutenant.

Albert Rupprecht—Wounded July 13, 1863, Cox's Plantation. Mustered out with regiment.

Anson Kinney—Wounded May 21, 1863, Plain Store. Mustered out with regiment.

Geo. N. Richardson—Mustered out with regiment.

Jacob Gammel—Mustered out with regiment.

CORPORALS.

Orville D. Laird—Transferred to Co. C, Oct. 1, 1862.

Wm. Muller—Deserted Oct. 19, 1863.

Charles Duke—Mustered out with regiment.

Wm. G. Dykeman—Killed May 27, 1863, Port Hudson,

Collins V. Smith—Wounded May 27, 1863, Port Hudson. Died April 19, 1864, Rochester, N. Y.

Herman Gentsch—Wounded Oct. 19, 1864, Cedar Creek. Discharged for disability, May 3, 1865.

Frank Lasso—Mustered out with regiment.

Wm. D. Cook—Mustered out with regiment.
Peter Krauskopf—Wounded May 21, 1863, Plain Store, and Oct. 19, 1864, Cedar Creek. Mustered out with regiment.
James F. Ryther—Mustered out with regiment.
Seneca Ackley—Mustered out with regiment.
David B. McDonald—Killed Oct. 19, 1864, Cedar Creek.

MUSICIANS.

Charles Rose—Mustered out with regiment.
James P. Phelan—Mustered out with regiment.

PRIVATES.

William Blau—Regimental Band. Mustered out with regiment.
John H. Ballinger—Wounded Oct. 19, 1864, Cedar Creek. Color Guard. Mustered out with regiment.
Jos. W. Ballinger—Died of disease, July 28, 1864.
Chas. Busch—Died of Disease, Oct. 5, 1863, Baton Rouge, La.
James Cameron—Wounded May 27, 1863, Port Hudson. Died Jan. 5, 1864, Franklin, La.
John Crowder—Killed Sept. 19, 1864, Winchester.
John Cook—Killed Sept. 19, 1864, Winchester.
Fred Cousindeer—Recruit. Died of disease, Oct. 10, 1864.
Asher Chamberlain—Killed May 21, 1863, Plain Store.
John Clark—Wounded Sept. 19, 1864, Winchester. Discharged for disability, May 3, 1865.
Louis J. Duval—Recruit. Transferred to 90th N. Y. Vet. Vols when 116th was mustered out.
Henry Favre—Deserted Oct. 19, 1863.
Cornelius Fitzpatrick—Transferred to Co. E, March 1, 1863.
Albert Fette—Regimental Band. Discharged for disability, May 3, 1865.
Reinhold W. Franke—Died of disease, Sept. 13, 1863, Algears, La.
Michael Faber—Mustered out with regiment.
Louis Fisher—Mustered out with regiment.
Frank Fuchs—Mustered out with regiment.
Benj. H. Grover—Mustered out with regiment.
Henry J. Groff—Recruit. Transferred to 90th N.Y.Vet.Vols. when 116th was mustered out.
Chas. B. Herold—Recruit. Transferred to 90th N. Y. Vet. Vols. when 116th was mustered out.
Jas. H. Johnson—Taken prisoner Oct. 19, 1864, Cedar Creek. Mustered out with regiment.
Anton Klipfel—Mustered out with regiment.
John Knecht—Mustered out with regiment.
Gustave Kappler—Killed Oct. 19, 1864, Cedar Creek.

Louis Kline—Wounded May 21, 1863, Plain Store, and Oct. 19, 1864, Cedar Creek. Died Nov. 15, 1864, Buffalo, N. Y.

Wm. B. Lathrop—Wounded July 13, 1863, Cox's Plantation. Died Aug. 5, 1863, Baton Rouge, La.

John Leinberger—Mustered out with regiment.

Hugo Loepert—Mustered out with regiment.

John Lutter—Wounded Oct. 19, 1864, Cedar Creek. Mustered out with regiment.

John Mischler—Wounded Oct. 19, 1864, Cedar Creek. Mustered out with regiment.

Valentine Merkle—Regt'l Band. Mustered out with regiment.

Payson Morrow—Killed May 27, 1863, Port Hudson.

James S. Maloney—Wounded May 27, 1863, Port Hudson. Mustered out with regiment.

Donald McGilvary—Transferred to Co. E, March 1, 1863.

Chas. F. A. Nichell—Promoted to Hospital Steward, Sept. 2, 1862.

Peter Nash—Killed May 21, 1863, Plain Store.

Matthias Nachbar—Mustered out with regiment.

Martin Ott—Mustered out with regiment.

Gustave Opitz—Mustered out with regiment.

Chas. Prebie—Recruit. Transferred to 90th N. Y. Vet. Vols. when 116th was mustered out.

Jos. H. Parker—Transferred to Co. G, March 1, 1863.

Henry Pries—Wounded May 21, 1863, Plain Store. Mustered out with regiment.

Fritz Pries—Mustered out with regiment.

Nicholas Rees—Wounded Oct. 19, 1864, Cedar Creek. Mustered out with regiment.

Curtis Rowan—Wounded Sept. 19, 1864, Winchester. Mustered out with regiment.

Gustave Reidle—Killed May 21, 1863, Plain Store.

Fred Richards—Wounded May 21, 1863, Plain Store. Died Aug. 1, 1863, Baton Rouge, La.

Theo. Robinson—Died of disease Sept. 19, 1863, Baton Rouge, La.

Chas. Rehlander—Wounded May 21, 1863, Plain Store, and July 13, 1863, Cox's Plantation. Discharged for disability, March 19, 1864.

Joseph Roff—Deserted April 10, 1864.

John Smith—Transferred to Co. I, Nov. 1, 1862.

Joseph Schweider—Discharged for disability, Jan. 16, 1864.

Edward Schneider—Discharged for disability, Nov. 27, 1863.

Philip Schneider—Killed Sept. 19, 1864, Winchester.

Chas. Schulz—Died of disease April 25, 1863, Baton Rouge, La.

Conrad Sauer—Recruit. Died of disease, June 20, 1864, Morgansia, La.

Jacob Schottler—Mustered out with regiment.

John D. Schlegel—Wounded Oct. 19, 1864, Cedar Creek. Mustered out with regiment.

Chas. Schwamyer—Mustered out with regiment.

Herman Schoy—Mustered out with regiment.

Jacob Tschole—Recruit. Wounded Oct. 19, 1864, Cedar Creek. Transferred to 90th N.Y.Vet.Vols. when 116th was mustered out.

August C. Unholz—Died of disease in New Orleans, La. Date unknown.

Joseph Veigh—Wounded May 27, 1863, Port Hudson. Mustered out with regiment.

Chas. Vanlievan—Mustered out with regiment.

Andrew Wuerstner—Regimental Band. Transferred to Vet. Reserve Corps, April 1, 1865.

John Wohlgemuth—Died of disease, June 6, 1863, New Orleans, La.

John Worden—Died of disease, June 12, 1864, Baton Rouge, La.

Chas. F. Wertsch—Died of disease, July 1864.

Bernhard Wein—Wounded Sept. 19, 1864, Winchester. Mustered out with regiment.

Jacob Zumsteim—Promoted to Hospital Steward U. S. A., Aug. 29, 1864.

William Zesch—Recruit. Transferred to 90th N. Y. Vet. Vols., when 116th was mustered out.

COMPANY I.

CAPTAINS.

Jefferson B. Stover—Resigned Nov. 8, 1862.

Geo. W. Carpenter—Wounded Oct. 19, 1864, Cedar Creek. Promoted to Major, Feb. 12, 1865.

William Tibbetts—Mustered out with regiment.

FIRST LIEUTENANTS.

Geo. W. Carpenter—Promoted to Captain, Nov. 8, 1862.

Edward Erwin—Resigned Oct. 14, 1863.

William J. Morgan—Promoted to Captain Co. C, April 12, 1864.

Chas. H. Curry—Mustered out with regiment.

SECOND LIEUTENANTS.

Edward Erwin—Promoted to 1st Lieutenant, Nov. 8, 1862.

Wm. J. Morgan—Wounded May 27, 1863, Port Hudson. Promoted to 1st Lieutenant, Sept. 14, 1863.

FIRST SERGEANTS.

Wm. J. Morgan—Promoted to 2d Lieutenant, Nov. 8, 1862.

Richard M. Hair—Wounded May 27, 1863, Port Hudson. Promoted to Sergeant-Major, July 18, 1863.

John Ream—Discharged for disability, March 15, 1863.

Jerome S. Griswold—Wounded May 27, 1863, Port Hudson. Mustered out with regiment.

SERGEANTS.

Addison A. Cole—Wounded May 27, 1863, Port Hudson. Transferred to Vet. Reserve Corps, March 15, 1865.

Vanness Fuller—Killed May 27, 1863, Port Hudson.

Willis H. Merrifield—Discharged for disability, Feb. 1, 1863.

Hiram H. Hines—Transferred to Vet. Reserve Corps, Aug. 22, 1863.

Wyvil B. Todd—Wounded July 13, 1863, Cox's Plantation. Mus-out with regiment.

Judson E. Leggett—Mustered out with regiment.

Thomas Nicholson—Mustered out with regiment.

CORPORALS.

Sanford Thomas—Killed May 21, 1863, Plain Store.

Albro Enos—Wounded June 14, 1863, Port Hudson. Transferred to Vet. Reserve Corps, Nov. 1, 1863.

Wheeler B. Curtis—Discharged for disability, July 3, 1864.

Hugo Bihler—Discharged for disability, Dec. 18, 1863.

Chas. F. Barry—Discharged for disability, Feb. 14, 1863.

William H. Gail—Discharged Dec. 19, 1862.

Augustus Cadugan—Wounded July 13, 1863, Cox's Plantation. Discharged for disability, 1863.

Lorenz Helfter—Taken prisoner April 9, 1864, Pleasant Hill. Mustered out with regiment.

Chauncy P. Van Antwerp—Wounded July 13, 1863, Cox's Plantation. Died July 24, 1863, Baton Rouge, La.

Frank Burlingham—Killed Oct. 19, 1864, Cedar Creek.

John Hiller—Killed Oct. 19, 1864, Cedar Creek.

Oscar E. Gail—Taken prisoner Oct. 19, 1864, Cedar Creek. Mustered out with regiment.

George A. Kogle—Wounded Oct. 19, 1864, Cedar Creek. Mustered out with regiment.

Jacob Winter—Died Oct. 17, 1864, Philadelphia, Pa.

Joseph Ferdinand—Mustered out with regiment.

Russell W. Button—Mustered out with regiment.

Frederick Schlichteisen—Recruit. Transferred to 90th N. Y. Vet. Vols. when 116th was mustered out.

MUSICIAN.

Julius L. Knapp—Promoted to Principal Musician.

WAGONER.

Henry Van Antwerp—Mustered out with regiment.

PRIVATES.

Thaddeus Anderson—Transferred to Vet. Reserve Corps, Aug. 22, 1863.

Frank Bartell—Mustered out with regiment.

Andrew Berger—Wounded May 21, 1863, Plain Store. Mustered out with regiment.

Curtis A. Brewer—Mustered out with regiment.

Josephus Barron—Discharged for disability, Nov. 18, 1863.

Henry R. Becker—Recruit. Transferred to 90th N. Y. Vet. Vols. when 116th was mustered out.

Chas. Berry—Transferred to Vet. Reserve Corps, Aug. 26, 1863.

Amos Barron—Died of disease Jan. 9, 1863, Fort Monroe, Va.

Geo. W. Blanchard—Killed May 21, 1863, Plain Store.

Matthias Bunk—Died of disease Aug. 28, 1863, Baton Rouge, La.

James Case—Deserted Aug. 9, 1863.

Daniel Carpenter—Died of disease Sept. 21, 1863, Buffalo, N. Y.

John Cundy—Recruit. Transferred to 90th N. Y. Vet. Vols. when 116th was mustered out.

Charles Curtis—Wounded Oct. 19, 1864, Cedar Creek. Discharged for disability, May 3, 1865.

Martin Drumb—Wounded May 21, 1863, Plain Store. Mustered out with regiment.

John Dormer—Killed May 27, 1863, Port Hudson.

William Everson—Sentenced to Ship Island for balance of term of enlistment, by general court martial, Jan. 7, 1863.

Frederick Ehlert—Recruit. Transferred to 90th N. Y. Vet. Vols. when 116th was mustered out.

Nathaniel C. Fuller—Deserted Aug. 9, 1863.

Delos W. Fowler—Wounded Sept. 22, 1864, Fisher's Hill. Mustered out with regiment.

Ignac Geitger—Wounded Oct. 19, 1864, Cedar Creek. Mustered out with regiment.

Lewis Grim—Transferred to Vet. Reserve Corps, Nov. 1, 1863.

Daniel Gundel—Recruit. Died of disease July 14, 1864, New Orleans, La.

George Hilbren—Died of disease Dec. 18, 1862, Fort Monroe, Va.

William Hilbren—Killed May 27, 1863, Port Hudson.

Charles Hillbury—Recruit. Died of disease Aug. 13, 1864, Philadelphia, Pa.

Robert Y. Hill—Killed May 27, 1863, Port Hudson.

Joseph Helmer—Transferred to U. S. Navy, May 10, 1864.

Michael Hanrahan—Transferred to 1st La. Cavalry, Feb. 9, 1863.

Andrew Hoke—Recruit. Wounded Oct. 19, 1864, Cedar Creek. Transferred to 90th N. Y. Vet. Vols. when 116th was mustered out.

Jared Hewett—Wounded May 21, 1863, Plain, Store. Absent sick in Hospital, Washington, D. C.

Robert L. Johnson—Wounded May 27, 1863, Port Hudson. Absent sick.

Delos P. Kapp—Transferred to Vet Reserve Corps, April 1, 1865.

Peter Kogle—Wounded June 13, 1863, Port Hudson. Absent sick.

Thomas King—Transferred to 1st La. Cavalry, Feb. 9, 1863.

Wesley Long—Transferred to Vet. Reserve Corps, April 26, 1863.

Pulaski L. Leggett—Mustered out with regiment.

Wm. Miller—Deserted July 6, 1864.

Henry Mutter—Killed Oct. 19, 1864, Cedar Creek.

George Margy—Died of disease June 15, 1864, New Orleans, La.

Joseph Masher—Died of disease Oct. 26, 1863, Baton Rouge, La.

Philip Merry—Killed July 13, 1863, Cox's Plantation.

Bryan McNamee—Recruit. Transferred to 90th N. Y. Vet. Vols. when 116th was mustered out.

Henry F. Myers—Recruit. Transferred to 90th N. Y. Vet. Vols. when 116th was mustered out.

Jacob Maue—Mustered out with regiment.

Edward Murphy—Mustered out with regiment.

Theophilas Moore—Mustered out with regiment.

Michael McDaniel—Absent in confinemet since April 2, 1863.

Davis Nye—Discharged for disability, June 15, 1863.

Wm. H. Pollett—Mustered out with regiment.

Ira J. Pratt—Wounded May 21, 1863, Plain Store. Died June 3, 1863.

Luke Pierson—Wounded May 21, 1863, Plain Store. Died Sept. 8, 1863, Baton Rouge, La.

Wm. Putnam—Wounded May 21, 1863, Plain Store, and April 8, 1864, Sabine Cross Roads. Died of disease, Nov. 28, 1864.

—. Pomeroy—Mustered out with regiment.

Jas. H. Ritch—Discharged for disability, Feb. 28, 1863.

Andrew Smith—Transferred to U. S. Navy, May 10, 1864.

John Shannon—Recruit. Transferred to 90th N. Y. Vet. Vols. when 116th was mustered out.

John Smith—Wounded May 21, 1863, Plain Store. Mustered out with regiment.

Joseph Swing—Wounded April 8, 1864, Sabine Cross Roads. Mustered out with regiment.

Hiram R. Sawyer—Mustered out with regiment.

George W. Stowell—Died of disease, Jan. 12, 1863, Carrollton, La.

Chas. Strong—Wounded May 27, 1863, Port Hudson. Died June 10, 1863.

Oliver A. Stevens—Died of disease, July 11, 1863, Baton Rouge, La.

Chas. Thayer—Wounded May 27, 1863, Port Hudson. Mustered out with regiment.

Samuel Tester—Transferred to U. S. Navy, May 10, 1864.

Michael Umberheim—Wounded Sept. 19, 1864, Winchester. Mustered out with regiment.

Jas. E. Vanslyck—Died of disease, April 8, 1863, Baton Rouge, La.

Wm. S. Van Campen—Mustered out with regiment.

Albert Weatherwax—Absent sick since Nov. 5, 1862. No notice of death ever received.

John Wilson—Transferred to U. S. Navy, May 10, 1864.

Thomas Wilson—Recruit. Transferred to 90th N. Y. Vet. Vols. when 116th was mustered out.

John Wohlgemuth—Transferred to Co. H., Oct. 1, 1862.

John Weatherlow—Discharged for disability. Date unknown.

John S. Whitcher—Wounded May 27, 1863, Port Hudson. Died June 10, 1863.

Henry Winkler—Recruit. Transferred to 90th N. Y. Vet. Vols. when 116th was mustered out.

Wm. S. Waldo—Deserted May 30, 1863.

Henry F. Yaw—Wounded Sept. 22, 1864, Fisher's Hill. Discharged for disability, April 10, 1865.

COLORED COOK.

Norman Byron—Recruit. Transferred to 90th N. Y. Vet. Vols. when 116th was mustered out.

COMPANY K.

CAPTAINS.

James Ayer—Died of disease, May 22, 1863. See page 296.

Warren T. Ferris—Mustered out with regiment.

FIRST LIEUTENANTS.

Philip W. Gould—Resigned Nov. 22, 1862.

Warren T. Ferris—Promoted to Captain, July 16, 1863.

John H. Dingman—Mustered out with regiment.

SECOND LIEUTENANTS.

John W. Grannis—Resigned Sept. 30, 1862.

Elisha B. Cottier—Died of disease, Aug. 21, 1863. See page 302.

Geo. H. Shepard—Promoted to 1st Lieutenant, April 12, 1864.

FIRST SERGEANTS.

Geo. H. Shepard—Promoted to 2d Lieutenant, July 18, 1863.

Daniel C. Conger—Wounded May 27, 1863, Port Hudson. Discharged for disability, May 2, 1864.

Chas. H. Ballard—Wounded Sept. 19, 1864, Winchester. Mustered out with regiment.

SERGEANTS.

Joseph W. Gould—Deserted Nov. 8, 1862.

Horace P. Ingersoll—Promoted to Lieutenant Corps d'Afrique, March 3, 1863.

Elijah P. Smith—Mustered out with regiment.

Valentine Doane—Mustered out with regiment.

Job B. Sherman—Wounded May 27, 1863, Port Hudson. Mustered out with regiment.

Henry W. Eno—Wounded May 27, 1863, Port Hudson. Mustered out with regiment.

CORPORALS.

Frank M. Judson—Wounded May 21, 1863, Plain Store. Died May 23, 1863.

Horace A. Paxson—Wounded May 27, 1863, Port Hudson. Transferred to Vet. Reserve Corps, Jan. 10, 1863.

Harvey M. Crawford—Wounded April 8, 1864, Sabine Cross Roads. Discharged for disability July 19, 1864.

John Dibble—Mustered out with regiment.

Joseph H. Baldwin—Mustered out with regiment.

William Naigel—Wounded Sept. 19, 1864, Winchester. Mustered out with regiment.

Austin Reifel—Mustered out with regiment.

David Weissenger—Wounded May 27, 1863, Port Hudson. Mustered out with regiment.

Douglass S. Taylor—Mustered out with regiment.

MUSICIANS.

Geo. W. Carr—Discharged May 18, 1864.

Leroy J. Russell—Mustered out with regiment.

WAGONER.

Bela Crawford—Died of disease, Oct. 27, 1863, New Orleans La.

PRIVATES.

Austin H. Ames—Transferred to Vet. Reserve Corps, Sept. 26, 1863.

Edwin Avery—Mustered out with regiment.

Richard H. Avery—Mustered out with regiment.

Ashael E. Ames—Wounded May 21, 1863, Plain Store. Mustered out with regiment.

Wm. H. Brewer—Mustered out with regiment.

Geo. W. Barker—Mustered out with regiment.

John E. Butler—Mustered out with regiment.

John M. Baker—Discharged for disability, April 10, 1864.

John Black—Wounded June 14, 1863, Port Hudson. Transferred to Vet. Reserve Corps, Jan. 10, 1865.

Chas. Bramiller—Wounded May 27, 1863, Port Hudson. Died Aug. 23, 1863, Baton Rouge, La.

Chas. E. Craig—Taken prisoner Oct. 19, 1864, Cedar Creek. Mustered out with regiment.

Josiah L. Claghorn—Promoted to Regt'l Com. Serg't, Sept. 3, 1862.

Wm. J. Cameron—Mustered out with regiment.

Daniel Crawford—Wounded May 27, 1863, Port Hudson. Mustered out with regiment.

Merritt Dean—Mustered out with regiment.

Chas. Dash—Mustered out with regiment.

John M. Dexter—Mustered out with regiment.

Cyrenus C. Dibble—Discharged for disability, April 19, 1864.

Joseph A. Ewers—Wounded Sept. 19, 1864, Winchester. Mustered out with regiment.

Wm. Ewers—Mustered out with regiment.

Reuben Eddy—Mustered out with regiment.

Ariel Evans—Died of disease, Jan. 11, 1863, Carrollton, La.

James H. Fails—Died of disease, Nov. 11, 1863, Evans, N. Y.

Lyman M. Frary—Died of disease, Nov. 21, 1862, Fortress Monroe.

James Frost—Mustered out with regiment.

Marshall A. Fairbanks—Mustered out with regiment.

George Fedic—Mustered out with regiment.

Nicholas Fedic—Mustered out with regiment.

Geo. A. Freeman—Wounded May 27, 1863, Port Hudson. Mustered out with regiment.

Jno. L. Flint—Mustered out with regiment.

Conrad Glosser—Mustered out with regiment.

John Glosser—Mustered out with regiment.

Frank E. Griffith—Wounded April 9, 1864, Pleasant Hill. Transferred to Vet. Reserve Corps, Jan. 10, 1865.

Milton H. Hill—Wounded May 27, 1863, Port Hudson. Died June 1, 1863.

Geo. H. Hawks—Died of disease July 10, 1863, Baton Rouge, La.

Stephen V. R. Hammond—Mustered out with regiment.

George M. Hill—Mustered out with regiment.

John A. Haggerty—Wounded May 27, 1863, Port Hudson. Mustered out with regiment.

Charles Iback—Wounded May 27, 1863, Port Hudson. Mustered out with regiment.

Loyal C. Ingersoll—Deserted Dec. 31, 1862.

Chas. E. Kingsley—Died of disease, July 26, 1863, Baton Rogue, La.

Alonzo F. Killom—Wounded June 14, 1863, Port Hudson. Mustered out with regiment.

Miner D. Lynn—Mustered out with regiment.

Lewis Ludlow—Wounded July 13, 1863, Cox's Plantation. Mustered out with regiment.

Chas. B. Mills—Wounded June 14, 1863, Port Hudson. Discharged for disability, March 9, 1864.

Wm. Matthewson—Promoted to Regt'l Com. Sergt., May 16, 1865.

Chas. Naigel—Mustered out with regiment.

Geo. N. Ostrom—Died of disease, Dec. 16, 1863, New Iberia, La.

Francis M. Phelps—Transferred to Vet. Res. Corps, April 28, 1865.

Albert D. Prescott—Mustered out with regiment.

William B. Page—Discharged for disability, Jan. 25, 1864.

Adrian Patrick—Discharged for disabilty, Dec. 14, 1863.

Peter Reifel—Wounded May 27, 1863, Port Hudson. Discharged for disability, March 30, 1864.

Warren K. Russell—Promoted to Regt'l Com. Sergt., Oct. 1, 1863.

Theodore Slater—Wounded May 27, 1863, Port Hudson. Died of disease Sept. 9, 1863, Evans, N. Y.

Franklin Sooy—Died of disease Aug. 9, 1864, Philadelphia, Pa.

James H. Smith—Discharged for disability, Jan. 25, 1864.

James Stone—Mustered out with regiment.

Morris Taylor—Mustered out with regiment.

Lafayette Taylor—Mustered out with regiment.

William Tromler—Wounded April 23, 1864, Cane River. Discharged for disability, May 17, 1865.

Wendell Tice—Wounded May 21, 1863, Plain Store. Transferred to Vet. Reserve Corps, Nov. 14, 1863.

Jno. A. Thomason—Died of disease July 18, 1863, Baton Rouge, La.

Wyman Vibbard—Mustered out with regiment.

Andrew Wuest—Killed Sept. 19, 1864, Winchester.

Horatio G. Whittemore—Transferred to Vet. Reserve Corps, Nov. 14, 1863.

Gurden F. Waite—Absent on sick leave since Sept. 2, 1864.

Ira White—Mustered out with regiment.

Philip Zeigler—Transferred to Vet. Reserve Corps, Oct. 3. 1863.

www.ingramcontent.com/pod-product-compliance
Lightning Source LLC
LaVergne TN
LVHW010205110826
845151LV00002B/608

* 9 7 8 1 4 2 5 5 3 6 1 7 6 *